THE road to INDEPENDENCE

101

women's

journeys

to starting

their own

law firms

Karen M. Lockwood
Editor

Defending Liberty
Pursuing Justice

Commission on Women
in the Profession
American Bar Association

Cover design by ABA Publishing/Monica Alejo.

The materials contained herein represent the opinions of the authors and editors and should not be construed to be the views or opinions of the law firms or companies with whom such persons are in partnership with, associated with, or employed by, nor of the American Bar Association or the Commission on Women in the Profession unless adopted pursuant to the bylaws of the Association.

Nothing contained in this book is to be considered as the rendering of legal advice for specific cases, and readers are responsible for obtaining such advice from their own legal counsel. This book and any forms and agreements herein are intended for educational and informational purposes only.

Printed in the United States of America.

15 14 13 12   3 4 5

Library of Congress Cataloging-in-Publication Data
Road to independence : 101 women's journeys to starting their own law firms / Karen M. Lockwood, editor.
    p. cm.
  Includes index.
  ISBN 978-1-61632-084-3
  1. Women lawyers—United States—History. 2. Women-owned law firms—United States—History. I. Lockwood, Karen M.
  KF299.W6R58 2011
  340.082—dc23
                        2011025995

Discounts are available for books ordered in bulk. Special consideration is given to state bars, CLE programs, and other bar-related organizations. Inquire at Book Publishing, ABA Publishing, American Bar Association, 321 N. Clark Street, Chicago, Illinois 60654-7598.

www.shopABA.org

From the Chair of the Commission on Women in the Profession

The Commission on Women in the Profession has long been concerned about the fact that women continue to face significant barriers and obstacles at law firms in this country. Women experience disproportionately high rates of attrition from law firms; confront disparities in compensation, which increase with seniority; are often subjected to implicit bias in assignments and evaluations; and are grossly underrepresented in the equity partnership ranks and in positions of real power and influence in law firms. Thus, it is hardly surprising that more and more women are opting to create their own firms.

Recognizing this growing phenomenon, the Commission decided two years ago to invite women from around the country who founded their own law firms to recount their experiences and offer their insights. *The Road to Independence: 101 Women's Journeys to Starting Their Own Law Firms* is a compilation of 101 letters from women who have taken the courageous and difficult step of creating a law firm of their own, either as a solo or with others.

The authors of *The Road to Independence* created their own firms for a wide variety of reasons. Some left voluntarily because they were disaffected with the allocation of client origination credit or because they felt that they were facing barriers to partnership or advancement in the partnership. Many grew tired of onerous billable hour requirements, inflexible work schedules, or the inability to achieve a desirable work/life balance. Other women wanted to focus their practices in a particular niche area or offer more creative fee arrangements to their clients. A few were laid off by firms because of the recession. But certain common themes emerge: the desire for autonomy and independence, the quest to be one's own boss, and the enormous personal and professional satisfaction of creating and building a practice you can call your own.

The letters compiled in this book reflect the voices of women who are happy with their practices, proud of their entrepreneurial spirit and business development skills, and eager to share their advice with others who may be emboldened to follow in their footsteps. We hope that *The Road to Independence* will serve as a catalyst, guide, and inspiration for other women who are contemplating the possibility of setting out on their own.

We are grateful to the chair of the Commission's publications committee, Marsha Simms, for her diligence in keeping this project on track. We also owe an enormous debt of gratitude to Karen M. Lockwood, who took the laboring oar to review and organize the letters, as well as write the introductions to each chapter and the conclusion. Karen's dedication, vision, and commitment helped to transform the idea for this publication into a reality.

We thank the members of the publications committee in assisting us with recruiting and working with contributors to this book. Special thanks also go to Ruthe Ashley for her review of the entire manuscript. In addition, we appreciate and acknowledge the staff of the Commission and particularly our executive director, Veronica M. Muñoz, and the Commission's publications manager, Barbara Leff, who shepherded the book through production.

Last, and most important, we thank the many authors of the letters that you read in this book. Thank you for taking the time to tell your stories and share your life experiences. Your vignettes and sage words of wisdom will inspire other women lawyers to explore the possibility of likewise blazing their own trail to success and fulfillment.

ROBERTA D. LIEBENBERG, CHAIR, 2008-2011
ABA Commission on Women in the Profession

Special Acknowledgment

In addition to all those previously thanked in the preceding message from the chair, the ABA Commission on Women in the Profession gratefully acknowledges Roberta Liebenberg for conceiving the idea of *The Road to Independence* and for her tireless effort in bringing it to fruition. This book is the direct result of her enthusiasm and leadership.

The Commission on Women in the Profession

Chair
Roberta D. Liebenberg

Members
Ruthe Catolico Ashley
Hon. Fernande R.V. Duffly
Patricia Kruse Gillette
Jim Goh
Lisa Horowitz
Denise F. Keane
Eileen M. Letts
Lorelie S. Masters
Gloria Santona
James R. Silkenat
Marsha E. Simms

Staff
Veronica M. Muñoz, Director
Alia Graham
Beverly Tate
Barbara Leff
Melissa Wood

American Bar Association Commission on Women in the Profession
321 N. CLARK STREET, CHICAGO, ILLINOIS 60654
PHONE: 312-988-5715 FAX: 312-988-5790
E-MAIL: abacwp1@americanbar.org
WEB SITE : www.americanbar.org/women

Any proceeds from this publication will go toward the projects
of the ABA Commission on Women in the Profession.

CONTENTS

- CONTENTS -

CHAPTER 6: 2005–2008
Accelerating into the Recession

Introduction

This book collects 101 letters written by women who have founded law practices. The project began with invitations to these women to write about their decisions, experiences, and reflections in letters to other women thinking about starting their own firms. When collected into a whole, these letters became so much more than just advice.

Whether the reader browses the set or digests entire chapters in a sitting, unmistakable consensus emerges. In their personal voices, the writers reiterate key themes: Of becoming businesswomen. Of choosing a practice area true to their passions and to the high character they bring to the bar. Of controlling not only their days, but also their destinies. Of ambition in action.

The ABA Commission on Women in the Profession, in soliciting these letters, anticipated that the insights and experiences of women who have pioneered in founding a law practice would be both inspirational and filled with practical advice.

What was not anticipated was the power and narrative that would be created when the letters were compiled historically. Grouped chronologically, this collection implicitly portrays the profession's growth, the society's evolution, the economy's fortunes, and the periodic changes in business models of private practice. Explicitly, the collection of letters unites to reflect not only the drive of these women to practice law, but also the impact of those cultural changes on women in private practice.

In their total effect, therefore, the letters present a picture of the legal profession that the reader may recognize on a personal level—a profession that underestimates the power and grit of women lawyers, who comprise the essential half of the profession's talent still not at the table in traditional firms.

The reader will see here the ambitious and imaginative leading edge of the profession exploding traditional ideas about how law must be practiced. Amid the marketplace speculation over future business models for traditional law firms, this collection of voices and ventures establishes the economic force of individual lawyers who create new practices in the image of their values and aspirations. These individuals find business forms in which they can control and manage all of their responsibilities and succeed at the highest levels of the profession. These women lawyers—some over 35 years in practice—exemplify clear-eyed plans and the determination to establish legacy firms.

The Origin and Arrangement of Letters

The Commission solicited letters through an open process, seeking referrals to women who have founded firms, using online resources and open announcements to identify women-owned firms, and providing an invitation to women who asked. While this method of gathering letters was not designed to be scientific, the result nevertheless produced a remarkably broad selection of firms whose origins span six decades.

The letters appear here chronologically according to the date each writer started her woman-owned law practice. If two or more writers started in the same year, their letters are arranged by the year of their law degrees. The entire set is then grouped into chapters, which uncover and track the themes emerging from each historical period.

This manner of organization reveals a startling acceleration in the rate at which women are starting firms. The '50s and '60s each claim just one woman founder among our writers. In the '70s, seven of our writers founded firms. We have eight founders' letters from the '80s. From the '90s, we have 27. In the 2000s, 57 of our writers started their first woman-owned practice. The crescendo is plain. Further, even *within* the most recent period of 2000–2010 (plus the first day of 2011), the number of women's letters grows sharply through time, as shown in chapters 5, 6, and 7. Thirty-seven of the 101 writers founded their firms in the last six years, the years 2005–2010, and one of them on January 1, 2011. Clearly, women are increasingly starting their own firms in order to do it their own way.

This arrangement of letters reveals another notable trend: increasing proportions of women starting firms are, in fact, seasoned women lawyers with significant practice histories. From the '50s through the '70s, nearly all of our founders started their own practices in the first decade after law school (chapter 1). The '80s hinted that more senior women would be doing so; three of our eight writers started their firms more than 10 years out of law school (chapter 2). By the '90s a trend had started; our letters in that decade come from 10 graduates of the '90s, 15 of the '80s, and two of the '70s (chapters 3 and 4). In the latest period from 2000 to the most recent 2011 writer, the founders graduated in years across all the relevant decades: 12 in the 2000s, 23 in the 1990s, 16 in the 1980s, and six in the 1970s (chapters 5, 6, and 7).

The economic success of founding a firm is more assured now, and the movement to found firms appeals to women lawyers across generations. The numbers reflect, for women-owned firms, a marketplace come of age.

Emergent Themes
The letters are highly individual in tone and content. The writers explain the individuality of their letters through the context of their own prior experience.

Writers who founded their firms as senior practitioners speak with a longer perspective, strategically using their experience in practice and confidence at the bar to plan their success. The clarity of a founder's reasons for breaking out seems to increase as the writer reflects back upon her experience from a greater distance.

Junior women founders—including notably the first movers whose letters start this book—have moved forward without preconceived notions, fashioning both their business models and their practices to meet their visions and their needs. Still new to their decision to start on the road to independence, they nevertheless show great resolve about their decision.

Women with law degrees from other countries appear and show their own angle on starting a practice. They move gracefully between countries and legal cultures, reminding us not to adopt a myopic view of American practice.

Not all of the writers still operate the firms or practices they describe here. Their reasons for moving on—acquisition, merger, change in direction, retirement, and others—bespeak the strength and lasting independence that is gained by having formed the new venture. Some who have moved on regard it as a profound experience, one that is individualistic, inspired, and instrumental to the formation of what followed in their careers.

Across the age groups, however, the strong majority of these writers remain in practice. Indeed, some continue into retirement, and some envision a lasting enterprise that continues after they as founders have stopped. The ambition of the population of founding women firm owners is obvious—and long-lived.

Across the individuality of these letters in tone and content, there appears a unifying arc of time, which marks changes in the profession itself. Assembling the letters by the year the women started their first firm—as described above—yields a remarkable set of insights. Popular movements, such as the equal rights movement in the 1970s, show their strong influence. Rises and declines in the nation's economic vibrancy are evident. The impact of law firm growth into very large organizations is palpable. But more than that, the resulting fabric of these writers' perspectives portrays the impact of that evolution on women. That impact is summarized in each chapter's introduction.

Collectively, against this backdrop of an ever-changing legal profession, the letters convey visionary insights, advice about using ambition, strength in understanding the power of independence, and frustrations about exercising that power in a largely male or monolithic organization.

Practical Advice

Throughout the book, the reader will find business-savvy tidbits and practical tips for starting and growing a successful law business. This collection does not try to be complete or authoritative on that subject. Manuals other than this book provide a comprehensive "how-to" compendium of the managerial steps to start a practice. Instead, the collection offers "nuts and bolts" of beginning and managing a practice in the words of the founders themselves. The reader learns those suggestions in the context of why it was important to the writer, as a part of her reflections about her decision to break out, and how she engineered her pathway toward success given her starting point.

The management suggestions in all of the chapters are of current interest because regardless of when a writer founded her firm, she composed her practical advice after the spring of 2010, using the modern lens of today's business environment. The reader is urged to review the entire collection for practical advice such as the following:

- collect information early, including sources of fees, market trends, and definitions of the new firm's practice scope

- start modestly with inexpensive offices; hire slowly
- carefully plan and budget, both before starting and throughout the business cycles
- technology is an important partner; invest in it properly and early
- creative financing is available; find good bankers and trustworthy advisors
- ask for business; use creative fee structures
- reach out to colleagues for advice, help, friendship, and coaching; prepare to be surprised at how many respect your work and want to help
- do not burn bridges
- develop the habit of communicating frequently to the marketplace and your contacts
- opportunities are everywhere; learn to see them.

The writers, offering these and other points of advice, thus tell how they created routines and reaped rewards.

Some Observations and Take-Aways

The implication of the collected letters is to urge the reader to proceed, to venture, and to plan as much as possible, but to unstintingly move forward in creating her own practice if that is her goal. These writers teach us that ambition, the need for more flexibility, the desire for control, and the excitement of creating a legacy drive women to found law firms. They tell the story of courage and of faith in the eventual success of their law firm businesses.

The letters also form the unmistakable impression that the profession will continue to see significant numbers of new practices founded by women— not only recent law grads, but also increasingly women who leave established traditional practices and big firms or who see a smarter, faster, more facile method of doing business.

These are the voices of women happy with their practices, grateful for what they have learned, proud of what they have achieved, and philosophical about their hard work. They find balance in the challenges, because they own their chosen solutions.

We hope you enjoy their letters.

CHAPTER 1

THROUGH 1979

The Pioneers and the First Advocates of Women-Owned Firms

"We were not only a women-owned business, but had as our primary mission establishing a firm that was dedicated to addressing issues affecting women, particularly issues of discrimination."

—Janice Goodman

Those who had nowhere to practice in the early years, and the feminists, anchor the letters from the earliest of our women founders.

Nine letters describe firms founded in the period from 1954 to 1979, including one in the '50s and one in the '60s. This powerhouse of writers starts with the second African American woman lawyer in the state of North Carolina, who discovered that law firms and corporations were not hiring female attorneys. The group also includes two letters by partners of "the First Feminist Law Firm," which grew out of the New York Law School Women & the Law Committee. Those writers were not just interested in a women-owned business but "were driven by a mission, namely, our belief that equal rights for women were to be achieved by litigation in the courts, if necessary."

An early founder adds her voice as one who began an independent practice immediately out of law school in the '70s, and—maintaining her practice—recently secured certification as a WBE (Women's Business Enterprise)-certified firm focusing on commercial litigation and executive employment.

Summarizing what must be true for all of these women, whether junior or senior, a 1955 law graduate who started her solo firm in 1968 writes: "Two approaches have kept my career vigorous for 54 years: willingness to adapt to changes in the profession and networking."

These writers inject the sense of mission and the resolve to bring about change. They remind us of our practice roots.

- ANNIE BROWN KENNEDY -

"I was the second female attorney and the first African American female attorney to practice law in Winston-Salem. . . . The only option I had when I began practicing law was to start my own law firm."

When I began practicing law in 1954, I became the second African American female attorney to practice law in the state of North Carolina. I was also the second female attorney and the first African American female attorney to practice law in Winston-Salem, North Carolina.

In 1954, the major law firms and corporations in North Carolina were not hiring female attorneys. My husband, Harold L. Kennedy Jr., joined me in 1955 in the private practice of law, and we became one of the first husband-wife law firms in North Carolina. The only option I had when I began practicing law was to start my own law firm.

The development and growth of my law practice involved several factors. First, I received widespread media coverage from local newspapers and radio because, in the light of the times, I was unique as a female attorney.

Second, I joined a large Baptist church where I was well-received and began participating in many church organizations. I was asked to write a monthly column entitled "This Is the Law" in another large Baptist church's monthly newsletter.

Third, I was highly sought after to give speeches at churches and community organizations. I developed a large client base by participating in church and community activities and speaking to churches and community groups.

Fourth, as my law practice grew, I was asked to serve on many community boards, such as the YWCA and United Way.

Fifth, I became politically active. I worked in many political campaigns and was asked by Governor Terry Sanford to serve on the North Carolina Commission on the Status of Women. I eventually was appointed to serve in the North Carolina House of Representatives, where I served for 13 years.

My legal clientele continued to grow because of my political participation. In addition, I received referrals from past clients and from other attorneys.

I concentrated early in my practice on family law. Very few lawyers were doing that type of legal work in the 1950s and 1960s.

My advice to women attorneys who wish to start their own law firms is as follows:

1. In addition to marketing their practices with websites on the Internet and with business cards, become active in church, community, and bar association activities;

2. Select mentors that you can go to for advice, especially other women attorneys who have developed their own law firms;

3. If you are a solo practitioner, consider associating with other attorneys in complex litigation;

4. Live a well-balanced life. By starting your own law firm, you can determine how you spend your time. Take the time to have a good family life.

I wish you the best in starting your law firms.

ANNIE BROWN KENNEDY is a senior partner in the law firm of Kennedy, Kennedy, Kennedy and Kennedy, LLP, in Winston-Salem, North Carolina, where she focuses on civil litigation, employment law, and personal injury litigation. She graduated from law school in 1951 and founded her firm in 1954.

- Noreen Saltveit McGraw -

"Two approaches have kept my career vigorous
for 54 years: willingness to adapt to changes in
the profession and networking."

The practice of law has changed dramatically since I started in 1956, a time when very few attorneys were women, and even fewer were trial attorneys. But I came from a family of trial lawyers—including my father, my grandfather, and my older brother, Bernie. On occasion, I even skipped class in high school to watch my father try a particularly juicy case.

Two approaches have kept my career vigorous for 54 years: willingness to adapt to changes in the profession and networking (through mentors and state and local bar associations.)

I started out in my family's firm in Medford, Oregon (population 30,000 at that time). Our practice was general with emphasis on litigation. About 40 lawyers practiced in the downtown area, and I started going to lunch two or three times a week at a restaurant where many of the local bar met. It was a great way to know my peers, find out the courthouse gossip, and pick up tips on trial tactics. It also taught me a lot of respect for the integrity and ability of these lawyers. If, however, one of them developed a bad reputation—for being unprepared, not forthright, etc.—it became known quickly and was very hard for that attorney to shake.

I moved to Portland in the '60s to improve my social life and concentrate on jury trials in a metropolitan area. I was surprised how large and impersonal the Multnomah County Bar seemed. However, by becoming active in bar committees and a specialized bar—Oregon Trial Lawyers—I was able to find mentors among more established and connected attorneys.

By that time, I had been practicing for four years with a fair number of jury trials and even some appellate work. But at the time, there was not one full-time woman trial lawyer in Oregon's most populous county; only two tried occasional cases. After contacting 35 law firms and interviewing with a dozen or so, I had only two job offers: one with a small firm doing collection work and another with the Attorney General's Workers Compensation Division. In 1960, the state had a monopoly on coverage but jury trials were allowed, so these cases paralleled personal injury cases, with the state as defendant.

As assistant attorney general, I tried cases on a regular basis against some of the top personal injury lawyers in the Portland area. Moreover, later—because of my work and trial record—I was allowed to practice half time (two or three days a week) while a babysitter watched my growing family.

By 1965, the law had changed, taking away the right to jury trial. By that time, I had gained invaluable skills and contacts, which gave me the confidence to go out on my own. I sought referrals from other attorneys, especially in workers' compensation cases, signed up for criminal appointments, wrote close attorney friends seeking any referrals they might send my way, etc. My goal was still to work half time, and I located a small firm with an unused office and a receptionist. The rent was modest and I had to take care of my own secretarial needs.

I also took on a pro bono case representing a group of migrant workers against a labor contractor and camp owner. This led to a federal court case largely in Spanish with an interpreter. (Since I had a degree in Spanish and had lived a year in Mexico, I could converse freely with the clients.) This case resulted in a victory for the migrants and a whole new group of Spanish-speaking clients.

Around this time, Ralph Nader—who had just burst onto the national legal scene with the publication of his book *Unsafe at Any Speed*—spoke at the Oregon State Bar convention, passionately challenging lawyers to advocate for the public good. My good friend Larry Aschenbrenner and I took up Nader's challenge, along with Charley Merten (then head of Legal Aid in Oregon) and Don Marmaduke (partner in a major law firm). Larry, Charley, and Don had all served in Mississippi in the '60s with the ABA project representing civil rights workers. We were all eager to use our skills and knowledge to provide access to the courts and improve the law in Oregon. Nader's impassioned speech had provided the catalyst.

Soon after, the four of us formed the first public interest law firm in Oregon, and I was able to apply the skills and knowledge gained in the migrant worker case to several class action lawsuits on behalf of minorities and women.

Two years later, when the Oregon State Bar certified us as a recognized public interest law firm, we could point to a number of significant cases we had handled involving civil rights and environmental and consumer protection issues.

The public interest requirement of 50 percent pro bono law reform work guaranteed us independence, but it created month-to-month financial anxiety since we all had children at home to support and educate. After four years, Larry and Don left. Charley Merten and I continued on as partners for another seven years, handling lots of law reform cases, but no longer as an "official" public interest law firm adhering to the fifty-fifty quota.

I became increasingly involved with class actions on behalf of women in this period. Some of these sought greater opportunity for women within large institutions such as Oregon's two largest banks, a packing plant, a newspaper, etc.

By the end of the '70s, the federal court had become more conservative, and it was harder to mount effective civil rights and environmental cases. Charley met, and eventually married, a young lawyer, and they wanted to start their own practice. I became more focused on personal injury and other cases that would help me get my children through college. So we parted, very amicably.

In order to keep costs down, I searched for a firm interested in renting out space and found an arrangement with four other lawyers with varying practices—domestic relations, criminal law, estates, etc. Because we were all compatible and respected each other, this arrangement worked well.

As the '80s wore on, I became increasingly involved in writing and editing projects for the Oregon State Bar and served as chair of the Continuing Legal Education (CLE) Committee. This proved to be a valuable networking tool, and my law practice thrived.

On the horizon, however, was a second massive rewrite of the workers' compensation legislation, which reduced the number of cases dramatically after 1990. I began to look around for another direction for my law practice to take and ended up shifting my focus to alternative dispute resolution, taking training in mediation.

In addition to retooling my practice, I became involved in both the Oregon and Portland bar associations to reestablish name familiarity and attract potential referrals. I also joined the United States Arbitration and Mediation service (USA&M) and joined state (Oregon Employment Relations Board) and federal (Federal Mediation and Conciliation Service) labor arbitration panels for cases.

This practice has served me well over the last 15 to 20 years, and today it allows me to engage in mediation and arbitration part time, as I wind down an active practice of over 50 years.

NOREEN SALTVEIT MCGRAW is a solo practitioner in San Diego, California, where she focuses on alternative dispute resolution, particularly pre-trial mediation through the provider United States Arbitration and Mediation. She graduated from law school in 1955 and founded her solo practice firm in 1968. *www.realchange.org/noreen.htm*

- Janice Goodman -

"A women's firm dedicated to representing women in the job market as well as others who have suffered from discrimination is a challenging business model that is financially viable."

The "First Feminist Law Firm," as we called ourselves (Bellamy, Blank, Goodman, Kelly, Ross & Stanley), was formed in New York City in the early part of 1973. The original partners were Carol Bellamy, Diane Blank, Janice Goodman, Mary Kelly, Susan Deller Ross, and Nancy Stanley. The firm grew out of the "Women and the Law" movement begun at NYU School of Law. We were not only a women-owned business, but had as our primary mission establishing a firm that was dedicated to addressing issues affecting women, particularly issues of discrimination.

Ours was a very unique experience. The feminist movement was at its peak in the late 1960s through the 1970s, and with that came a substantial increase in the enrollment of women at law schools around the country. By 1970 close to 40 percent of the enrollment at NYU was female, and the numbers were increasing nationally. We at NYU formed a Women & the Law committee, which, among other things, opened up the prestigious Root-Tilden full tuition and board scholarship, which was previously limited to men only; introduced the first Women and the Law course; convened the first national Women and the Law convention; initiated litigation against white shoe law firms that discriminated in their hiring practices; and brought an action that resulted in the desegregation of the New York State Bar exam.

Four of us (Blank, Goodman, Kelly, and Ross) were students together at NYU initiating these various actions. We graduated in 1971. Bellamy was a supportive graduate of NYU, and Stanley was a close friend at a law school in DC. At about the same time that we established our practice, others were also emerging. Those included Equal Rights Advocates (a 501(c)(3) organization) in San Francisco, a feminist law firm in Boston and one in Philadelphia, and a women-run law firm in New York City. All of us were young and inexperienced but completely dedicated to helping develop new law.

Although we did jump into this endeavor with limited background, we were aided by the times. There was a strong women's movement and a surge of women wanting to be represented by women. As a consequence of this feminist activity, our law firm, though a for-profit institution, was able to obtain a significant grant from the Sachem Foundation for two litigation projects: (1) challenging mortgage lending practices that discounted the income of married women since it was presumed that they would leave the workforce once having had children; (2) challenging divorce laws that denied women equitable distribution of property acquired during marriage.

The funding from these suits, which ended in successful results, helped keep us afloat at the very beginning. But the fact of the matter is that we never suffered from lack of potential clients. Because women's issues were newsworthy at that time, and because our mission was so unique, we received a fair amount of publicity, including an article in the *New York Times*. As a consequence, from the day we opened our doors there were women clamoring for services. A problem, however, was that many of these women did not have the funds for legal service. We were primarily sought after to represent women suffering from job discrimination where we had to rely on court-awarded fees if successful and women in matrimonial matters where we would have to rely on fees from the husband. We represented women in several high profile employment discrimination class actions—most notably *Women's Committee, et al. v. NBC* and women at *Newsday*.

In addition to the usual issues confronting young law firms, we also had to confront some difficult political issues—one of the hardest being would we represent men in divorce actions. Yes was the answer, but there were many caveats regarding under what circumstances we would take on such representation. Another difficult issue—what happens when two or more partners become pregnant at the same time. There was never any question that we did not represent employers defending discrimination law suits.

Our novel experiment lasted five years and dissolved for reasons not dissimilar to the breakup of traditional small firms. Some of the partners simply did not like private practice—the hustle for billable hours and paying clients. One partner became a prominent public official spending little time on the firm. There were issues regarding how to divide the high profile cases. There were increasing money issues, in part relating to having to wait up to five years for fees on successful employment cases. We were involved in an emerging field of law, which made many cases a long-term battle. Finally, there were the difficulties in dedicating a private practice where most of our clients had little discretionary income.

It is hard to translate our experience into how women can start their own law firms today. As described above, we were not just interested in a women-owned business replicating what male firms do, but rather we were dedicated to a civil rights practice to advance the position of women. I believe that is still a viable model, particularly if the practice is dedicated to the area of employment discrimination. When we formed, the antidiscrimination law was just emerging, and there was only one other private practitioner in New York City practicing employee side representation. There were only a handful of lawyers around the country practicing in the field. These were uncharted waters, and almost every issue was novel—from how much discovery would be made available to how broad a class of women could be represented in a class action.

Today employment discrimination law has significantly expanded, and the number of practitioners has increased manyfold. A women's firm dedicated to representing women in the job market as well as others who have suffered from discrimination is a challenging business model that is financially viable. Such a firm, unlike ours, would not be fending for itself in unchartered waters. After our feminist law firm closed, I continued, to this day, to practice successfully in the field of employment law, in both a partnership situation and as a solo. I have continued to dedicate my practice to the representation of employees while earning a living. There is now a substantial bar ready to help, and although new, challenging issues continue to arise, there is a significant body of law to build upon.

JANICE GOODMAN heads the Law Offices of Janice Goodman in New York, New York, where she practices employment law representing individual employees and class members in discrimination and contract matters. She graduated from law school in 1971 and founded her firm in 1973.

- MARY F. KELLY -

"The pivotal values for me, in hindsight,
were resilience, professional commitment to the law,
and the desire to help clients."

We started Bellamy, Blank, Goodman, Kelly, Ross & Stanley, the first feminist law firm in New York, in February 1973, and our firm lasted for five years.

Fifty percent of our partners formerly were practicing in traditional law firm settings. The impetus for starting our law firm dated from our law school days: five of us had attended NYU School of Law. We were charter members of the NYU Women's Rights Committee, a seminal law school organization that created a regional law school coalition that helped to shape law schools, and women in the profession, for 20 years after our graduation in 1971.

In my case, my initial career experience immediately following law school graduation was as an associate at a Wall Street law firm. I was the first woman in their litigation department, and while my presence challenged the traditionally minded male litigators, I gained invaluable training in litigation skills that were necessary once we formed our own firm.

There were many benefits derived from forming a feminist law firm. There was an unusually high degree of commitment and perceived responsibility to the principles of feminism from 1968 to 1973, during the time that we made plans to start such a law firm. Those shared principles formed an important part of our firm and actually were the basis of it. We were driven by a mission, namely, our belief that equal rights for women were to be achieved by litigation in the courts, if necessary, to secure such rights.

We immediately experienced financial challenges. First, we had no natural client base. Quite the opposite: instead of having, for example, business entities or individuals who engaged our representation for a retainer fee, our clients were based upon statutory-based, court-awarded fees (e.g., Title VII or section 1983 cases), which depended upon judicial discretion. Thus, we had long stretches (two to five years) to wait for fees to be awarded. Our personal lives were directly impacted. We had to rely upon savings and partners/husbands to sustain us over the dry period. This is a serious challenge to the survival of any firm.

What mitigated in our favor was a secondary group of clients that we cultivated to sustain our viability, namely, matrimonial matters. Most of those clients were women, and while many of these clients also faced financial stresses, the relationship netted us up-front retainers and/or monthly payments, which sustained us.

After leaving the feminist firm (and passage of a few years for raising my family of four children in the early years of my children's lives), I created a two-woman partnership, Kelly & Knaplund, based in Westchester County. My partner, who was a part-time village justice, was happy to concentrate in matrimonial practice, while I engaged in a general practice, including matrimonial, adoption, small corporations, and residential real estate transactions. Our partnership lasted 12 years and terminated only because my partner felt compelled to withdraw in order to join her retired husband who wanted to move out of state.

One of the operating principles of Kelly & Knaplund that stabilized our practice was the decision to share office expenses on an equal basis, regardless of clients or income production. Thus, we knew what percentage of (and amount of) office costs we were each responsible for, and since our clients were individual (unless we otherwise designated the client or clients as joint), we could earn disparate levels of income without the tension of worrying about who was producing more revenue.

Once this partnership ended, I created a solo practice. I was fortunate, because of location and living space, to be able to create a residential-based law practice, which has lowered my direct office expenses and captured favorable income tax benefit. Combining a solo practice with a secondary office in White Plains, shared with other attorneys, has proven to be the current successful model for me. The shared office in a desirable location has allowed me to choose the best venue to see clients, to share the ongoing expenses of law publications and a law library, and to experience the valuable collegial interchange of ideas and legal issues and dilemmas with colleagues. It also provides a base for mutual referrals.

The pivotal values for me, in hindsight, were resilience (being able to adapt to the changing and sometimes challenging circumstances of the different models of law practice), professional commitment to the law, and the desire to help clients. Those values were the core of each form of law practice in which I engaged.

MARY F. KELLY is an attorney in private practice at Kelly & Knaplund in White Plains, New York, concentrating her practice in matrimonial and family law. She graduated from law school in 1971 and founded her first firm in 1973 with letter contributor Janice Goodman and others. She founded her current firm in 1984. *www.kellyandknaplund.com*

- KAREN DeCROW -

"Not every woman has babies, but most do. So until we stopped the exclusion of pregnant women from the work place, we could not eliminate discrimination against women."

My gardener tells me he brought his daughter with him. She wants to be a lawyer. She is 15 years old.

I prepare for a conversation. My fantasy is that she has developed a passion for justice, thanks to a good class in high school. I imagine that she will tell me that she wants to create equality for all.

"Your dad tells me you want to be an attorney," I say, smiling. "Tell me why."

"Because I want to live in a house like yours," she says.

I was admitted to the New York state bar in 1974. When I started out—in solo practice—there were not many alternatives. One could say I was in private practice by default.

At the time, what large law firm would hire me? Two strikes against me: I am female. I am well known as a feminist. I had been active in the National Organization for Women (NOW) since 1967. In 1974 I was elected as the national president.

Today, being active in NOW would not be a bar to being hired by a law firm. It might even be a plus. Then, it certainly was not an item on a curriculum vitae to attract the hiring partner.

I did have a tempting offer to work for a government agency in Washington, DC. But I had many ties in Syracuse, New York, and did not want to move.

Everything changed in a few decades. Many women lawyers now work for large firms. This refashioning is a product of our success. We have rewritten the culture: women are welcome in law schools (I was the only female in my class) and on the job.

Although I have enjoyed 36 years of practicing law by myself, I am always careful to tell law clerks, interns, and other lawyers that this may not be a pattern that can be imitated.

The specific purpose for my going to law school (I had a career for 10 years as a journalist before I enrolled) was to practice discrimination law. When I graduated from the Syracuse University College of Law there were hardly any lawyers doing discrimination work. Most did not know the field existed.

So, I could carve out a national practice doing what I loved. Because of my high profile, clients called me. A good way to establish a practice is to do something no one else is doing.

New challenges emerged: It became apparent that I would have to delve into issues that were not so obvious before. When I started practice, most opposing counsel, and most judges, did not know what I was talking about. When I would carefully outline the differential treatment experienced by my client, the usual response was not "she is being treated like other workers." No one claimed that. What they said with regard to her being underpaid or not promoted was "What is wrong with that?"

I have a sense of the human story. At the risk of sounding boastful, I will say that I knew we were on the right side of history. I knew that sex discrimination was on the way out, or at least, was going to become paler and paler.

I recall a public meeting at which I testified that according to a city budget, there was $200 a year being spent on after school sports for girls and $99,000 being spent for the boys. I was told "What's wrong with this?"

As I travel around the country I see pregnant women performing every job imaginable. It makes me happy. I think about my countless cases on their behalf. Don't fire her, I would insist. Let this be a matter between her and her physician. (Bringing a lawsuit is no longer necessary thanks to passage of a federal law.)

Not every woman has babies, but most do. So until we stopped the exclusion of pregnant from the work place, we could not eliminate discrimination against women.

Teachers had to resign when they were pregnant. The (nutty) theory that school children had never seen a pregnant woman was cited as the reason.

A pregnant cocktail waitress case gave me particular pleasure. Her doctor had said she shouldn't wear spike heels. Her young male manager fired her, stating that sexy shoes were part of the job. Not so, we argued. The job is taking drink orders and serving the correct drink. After we prevailed, I paid a visit to the restaurant and watched with joy, my by-this-time very pregnant client, in her flat shoes, serving drinks.

How did my career evolve into who I am now and what I do now?

It was somehow inevitable because I read Betty Friedan's book, *The Feminine Mystique* (1963), on the way to the liberation of women. As is well known, Friedan had a great deal of trouble getting that book published. When it finally was accepted by a publisher, they ordered a small printing. Some surprise. It became an international best seller.

She and I were friends for decades and worked together on countless feminist projects. A fond Friedan memory I have is visiting her apartment and seeing shelf after shelf with copies of *The Feminine Mystique*, in dozens of languages.

I was also very influenced in my thinking by reading *The Second Sex* by Simone de Beauvoir, when it was published in the English translation in 1953.

Is my firm still in business?

Of course. It is thriving. I have clients from all over the country.

What benefits and advantages have I gained?

Freedom, freedom, freedom. No senior partner tells me what cases to accept, how to approach them, and what I can say or not say. This is a luxury had by few professionals, and I am grateful for my life.

One downside is that although I am comfortable (see comment from the gardener's daughter), I will never get wealthy. Partners in major firms earn millions of dollars, I am told. They also used to have job security. This is no longer the case. They are getting fired right and left. As for me, I will never fire myself, so job security is assured.

What do I wish I had known before I began?

My approach to work and to life is, hopefully, rational and logical. Practicing law—dealing with clients and opposing counsel and judges—is anything but logical. As I tell my law clerks after a particularly exhausting deposition, now you see it. This is what the practice of law is all about. Very different from law school and those fascinating law books.

I am lucky to be able to work in a practice that I love. Every day is different. Every case presents a new set of intellectual challenges. At 72, I have no plans to retire. I hope my health allows me to practice until I am 150 years old.

KAREN DECROW is in private practice in Jamesville, New York, where she focuses on representing plaintiffs in employment law matters and handling civil liberties matters. She graduated from law school in 1972 and started her firm in 1974, the same year she was elected national president of the National Organization for Women (NOW).

- LAUREL G. BELLOWS -
&
- FRANCINE BAILEY -

---

*"Move beyond the gender advantage, and focus
on what it takes to be a successful business owner.
The success of a firm begins and ends with the passion
and dedication of its leaders."*

It's Not Just Business...It's Personal

Looking back, I wouldn't have it any other way. Being at the helm of a woman-owned law firm is challenging and personally satisfying. Independence provides the opportunity to tailor work/life chaos to my shifting priorities and preferences. Yet, I quickly learned that as your own boss the ability to personalize your office and life does not soften the realities of running a business.

Put Your Business Hat On

Clients will be interested in your firm's woman-owned status. But at the end of the day, your law firm is a business. As Francine likes to say, you don't get extra credit for having two X chromosomes. Are you cut out to be an entrepreneur? Are you ready to move outside your comfort zone? Are you a self-starter? A risk taker? Are you able to set aside a year of expenses? As owner, you are the decision maker, the hirer, the firer, the person responsible for emergencies whether triggered by a client or a computer meltdown.

Be prepared for round-the-clock commitment. You can choose your clients and when, where, and with whom you work. But be prepared to exchange your free time for the freedom of personalizing your firm. You can select your environment, but you can't control it. Owning your business is a daily combination of unpredictable events.

You may choose to share the ownership burden with like-minded partners. Partnership is a subject for an entire treatise, but must be considered as carefully as marriage, since firm divorce is just as painful, expensive, and messy. Should you opt for partnership, be ready to harmonize varying perspectives on work/life balance, contributions of money/time/expertise/clients, and personality quirks that abound.

Francine says being a woman-owner is not enough to catapult you into success. Move beyond the gender advantage, and focus on what it takes to be a successful business owner. The success of a firm begins and ends with the passion and dedication of its leaders.

Choose a Space

Your office location is a reflection of you. You might match your location and expertise with a particular neighborhood, choose an office in an ethnic community to build a client base where you have roots and language facility, or perhaps select a convenient neighborhood location that attracts clients who appreciate evening hours.

We chose a downtown office location on LaSalle Street, easily accessible to our business clients and providing the footprint to compete with downtown firms. We opted for The Rookery, a landmark building that combines the talents of Frank Lloyd Wright and Daniel Burnham—a building highlighted in the best seller *Devil in the White City*. Clients bring their teams on field trips to see our building. Architecturally unique, the Rookery sets us apart.

Surround Yourself with a Good Team

Clients are calling. Who in addition to you is providing legal services? Who is answering the phone, providing administrative support, helping with books and payroll, fixing frozen computers, sweet-talking printers, and greeting clients?

As the owner, you will spend more time in your desk chair than in your armchair at home. Attracting and retaining both professional and support talent are essential to establishing credibility and maintaining a reputation for excellence. A small firm offers hands-on experience, lower billable hour requirements, and individual mentoring that associates may not find elsewhere.

Spending countless hours at the office is infinitely easier if you are surrounded by an enthusiastic team. Look beyond the résumé. A person with the best credentials on paper may not have the personality to fit the culture of your firm. Create a team of zealous advocates that work well together.

Keeping the team together is equally important and requires strong leadership and management skills. Management is a key ingredient to maintaining stability. A good manager is organized, efficient, and delegates. Having a sense of humor and optimism is imperative. A good leader values team members, embraces ingenuity, and acknowledges employee achievement. Your team is your most important asset.

Getting the Clients

You have perfected your business plan and built a team. Now, it's time to make the cash register ring. There are countless ways to find clients and develop business.

Your clients may be attracted to your firm because of its status as a women-owned firm. Use that status to your advantage. Corporate clients have diversity initiatives that require at least some corporate services to be provided by women- or minority-owned firms. But remember: being a woman-owned firm may be an initial advantage. Ultimately, it is the quality of service and your reputation that bring referrals and return clients.

Position your firm to acquire the cases and clients you want to represent. Identify specific goals. Will your firm be a general practice firm? Or will your boutique capitalize on a single expertise? Many women in large firms develop a specialty that is an excellent base allowing them to pursue a niche market and open a boutique firm. Clients will follow from the large law firm, hoping for lower fees with more personal attention.

Alternatively, many potential clients bemoan the slow extinction of the general practitioner. Forming a general practice allows a woman-owned firm to market itself as the one-stop for small businesses. At The Bellows Law Group, we have found that creating a mix of general practice and expertise works well. We serve as the general practitioner for business owners. Yet we are known for expertise in business litigation and executive compensation. Negotiating employment, separation, and buy/sell agreements, giving employment counsel, representing joint ventures, and litigating non-competes all blend together to support our clients as businesses grow and change—and cement personal relationships to identify additional client needs.

Involvement in local bar organizations and community events not only is good for the soul, but also creates a referral network. Become an event co-chair or speak at a CLE program to increase your profile within the community and build credibility. If you are of a particular ethnicity or speak a second language, you have a unique advantage. Attend events that cater to your ethnic community and develop a name for yourself. Build a referral network with other professionals (insurance brokers, financial planners, accountants) who share a similar client base. Participate in political events, neighborhood groups, church and not-for-profit boards. As an associate, Francine fills her evenings with American Bar Association and Wisconsin Bar Association activities, planning CLEs, speaking, and finding clients on sports rec leagues. Although she is not an owner of a woman-owned firm—yet—it is great preparation. Choose networking activities you enjoy, because building your business is how you spend your "free" time.

Enjoy the most satisfying way to get and keep business—entertaining! Build personal trust through informal entertaining. A savvy law firm owner knows that attracting clients is about building relationships over the long term. Use lunch, coffee, and weekend brunch to nourish your body and your business.

Be creative. Impress your clients with your ability to propose the unexpected. Suggest concerts, theatre, university lectures, sample sales, or spa days that blend with your client's interests. Join a sports team with a client and bond once a week over an entire season. Planning a special outing that caters to your client's interests shows you care, listen, and are willing to spend the extra effort, which, in turn, translates to the personal attention you would provide as their lawyer. The entertainment you plan speaks loudly about who you are and the variety of perspectives and strategies you bring to the practice of law.

Owning your own firm offers the luxury to create a business that is a reflection of your personality, expertise, and business goals. Take the time to create a plan and map your course of action. Make choices that work for you. Let go of alternatives that aren't aligned with who you are and where you're heading.

Don't just build *any* firm. Build *your* firm. Because, it's not just business… *it's personal.*

LAUREL G. BELLOWS, a principal of The Bellows Law Group, P.C. in Chicago, Illinois, represents senior executives and corporations on employment matters, employment and severance agreements, executive compensation, and workplace disputes. She graduated from law school in 1974, joined her husband in practice in 1975 at Bellows & Bellows, PC, and founded her women-owned firm in 2009. **FRANCINE BAILEY**, an associate at The Bellows Law Group, P.C., focuses on business and employment law, litigating/negotiating employment agreements, severance agreements, and discrimination claims. She graduated from law school in 2006. *www.bellowslaw.com*

- Jo Benson Fogel -

"It was clear that those with whom I worked . . . could not afford to pay associates what they were worth . . . and that they really had no intention of considering a woman as someone with whom they would share a business interest."

In your early thirties? Have young children? Is there an upside to going out on your own? From the clarity of the rear view mirror, here goes....

Admitted to practice in 1971, the move to start a practice of my own occurred in 1977. It was clear that those with whom I worked had such big personal overheads they could not afford to pay associates what they were worth in terms of work performed, and that they really had no intention of considering a woman as someone with whom they would share a business interest. Despite statements to the contrary, they would look askance at me if I arrived at the office at 9:30 after driving carpool, while they had no compunction about leaving the office on a weekday to go to play golf with potential clients. For the most part they were good lawyers, fair businessmen, and helpful colleagues. At the time, I was too naïve to be angry about their financial myopia toward me and my work product. Not likely they would have been receptive to any ideas I might propound.

The biggest impetus to the self-confidence I needed to start my own litigation practice was the excellent experience I gained as a judicial law clerk.

TIP: If you believe that you are interested in trial/court work, do apply for a trial court judicial clerkship—early and often. For state courts, research the judges who attended the law school (or undergraduate school) that you attended.

Business Development
I did work for one national corporation that considered my status as a woman-owned firm an important part of their statistics, but I had been doing work for them because of my lower fees and local connections long before

they saw the "advantage" of reporting, when necessary, that I was a woman-owned firm.

The focus of my practice has become family law. I often attended and continue to attend programs presented by mental health professionals. Frequently, I was the only lawyer in attendance, which resulted in my receiving many referrals, while at the same time learning to manage myself in difficult situations so that I could provide the best legal services for clients under extreme stress. Business development seems to be easiest when you are amongst those who aren't around lawyers day in and day out.

Business Models

Because there were no courses in law school about running a business (and I doubt that I would have known to be interested), mastering the learning curve of running a business is crucial.

TIP: The American Management Association has business operations training for businesses of all sizes. The concepts and implementation of long range planning and developing business plans are core elements that must be learned if one is to have a law practice that sustains the owner and employees. The American Bar Association and, more recently, all state bar associations have law practice management training for lawyers. The advantage of a non-lawyer training is that you also gain some insight into the best business practices for your potential clients, and you may well meet potential clients as you start out with such seminars and training. Anecdotally, I have received a lot of referrals to my core practice because I understand how business obligations and family interactions affect all aspects of the client's life.

TIP: Budget a lot of time and money for state and local bar association activities. In these activities, there are many resources for business development, and the associations always have openings for volunteers to do worthwhile work, which sometimes brings productive peer recognition.

As work expanded, I spent a lot of time working on an office procedures manual and hiring techniques. I became active in the state bar Law Practice Management Section and joined the ABA section so that I could receive the ABA Law Practice Management publication. There were always helpful articles and meeting information that were of assistance to me.

TIP: Allocate at least 10 days a year for continuing law practice management education for at least the first five years. The time and money are formidable with a start-up but will provide great rewards if you find you like being your own boss.

What I Wish I Had Known and Might Do Different Today

I wish I had known more about opportunities to decide about useful partnerships or collegial affiliations. I think that these opportunities exist today, and were it not for my age, I would be much more active in seeking out financial and office arrangements with peers equal in competence, practice goals, and interests. In retrospect, I would be more active in that arena, because today I am facing the possible winding down of my practice and looking for ways to be compensated for bringing business to colleagues while cutting down on the administrative and business operations responsibilities required in an active local practice. I am still seeking a successful strategy for getting the most out of my prior efforts while carving out more time to enjoy this time in my life.

TIP: Attend any nuts and bolts courses offered by local or state bar associations and stay in touch with the lawyers who put on the program. We began the "Nuts and Bolts of Starting a Law Practice" program in my state while I was on the Law Practice Management Section Council. I have noticed that a number of "graduates" of that program have gone on to conduct successful practices, and I learned a lot from the other presenters whenever I was on a panel. Lawyers are very generous with their colleagues, and they are usually very useful in helping the new business owner avoid reinventing the wheel.

TIP: Look into financing early and often. Apply for a line of credit or equipment loan even if you do not need it, so that you can establish a business credit history. When you are considering expansion, you may have more obligations than you can afford without a line of credit. Comply with the disclosures. Find a savvy and energetic loan officer similar in age to you who is looking to establish credibility at his or her employer, and develop a good business relationship. If the bank you are working with is not open to your new proposals for financing, look for another one, but don't leave one until you have another lined up.

The Rear View Mirror

I wish I had gotten on the road to independence sooner. I know that start-up costs are higher now than when I began, but the psychic costs of being where you do not want to be and the psychic benefits of finding your own strengths far outweigh the anxiety of the start-up. Five years out, I had discovered my strengths and what I enjoyed in the practice of law. I should not have waited quite so long to "just do it." There were many on the road to independence long before the ABA finally realized that the establishment of a Commission on Women in the Profession might really be important to the profession. It is heartening to see the masthead of this august group, but I know that each of them had to be an advocate for themselves in uncharted professional territory.

Looking Out to the Future

I see that I could go on professionally for many more years in various environments as long as my brain and health remain at least at today's level. I am still operating under the same business model and have a weakness for hiring complementary people, not succession people.

Minor Regret

I have very little turnover but no one interested in taking ownership responsibility.

Do it, if you love to learn and are forever interested in the people from whom you learn, such as colleagues, clients, vendors, and adversaries of all kinds. Perhaps it is not the road to independence but the route to interdependence that has made this professional journey so interesting and mostly rewarding. Have Phun!

Jo Benson Fogel is the president of Jo Benson Fogel PA in Rockville, Maryland, where her trial practice focuses on family disputes, including divorce, custody, property disposition, guardianships, and contested estates. She graduated from law school in 1970 and founded her firm in 1977. *www.jobensonfogellaw.com*

- JANET RUBEL -

*"I was overcome with morning sickness in the midst of a motion call,
and the judge failed to pass my case. . . . For the next five years that
judge offered me his private bathroom and chambers
every time I walked into his courtroom."*

Hanging My Shingle or How I Went into Labor During the Bar Exam and Became a Solo Practitioner

I married my first and only husband during the first year of law school in
1976. We became engaged shortly before I began classes in January. To be exact, he asked me to marry him after the first date. I, well, my mother, wanted
a June wedding so I became a bride a few days after completing first semester
final exams.

This background is necessary to set the scene for my decision to go into private
practice after graduation. There were not too many job interviews for pregnant
women. The few interviews I managed to arrange before I was pregnant were
not promising. At one memorable interview with a Big Law firm I was told I
smiled too much to be an effective lawyer. At another Big Law outfit interview
a male attorney noted I was married and asked what kind of birth control I
used. That session ended abruptly when I told him what I thought of him and
that question.

It occurred to me that maybe a law firm job was not in my future. I come from
a long line of self-employed business owners who had told previous boss-
wannabes what they could do with their jobs.

I went into labor during the bar exam. Shortly afterward, my first daughter,
now an attorney practicing with me, was born. We had just built a home in a
new area, which was rapidly filling with new residents of mostly young families.
This seemed to be a promising site for a young attorney to open a practice.

After a brief partnership with a young male lawyer, I decided to fly solo. I shared space with another young attorney whose practice focused on business matters. I decided to concentrate on family law but did take a few detours into bankruptcy and a few other areas.

What does a young attorney just starting out in the law do without funds to hire a secretary? She hires her mother! Mom would not take any money. She decided to dress the part and went on a shopping spree for "career gal attire." No slacks for this office! I was fortunate she had only recently relaxed her hats and gloves policy—for both of us.

After my mother purchased the wardrobe required of my Della Street (and if you have to ask who she was, your legal education is sadly lacking; you need to watch *Perry Mason* reruns or the great old movies starring Warren William, who really did study law before embarking on an acting career), we were ready to welcome our first clients. Unfortunately, there weren't any.

My mother was quite the efficient receptionist/secretary. She mothered the clients and offered such a sympathetic ear that they wanted to sit in the outer office and chat with her instead of consulting me. I learned that she was such a good listener that the clients frequently decided to reconcile with their spouses instead of divorcing.

The end of my mother's well-intentioned tenure in my office was partly my father's fault. My parents, as aforementioned, ran their own businesses from their nearby home. This afforded them lots of time to hang out in my office. As my father, notoriously tight with a dollar, pointed out to me with some glee, it was cheaper for him to sit in my air-conditioned office than to turn his air conditioning on at home.

My father liked to sit in the office and kibitz with my mother, reading my newspapers and magazines, tearing out articles for his future reference, drinking my free coffee and tea and eating the occasional cookie (when my mother wasn't looking), and schmoozing with the clients.

At the time, I was taking simple bankruptcy cases. (How I hated those multi-set carbon copy typed filings; even with the snazzy state-of-the-art IBM Selectric II self-correcting typewriter my parents gave me when I graduated from law school, it was a pain to type those.) I could not figure out why potential clients called for bankruptcy consultations but never made it in the door to my office. Then one day I happened to walk into the reception area to find my father lounging on the couch and loaning a possible bankruptcy client a few dollars so he wouldn't have to file. I learned that this was a frequent occurrence.

I don't know if my father was ever repaid by my erstwhile bankruptcy clients or if my mother was able to repair broken marriages in my waiting room, but the handwriting was on my office wall: "Parents must go!"

After my parents retired from their daughter's practice of law and moved over to "help" at the law office of one of my brothers, I tried to hire a new part-time secretary. This began an endless stream of unemployable people: those who were very late for the interview, those who came drunk or high, those who took more breaks than they worked, secretaries who would not type or answer my phones, secretaries who tried to make dates with male divorce clients, and others who had no filing, typing, or office skills. My parents' return to the office began to look appealing.

Before the Internet, websites, cell phones, and other marketing tools, there was good, old-fashioned face-to-face contact. Now, I like sitting at home in my pajamas and practicing law as much as anyone else, but there is no substitute for getting out to bar association meetings, community groups, social clubs, and the local schools your children attend to press the flesh. I must emphasize that while meeting fellow lawyers is vital, it is equally important to meet actual, paying, possible clients.

Cultivate friendly relationships with colleagues. Clients come and go, but fellow members of the bar are around for a long time. Experienced attorneys can be a great source of help to a fellow lawyer starting her own practice. Some of the best advice I received was from older male attorneys (there were very few women attorneys in private practice then) who prefaced their advice with "Sweetheart," "Doll," or other now politically incorrect terms of address. I ignored the words because no insult was intended, and focused on the very useful information.

You may receive referrals and overflow work from other attorneys, but there is no substitute for your own clients. The responsibility is great but the rewards are commensurate. It is imperative to choose your clients carefully. There will be many characters that darken your doorstep and waste your time. Many lawyers offer free consultations. I offered them, too, until I realized I was spending entire days giving free consultations. This did not help the bottom line.

Practicing law and having children is possible, but not easy. I made my own hours. Once at a bar association luncheon, I caught myself cutting my colleague's steak into small pieces for him. I was overcome with morning sickness in the midst of a motion call, and the judge failed to pass my case. You can imagine what happened next. For the next five years that judge offered me his private bathroom and chambers every time I walked into his courtroom.

One morning my babysitter called in sick at the last minute. My parents were very helpful about watching my daughters but were not available that morning. I had to be in court so I dressed my toddlers and took them along with me. The jail matron watched them for me in the administrative offices. Yes, I have the only toddlers who have done hard time.

The best thing about solo practice is that there are no staff meetings, no office politics, and no lay-offs. You can hire your sullen teenagers for summer jobs answering the office telephones. Maybe you will have better luck than I did getting them to roll out of bed in time to be at the office by 8:30 in the morning. (Perhaps your offspring can learn to answer the phones, "Hello, law offices," instead of, "Yeah.") One of those reluctant law office employees may even become a lawyer.

Opening your own law practice is very challenging, frustrating, and nerve-wracking. I recommend it highly.

JANET RUBEL is a solo practitioner in Northbrook, Illinois, where she focuses on family law. She graduated from law school in 1978 and founded her practice in 1979.

- Elizabeth J. Cabraser -

"You will gain something far more valuable than dollars: respect and admiration from your professional peers, especially your women colleagues, and that intangible sense of integrity and credibility that comes from striking out on your own, unbeholden to a larger institution."

I understand that you are considering forming your own law firm. Congratulations! I wish you every success and satisfaction in forming your own firm and in forging your own career.

Thirty-two years ago, I made a similar decision. I had just graduated from law school and was clerking for a solo practitioner in Sonoma County, California. My boss, Robert Lieff, had by age 40 achieved a successful career, including a stint as law partner to a famous plaintiffs' trial lawyer, and had decided to scale down his practice to pursue his longtime passion for viticulture. He had moved to Sonoma to restore an old winery and plant a vineyard. My initial task was to help him close out his files, after which I would be free to pursue my legal career—elsewhere. I so enjoyed the independence of working in a small (two-lawyer) firm that I could not bring myself to interview with a large firm or work for a "real" boss. Somehow, I managed to persuade Bob to continue as a lawyer, so that I could continue to work for him, doing what I loved: representing plaintiffs in a wide array of cases. To make a long (and improbable) story short, we continued the law firm. Bob was gracious enough to underscore his faith in my abilities (or at least in my potential) by making me a full and equal partner in our little firm, and we soldiered on.

Today, Lieff Cabraser continues to represent plaintiffs in litigation in the federal and state courts, with an emphasis on complex litigation in the fields of securities and investment fraud, antitrust, consumer class actions, product liability, employment rights and human rights, and mass torts. We continue to work on a contingent basis only, relying on private contingent fee agreements, or, more frequently, court-awarded attorney's fees. It continues to be a wild ride: risky, exciting, exhilarating, intensely interesting, and, we hope, worthwhile. We have managed to survive, and often prosper, notwithstanding the increasing cost of litigation and the increasing burdens of high overhead.

While Lieff Cabraser has grown to three offices (our "mothership" in San Francisco, plus New York and Nashville), we are true to our roots. I am fortunate to be surrounded by extremely talented colleagues. Over 40 percent of our partners are women. Our longstanding commitment to diversity and equal opportunity is self-serving: we know that those principles will attract the best and brightest to our firm. I have no business training and, quite frankly, little business or organizational aptitude. If I could make a "go" of a litigation boutique, a contingent fee-only law firm, and a plaintiffs-only law firm, so can you. In fact, you'll probably do much better, notwithstanding the growing challenges of law practice.

To give you the pitfalls and the "would've, could've, should've" laments first: of course having basic business training, including bookkeeping, would have stood me in good stead. I would also advise, despite my notoriety as a Luddite, that you stay on top of computer training, utilize the tremendous resources now offered online, and be unafraid of new gadgets and technologies. These level the playing field between big firms and solo practitioners to an amazing extent.

A business plan is particularly important, since you are likely to be surviving on a line of credit. Be realistic, and take the time to find a sympathetic banker. Many banks, including Citibank and First Republic, have private banking departments that specialize in lawyers and law firms. They will understand your issues and your needs.

In addition to becoming technologically adept and having a basic business plan, learning to be a politician and diplomat, in the best sense of both words, is essential. I know you don't want to hear the word "networking" one more time, but it is important to get yourself, and your talents, widely known. Do join and stay active in your local bar associations and not-for-profit organizations that have attracted other legal professionals and judges. Share what you know by being a speaker and writer for CLE programs. Yes, these are investments of precious time and energy without financial remuneration (except for those ever-essential CLE credits), but they are uniquely valuable investments in your professional development, visibility, and ultimate prosperity.

Do not undervalue yourself. If you are working on an hourly basis, resist the urge to deeply discount your hourly rate. Charge what you are worth: what attorneys of similar experience, in your field, charge in the small/medium law firms in your area. No, you won't charge big-firm rates, because you don't have big-firm overhead, and good value is an attribute that will set you apart. But do not set your fees unrealistically—and unprofitably—low.

Another asset you have, that larger or more institutional firms don't, is client attention. Big firm attorneys can often not give sufficient attention to clients, because this "hand holding" is not billable. You are now free of many of the pressures of the billable hour and can choose to utilize your time to communicate with your clients. They will appreciate the attention, they deserve it, and they will be especially grateful for not being charged for the time you are investing in understanding them and their concerns.

None of these ideas are unique, new, or startling. The key is to implement and practice them consistently. You will likely be struggling financially, for more than a few months, or perhaps more than a few years, as you establish your practice and your name. Be not afraid. Financial success is not necessarily the sole mark of favor or merit. You are investing in yourself, and you are worth the financial sacrifice that it takes to establish and develop your own firm today. In the process, you will gain something far more valuable than dollars: respect and admiration from your professional peers, especially your women colleagues, and that intangible sense of integrity and credibility that comes from striking out on your own, unbeholden to a larger institution. This asset will not only stand you in good stead and ultimately pay dividends in the success of your practice; it will enhance your clients' causes and credibility as well. That alone makes the endeavor worthwhile.

Finally, do not hesitate to bend the ear of more experienced practitioners who are making a go of it with their own firms. Yes, they may be your competitors, but they are also willing to help you and share specific stories and tips that are pertinent to your geographic and practice area. Just remember to return the favor, via professional courtesy, and be ready and willing to help them out in a pinch. We are all in this together. That is the secret to professional satisfaction and success.

All the best.

ELIZABETH J. CABRASER is a founding partner of Lieff Cabraser Heimann & Bernstein, LLP in San Francisco, California, where she focuses on class actions, products liability, and complex consumer litigation. She graduated from law school in 1978 and, beginning in 1978, worked with Robert L. Lieff to encourage that they both remain in practice together; she became partner in 1980. *www.lchb.com*

CHAPTER 2

1980–1989

The Early Movers— Experimenting with Individual Reasons to Strike Out

---

"There was a time, back in the early '90s, when I was told we were the largest women-owned law firm in the state of Illinois. I'm glad that there are many more majority-women firms now, including a number that are larger than ours."

—Fay Clayton

This decade's letters mark the onset of women drawn toward alternative practice forms for highly individual and personal reasons. There are eight letters in this group.

The five writers who had graduated from law school in the 1970s did not start their firms until four to 12 years later. One such writer, only four years out of law school, saw in 1976 that firms were reluctant to hire women and decided "to determine her own destiny" and to "show that women could run a business." Another, who started her firm after 12 years of practice, worked in a close husband/wife team to accomplish balance. She believed that a working parent could "have it all." This theme is crystallized by a writer in practice in France, who recalls her woman friend and colleague saying at lunch, "I am sick of working for others. What do you think of starting a firm?"

The three who graduated in the '80s started firms within the first four years after graduation. One of them continues in her solo practice today, and one practiced while earning her LL.M. in taxation. The third continued for years and recently merged into a larger established firm. To her, one of the proudest days of her life after gaining citizenship was opening her own firm in 1988.

In this decade, women who believed it possible to start a successful law practice did so for varying purposes. Their reasons—from proving women could run a firm business to finding balance—forecast issues that women would continue to confront in traditional practice two decades later.

- MARGARET L. BEHM -

*"Our office became a place for proactive pursuits and
socializing. These meetings kept our firm on the minds
of many and are part of the fabric of history of the
women's movement in Nashville."*

I grew up in Murfreesboro, Tennessee, in the 1950s and 1960s. The town
revolved around the courthouse square, one high school, and a small town
university. Despite prescribed roles for women, my parents' example fostered
my road to independence.

My parents were fiercely independent. Although early marriage was the norm
in their time, they spent their twenties as working, single adults and married
in their thirties, in 1950 after World War II. My mother, Adeline Dismukes,
traveled as a young woman to DC to work on the Manhattan Project and,
after the war, was secretary to the Allied Commander in Berlin. My dad,
Howard Behm, was brilliant at math and was captain of an artillery unit that
marched through the Hürtgen Forest. My parents met in Berlin, first settled
in New York, and after I was born, moved to Murfreesboro. My twin sisters
were born 11 months after me.

My father, now dubbed a Yankee in Murfreesboro, was viewed as an outsider.
As I grew up, I was one of the few students whose mother had to work. My
mom was a legal secretary who was as bright as the lawyers. She knew all the
legal players in town and ran the office. When I was at the law office after
school, clients would leave the office thanking lawyers for helping them.
My dad had several jobs, but after working as a nursing home inspector and
being troubled by what he saw, he used his math acumen to help an entrepreneur start and run a successful group of nursing homes. Both parents liked to
take charge, but they weren't their own bosses. After listening to their frustrations through the years, I knew I needed to develop the skills to determine
my own destiny.

Thankfully, the law school doors opened for women. After I graduated from the University of Tennessee College of Law in Knoxville, I was lucky to get a job at Legal Services in Nashville, thanks to my future husband who knew the director. I was one of a few lawyers from the University of Tennessee in a city dominated by Vanderbilt lawyers. Firms were reluctant to hire women, unless they were at the top of Vanderbilt's class, or well-connected, or both.

After four years at Legal Services, I knew I wanted to be in private practice in Nashville, but I also knew I didn't want to be in a large firm. The opportunities were limited. In addition to having a desire to control my own destiny and not be pigeonholed, I also had an inner passion to demonstrate that women could run a business. Even without a business background, I wanted to give it a try.

I decided to find a law partner who was well-respected in the community. Marietta Shipley was a district attorney handling child support cases. In 1980, we formed Shipley & Behm, the first women-owned law firm in Nashville. We practiced together until Marietta became a trial judge in 1990. In 1988, we had merged with my husband's law firm. Now the firm is called Dodson Parker Behm & Capparella, P.C., and sometimes Behm & Them! We have 12 lawyers, and seven of them are women.

Today, 30 years later, I'm grateful I took the plunge—and believe me, it is a plunge. When we started our firm, we had no client base because our previous clients qualified under poverty guidelines. What we had, however, was an incredible, supportive group of male and female lawyers who wanted to see us succeed. These lawyers and our friends were our top referral sources. In fact, today lawyers and community leaders still comprise about half of our referral sources. Client referrals, which started at zero, now represent the other half of our referrals.

Getting started, Marietta and I were active in many organizations, especially women's organizations. Our office became a place for proactive pursuits and socializing. These meetings kept our firm on the minds of many and are part of the fabric of history of the women's movement in Nashville.

In developing our practice, we took cases in which we had no prior experience and found prominent lawyers in the field to help us. We kept in touch with these lawyers, and down the road, we received referrals from them. These

lawyers also helped us understand how to charge for our services. I found myself telling folks I handled cases that I wanted to handle, not just the actual
type of cases I was handling. This both increased our business and helped me
develop a practice around the areas of law I enjoyed most.

Getting financing for our new business was tough. Male loan officers were
not accustomed to women starting businesses. Worse, interest rates were
hovering around 18 to 22 percent. Eventually, we decided to diligently search
for a woman commercial lender and found one! We obtained a $25,000 line of
credit, secured by Marietta's certificate of deposit—in a larger amount. All I
could have put up as collateral was a used vehicle worth $1,000 at best.

I was fortunate to start a business without debt. After a couple of years, our
firm no longer needed the line of credit. Since then, we have never taken
out a loan to finance operating expenses. We survive by eating what we kill
every month. When we have a good month, we save, and then we take a nice
draw. We have used multiple methods of billing, including value billing, for
years. With this method of cash flow, the firm has survived with relative ease
through four recessions, including the current Great Recession.

One of the biggest factors in our success has been the quality and loyalty of
our staff. Probably due to watching my mother, I especially view our staff
as essential to our success. Our office manager has been with us for over 25
years, and the paralegal with whom I work has been with the firm for 12
years. Also crucial to our success has been our responsive and innovative
technology contractor.

As for lawyers, we look for certain types. Our lawyers do interesting things
with their lives, things which may be wholly unrelated to the practice of law
but which demonstrate uniqueness of character. We look for a passion and
commitment to community service. Finally, we find that those who understand the entrepreneurial spirit are quicker to understand how to function
in a small law office. These qualities demonstrate a commitment to service,
and this responsiveness to clients from our staff and lawyers is the key to our
success.

From a management point of view, we have to stay on top of issues, even
though we can tire of addressing the same ones repeatedly. However, if these
issues aren't addressed directly and quickly, more damage is done, and more

nonbillable time is needed to fix the problem. Like all firms, we face the challenge of keeping good lawyers and allowing for flexibility while meeting expectations. My biggest pet peeve is dealing with annual health insurance rate hikes, which, according to the insurance companies, are triggered because we employ so many women of childbearing age. Thankfully, we are healthy overall, but our commitment to insuring our small group is a challenge.

As I look back, my joy in owning my own business is intertwined with my love of practicing law. The skills I use for problem solving in the business are the same skills I use for solving the problems clients bring to us. As with all law practices, there have been tense times and intense periods of work. But, I make good money and have the freedom to practice in the many areas I enjoy, areas that change through the years. As a business owner, I understand my business clients. Additionally, I have had the flexibility to teach at the law school, work in political campaigns, and assume leadership positions in the community. Most of all, I have had the independence that has allowed me to be a Girl Scout leader, coach my children's sports teams, and attend those important childhood events.

Thirty years ago our firm needed a line of credit to rent some affordable space. Now, we own a beautiful building in quaint Germantown, close to downtown Nashville. Like the courthouse square in Murfreesboro, there are sidewalks, restaurants, a mix of businesses and residences, and plenty of street parking. We are in a new space, but we still operate under the same old business model—a model that allows clients to leave our office thanking lawyers for helping them. What a great place to go every day.

MARGARET L. BEHM is the managing principal at Dodson Parker Behm & Capparella, PC in Nashville, Tennessee, where she focuses her practice on business transactions, employment law, commercial litigation, and municipal law. She graduated from law school in 1976 and founded her firm in 1980. *www.dodsonparker.com*

- PHYLLIS HORN EPSTEIN -

"In years gone by, there was a perceived stigma attached to solo and small firm lawyers, often thought of as lawyers inferior in experience to their large firm colleagues who engaged in specialty practice."

I started practicing law as a solo right after law school while teaching contract law at La Salle University and attending night school for a masters degree in tax law at the same time. In a short time I had a breadth of legal experience, was quick to learn what I loved and what I didn't love in the practice of law, and realized how law school had failed to prepare me for the nuts and bolts of practicing law, running an office, and experiencing a satisfying lifestyle.

I became an associate in a small firm in my city, Philadelphia, and eventually a partner. Today this is the office my husband and I work at full time in the practice of tax law. A small firm where I am partner has been, for me, the best way to practice law. When your name is over the door there is enormous freedom to control the important aspects of a practice: which clients to take on, which to let go, what to charge, when and to what extent to work pro bono, what cases to pursue, what specialty to apply, and what bar activities in which to participate.

In a small firm I have the independence to pursue work that is satisfying in an office I enjoy, doing work that is challenging and professionally satisfying, with the flexibility to balance the scales with family, friends, and individual pursuits. While some time is spent on office management, the decision to partake in bar-related and community-related activities, or even to write a book, requires no one else's approval. Perhaps the best reason for having my name on the letterhead is the flexibility I have, and have had, to be a mom who is able to drop off her son at the beginning of the school day and pick him up at the end, and to be there for those special events or illness. I've been to the pet parade, the Halloween parade, school plays, orchestra performances, class trips to historic sites, doctor appointments (planned and emergencies), play dates, lunches with my mom and friends, and vacations with the family without the enforced pressures of billable hour requirements. I even have the flexibility to leave the office to pick up dinner for my family. I wouldn't have missed any of it.

In years gone by, there was a perceived stigma attached to solo and small firm lawyers, often thought of as lawyers inferior in experience to their large firm colleagues who engaged in a specialty practice. In those days we were sometimes thought of as lawyers who would take any case in order to get business. But those days are long gone. Today solo practitioners and small firm lawyers often limit their practice to one or more specialties and their practices are considered to be boutiques. My firm, for example, has a practice largely limited to corporate, estate planning, probate, and tax planning and tax controversies. Other matters are generally referred to other boutique firms who practice in an area that we do not, or to larger firms who have a specialty that our clients require, so that our clients can rely upon us to provide them with the close attention that they could rarely expect to receive as a small fish in a very large pond. That approach, along with the benefit of today's technology, permits me to maintain an expertise and professionalism while, at the same time, allowing me the freedom and control that makes my professional and private life so rewarding.

PHYLLIS HORN EPSTEIN is an owner at Epstein, Shapiro & Epstein, P.C. in Philadelphia, Pennsylvania, where she focuses on tax planning, tax litigation, estate planning and gifts, nonprofit organizations, and commercial transactions. She graduated from law school and became a solo practitioner in 1980, eventually moving to become a partner in her small firm in 1985. *www.eselaw.com*

- LESLIE J. LOTT -

"It was terrifying to start a solo practice,
but that was, to me, the only way forward.
The basic plan was to work like hell and not look back."

You have been kind enough to ask about how I came to found my law firm and what the experience has been like. Thank you for a welcome opportunity to look back on the past 27 years and reflect on all that has happened.

In 1983, I left the Miami general practice firm where I had been working as a litigation associate, and started a solo intellectual property practice.

I had graduated from law school nine years earlier, started my professional life with the United States Patent and Trademark Office in Washington, DC, and then moved to New York City and a 100-year-old intellectual property firm. During my time there, I traveled to the Kingdom of Saudi Arabia on a two-year leave of absence and practiced with a firm in Jeddah, where I learned what it is like to be in the minority not only due to my gender but also my religion, my ethnicity, my culture, and my national origin—but that is another story.

On my return from Saudi Arabia, I moved to Miami, Florida, with my husband, Michael Moore, a maritime attorney, and our aging but loveable beagle. I worked with a terrific general litigation firm whose lawyers were almost an exact one-to-one match with the characters on *L.A. Law,* a television show that was popular at the time.

I had assumed I would arrive and land a job with the best intellectual property firm in Miami. I had practiced intellectual property law in three world-class cities on two continents. I had worked in the Patent and Trademark Office itself, arguably the best possible post-graduate training. The only trouble was—there weren't any intellectual property firms in Miami. There was a small patent practice, but that was about it.

It was terrifying to start a solo practice, but that was, to me, the only way forward. The basic plan was to work like hell and not look back. My natural fiscal conservatism greatly affected the business plan, such as it was. I started practicing out of my home in Coral Gables. Personal computers had just come on the market (I knew one lawyer who actually had one) and they were not user-friendly. It is difficult to even remember the old DOS operating system, but I calculated the cost of hiring a secretary as opposed to buying a PC, and there was no comparison. A good friend from law school had an office nearby, and he let me use his conference room when I needed to meet clients.

The practice grew day by day, week by week, and client by client. I became actively involved in just about anything that touched on intellectual property. I represented local restaurants, clothing stores, and even a roofing contractor, registering their trademarks and sending out cease and desist letters when others came too close for comfort. I worked with inventors, songwriters, designers, artists, and a puppeteer on patents and copyright matters. I tried federal trademark and patent cases, ranging from outboard engines to windshield protectors.

I also became active in the International Trademark Association (INTA), the Florida Association for Women Lawyers, and the Florida Bar. On the Florida Bar Intellectual Property Committee, I chaired the subcommittee responsible for writing the trademark examination manual for the Florida secretary of state. This resulted in speaking engagements around the state. By then, I was also expecting our first child.

In time, I became vice-chair and ultimately chair of the Florida Bar IP Law Committee, titles which brought with them a seat on the Florida Bar Business Section Executive Council. Colleagues from the council who practiced in other areas of business law (bankruptcy, commercial litigation, banking, etc.), in many, much-appreciated instances, referred intellectual property work to my firm.

I wrote an article on the basics of patent, trademark, and copyright law that was published in the *Florida Bar Journal*. Years later, referring counsel were still citing the article to me as the reason for their call. They had kept it in their offices, in case they had an intellectual property question in the future.

INTA was equally helpful. I served on and chaired a number of different committees, was appointed to two terms on the board of directors, and made close friends among many in-house trademark counsel, including counsel for one company whose trademark counterfeiting litigation we handled in South Florida for years. I was fortunate to have been named to the Panel of Distinguished Neutrals for the Resolution of Trademark Disputes.

One thing that I did not expect: it turned out that sometimes being a woman could be a significant advantage. When I practiced in New York, a few years before starting my own firm, there were many meetings I attended, let alone court appearances, in which I was the only woman in the room. Women lawyers were enough of a novelty in those days that we were noticed—never a bad thing when you are trying to build a practice.

My first associate was another woman, and at one time, the firm was an all-women shop. But soon, as the practice grew, we brought in a young patent attorney and litigator from an Atlanta firm, a man who had clerked for me during law school. The young patent associate, David Friedland, became my name partner, and we have since brought in more partners (including a trademark litigator and another patent attorney) and we currently have four associate attorneys and three paralegal assistants. Our numbers have fluctuated very little with the boom times and the recessions we have experienced over the years. We have essentially been a 10-lawyer firm, and that has been a comfortable size for us. Our hiring has always been client-driven. From time to time we have brought in lateral hires, but our biggest successes have come in promoting lawyers from within the firm.

I hope you will forgive my saying so, but I am very proud of our firm. Our lawyers have consistently been recognized for excellence including Best Lawyers "Lawyer of the Year" of 2010 in Intellectual Property Law for the Miami Area; Florida Bar Board Certification in Intellectual Property Law; "The Best Lawyers in America" since 1995; *South Florida Legal Guide's* "Top Lawyers in South Florida" since 2001; *Florida Trend's* "Florida Legal Elite" since 2004; "Florida Super Lawyers" since 2005; *Guide to the World's Leading Trademark Attorneys* since 1998; and *World Trademark Review* "Trademark Experts' Experts" since 2007.

I continue to practice with the firm and enjoy it very much. It continues to be a wonderful experience and a wonderful professional life, and there is nothing I would change, especially my excellent choice of law partners, if I do say so myself. As new associates come in, I tell them we have three rules: (1) the client comes first; (2) always give us your *best* work; and (3) *never* come into my office without a legal pad.

That brings to mind another three-part recipe for success. For clients to hire a lawyer, they have to know you, they have to like you, and most importantly, they have to believe you can get the job done. The rest is up to you. Good luck and God bless!

LESLIE J. LOTT is the founding partner of Lott & Friedland in Coral Gables, Florida, where she focuses on intellectual property law. She graduated from law school in 1974 and founded her firm in 1983. *www.lott-friedland.com*

- SALLI ANNE SWARTZ -

"For me, the practice of law is most fulfilling when the environment is the most satisfying. . . . [S]tarting a firm is one of the best ways to be successful and self-fulfilled."

My story is one of the most unlikely you may read in this wonderful collection, but I would hope that its underpinnings will give you the insight and courage you may need to go out there, be your own person, and start your own firm, either alone or with others.

I had been practicing international arbitration and corporate and commercial French and international business law in Paris for eight years with three different firms, including a big accounting firm, before I jumped off the cliff.

The mover in this venture was my French woman friend and colleague Caroline, who had moved firms with me each time. Frustrated with the big accounting firm mentality and having just passed the French bar and been admitted to practice as an *avocat*, she said to me over lunch one day: "I am sick of working for others. What do you think of starting a firm?"

Not wanting to insult her evident enthusiasm, I gently asked her if she had any clients who would support this new venture because, I quickly added, I had none, had no idea how to get any, had no social contacts in France (or elsewhere for that matter), and was generally at a total loss as to how to go about starting a firm anywhere, never mind in a country where I did not have citizenship.

To my utter astonishment, she said: "Don't worry. I am sure we will find clients and figure out how to practice together."

That evening I put the idea on the table at the same time as dinner. Another astonishing reaction from my husband: Yes, definitely, go do it!

So in the space of 24 hours, I decided to start a firm with another woman.

We had no idea what we were getting ourselves into, but I can reassure you that we were a success from the start.

The first steps were either difficult or easy depending on whether you are a glass half-full or half-empty type of person.

To start with, neither Caroline nor I ever thought we were doing anything bizarre; it never occurred to us that we were in any way different from two male lawyers who were starting a law firm. We didn't read any books or go see experienced attorneys to get advice. Neither of us had mentors, and neither of us were independently wealthy. We just decided to create a small boutique firm specialized in international business. No one discouraged us. To the contrary, our immediate entourages were very encouraging and so were our male colleagues.

For instance, when we went shopping for a banker, we used a banker who came highly recommended from a fellow (male) law firm entrepreneur. Our banker was very instructive and helped us put together our first business plan and helped us with our first purchases of equipment and furniture, as well as other financing later.

Nor was it difficult finding the first clients. In fact, contrary to what I believed was Caroline's home state advantage, I brought in more clients than she did. I suspect this was due to my having the title of "American" attached to my name, which attracted clients who were doing business with the United States and more generally internationally. I started by doing their international work, and then when they saw my capabilities, they entrusted me with their French corporate work. This is not how it usually happens, but it worked!

Where it became a bit more difficult was in developing the credibility we needed to compete for the "big clients": the banks, the Fortune 500 companies, and the like. And this is where, in my opinion, we were at a major disadvantage, not necessarily only because we were women, but also because we did not have the gravitas of age nor the protection that clients perceive comes with a big firm name.

To be specific, and this may be particular to France, family and school contacts are everything. You will not be admitted to the networking social circles if you do not have the family relations and/or school diplomas of those in the same networking social circles. There is little or no crossover between social classes or evolution between them.

Caroline and I had neither advantage. But since we were making money, we really did not bemoan the situation right away. After the first year, we did take stock to analyze how we obtained our first clients and what type of marketing would work best for us. We decided that there was no purpose in hitting our heads against the wall and trying to get clients that were likely never to treat us on par with the big boys. What we decided to do is to investigate markets where we could make a difference and differentiate ourselves from the competition.

We did this in several ways.

First, we marketed ourselves as capable of rendering the same services we would render if we were still with our prior prestigious law firms but at greatly reduced billing rates: clients would get the same work product for at least 25 percent less than the client would pay at a bigger, more prestigious firm. Since we had the big firm credentials, all we needed to do was gain access to the clients and render ourselves credible. We did this by publishing articles, joining chambers of commerce, and for me, joining the ABA Section of International Law.

Second, we decided small was beautiful and that our goals were not growth, power, and making lots of money on the backs of a pyramid of associates. Rather, our goals were independence, self-sufficiency, and a good lifestyle. This could be accomplished by being efficient and productive and having good, reliable, and loyal staff. We worked late nights, weekends, and holidays when the acquisition or arbitration required it, but when it didn't, we did not pretend that we were overworked and overloaded. We went out and had a two-hour lunch, prospected potential contacts, and went shopping or to the gym (or both). We did not pretend to be anything other than what we were: smart, productive, and creative (international) business lawyers who were flexible and willing to work with a client to get the job done in a cost-effective manner.

Third, we decided that technology was an important partner in this venture, and we did what our budget permitted to get the highest quality technology available, such as laptops for working from home and travelling, telephone transfer services, e-mail and computer fax services, and the like, which was somewhat unusual for small firms in Paris in the early 1990s.

Did we encounter particular prejudices when starting the firm or thereafter because we were women and only because we were (and are) women? I would say that if either of us did, I remain unaware of it. In fact, I was subjected to more nasty remarks and prejudicial behavior when working for male-dominated French and international law firms than from clients and suppliers once I was in an independent firm.

What do I wish I knew before I began the firm? Would I have done anything different if I could do it all again?

I am not sure I would have done anything drastically different, but it would have been nice to have had a mentor who could have shared business plan drafting, budget ideas, and marketing ideas with us. I also would have joined the ABA much sooner, as it is a terrific forum for networking and learning.

Finally, perhaps if I had planned my career path and knew that after a certain number of years in a big firm I would be going out on my own, I would have made more of an effort to court clients when I had the possibility to do so in my prior firms.

What is clear is that if I could do it again, I would, and I have absolutely no regrets whatsoever about creating the firm. The only regret I have is that my partner Caroline left the law to become president of her family business. But as with most changes, life goes on, and I continued and still continue to grow my client base and have joined forces with other attorneys in order to give clients a full-service operation.

For me, the practice of law is most fulfilling when the environment is the most satisfying. I fully support women finding creative solutions to the practice of law and firmly believe that starting a firm is one of the best ways to be successful and self-fulfilled.

SALLI ANNE SWARTZ is a partner at Giraud Naud Amiot & Swartz in Paris, France, where she focuses on transnational business deals such as joint ventures, mergers and acquisitions, consortia, distribution, oil and gas projects, commercial and corporate mediations, and French commercial corporate labor law. She graduated from law school in 1977 and founded her firm in 1988.

- BRIGID A. DUFFIELD -

*"I fantasize that it would be nice if I didn't have
to pay for my medical insurance and if I had a regular paycheck.
Truth is, that is folly."*

What an exciting challenge you are considering taking on! As you contemplate this important decision, I hope you will find the answers that make the most sense for you, your family, and those you care most about, as well as provide you with a satisfying career that will last your lifetime.

Starting my own practice was not something I gave a lot of thought to. Although it was the path that, 25 years later, has worked well for me, doing it without giving it a lot of thought is not the way I would recommend anyone do it. I made a lot of mistakes along the way. Thankfully, I had countless wonderful mentors and friends who helped me both when I did and when I didn't need it.

My decision to start my own practice was made when I needed to leave a great job. It was "the job of a lifetime." When I left the corporate world, I knew myself well enough to know I don't always work well or play well with others. Having my own business and being my own boss and the boss of others fed my needs and ego in a way working for someone else couldn't.

That is not to say that when I opened my office, I was financially sound or even making money. That took time. I am financially conservative, and my debt tolerance is low. So though I wasn't making money, I wasn't losing my shirt or compromising my family's financial well-being. For most of my professional career, like so many of us, I have been the primary if not sole financial support for my family.

One of the challenges for me was my own arrogance. It was hard, sometimes impossible, for me to ask for help and really to trust that if I asked for help, my peers would not think I was stupid, make fun of me, or use my ignorance against me at a later date.

Men encouraged me and pointed me to the supportive women. These men under-stood that women playing in a man's world needed to share common experiences with other women. I am incredibly grateful to and still blessed by the men men-tors in my life and the women mentors who made it safe for me to ask questions and to be vulnerable. Today, I still count on those same mentors. I trusted these professionals, whom I credit with helping me to reach success in my practice—success that I have been able to nurture and sustain for more than 25 years.

Advice came from men and women, lawyers and non-lawyers. Of course, every-one had an opinion.

My best advice to anyone contemplating the decision to open a practice is, trust your gut. You will make mistakes...we all do. But being self-supporting, self-suf-ficient, and succeeding or failing because of the risks you decide to take and the ones you don't will be the most empowering business endeavor you will make.

Being a solo, in private practice, has afforded me the luxury of being able to modify and change my practice as I evolved and as my life and my needs changed. That is still true to this day.

Before I started in private practice, I was a lobbyist for a trade association, representing small businesses. I mistakenly believed that when I left my dream job, those business clients would follow me. I was so wrong. I rented space from a criminal/personal injury lawyer, then mentor, now judge, who began sending me his divorce cases. I never intended to do divorce, but I can. I was incredibly blessed to have found the career path that was the perfect fit for me. Domestic relations/family law is the kind of practice that evolves.

A year into my practice I married. My first year of marriage was challenging. Be-ing a divorce lawyer did not help. I would go home and think, "People get divorced over less things than go on in our home." I realized that though I enjoyed litiga-tion, I had to do more than just litigation, or I wouldn't stay married. Mediation gave me the opportunity to diversify within the family law practice area without losing my mind or compromising my marriage.

Over the years, my practice included divorce litigation, collaborative law, media-tion, and training lawyers and mental health professionals to be mediators. I am a teacher trainer by education and experience. I was approved by the Association for Conflict Resolution as one of a handful of approved mediation trainers in the United States. I became an approved MCLE provider. Both of these avenues allowed me to combine my teaching skills into my practice and expand doing things I enjoyed.

In August of 1990, I gave birth to my daughter. Private practice gave me the flexibility to work full time and still be a room mom and attend her Irish dancing recitals and basketball games through all her school years.

In May of 2008, as a solo practitioner, I was able to make the decision to modify my practice and care for my mother who was dying of pancreatic cancer. I withdrew from all of my litigation files, took on more mediation files, and became her primary caretaker until her death three months later. Being a private practitioner I was able to make that decision, one that I will never regret and one that had I been in a traditional law firm, I likely would not have been able to make.

In October 2009, I was diagnosed with breast cancer. As it turned out, though I am in and will remain in chemotherapy until February 2011, I have been able to continue to work full time and set my schedule and work around the surgeries, the treatment, and the side effects.

During challenging times, I have thought of "getting a real job." The funny thing is, these many years later, I sometimes think it's not a real job. I fantasize that it would be nice if I didn't have to pay for my medical insurance and if I had a regular paycheck. Truth is, that is folly.

As I look to the future, I see my firm continuing to succeed. I love the flexibility of working for myself, the joy of succeeding, the lessons learned from failure, and the freedom to move in directions that I want, whether or not it makes sense to anyone else.

So, my advice is follow your heart, trust your gut. No matter what you decide, make sure the path you choose is the right path for you. Only you know what you want your legacy to be. If you succeed, fabulous! If you fail, fabulous! But if you are thinking about opening up your own firm and never try, you will look back with regret, and in the end, that would be a tragedy.

I send my best wishes for your success as you contemplate your journey.

BRIGID A. DUFFIELD is an attorney and mediator at The Law Office of Brigid A. Duffield, P.C. in Wheaton, Illinois, where she focuses on family law and domestic relations issues. She graduated from law school in 1984 and founded her firm in 1988. *www.brigidduffield.com*

- DEBORA FAJER-SMITH -

"Whatever the chosen field, don't go out on a limb until you know you have either a loyal following or an unshakeable group of referrals."

My mother tells the story that really sums up my love for this country and the practice of law: When I was four years of age, my parents and I emigrated from Sao Paulo, Brazil to Worcester, Massachusetts. My father, a physician and scientist, was invited to work on research for the "Pill." Since it was the 1960s, adults would ask me, the little daughter of a physician, "Debora, when you grow up, will you be a nurse?" [Note: Not a doctor!] Mother says I would pause, look them sternly in the eye, and say, "No, I want to be an American!"

The reason I recite this anecdote is to make the point that after becoming an American citizen in 1974, opening my own law practice, July 1, 1988, was one of the proudest days of my life. [Note: You have to want it.] I was single. I had clerked in a private firm with a great mentor, and after passing the Maryland and Washington, DC bar exams, I stayed with the firm for three years. [Note: Make sure you have at least three years in the practice area you want for your new firm.]

Those three years gave me the opportunity to learn my trade from some of the best lawyers, to save money, and to build a network of important contacts and clients. My mentor in law was actually a male role model. I knew that once I left on my own, it would be my reputation that would be evaluated, not the firm's! I knew I would have to be committed to this great adventure and had many long days ahead. I welcomed the challenge to help others, establish myself, and hopefully, leave a lasting legacy. [Note: I worked in assisting the disabled, those injured in the line of duty, and those crippled by the negligence of others.] I carefully chose my old hometown of Bowie Maryland as the site of my new firm. I had roots in the community, and it was only a short drive from the law firm where I started. [Note: Do your homework—make sure the location actually supports your field of law.]

I worked on contingency cases, meaning I did not get paid unless I won. There were no monthly "billables" to count on. Fortunately, approximately 85 clients came with me from my old firm. I made an amicable departure, and the partners were very helpful. [Note: Do not burn bridges. Find the good part of every relationship.]

It was an exciting moment, but a scary one as well. I did not want to lose my townhouse. I had to pay the mortgage and student loans. However, it was the right time. [Note: You must set up the best economic conditions for your type of practice, secure very reasonable first year expenses, such as a good deal on rent, and secure at least a line of credit.]

Bowie, Maryland, a suburb outside of Washington, DC, was a family-oriented community, but it was also a hub for transitory government-related workers. Therefore, although I was able to keep increasing my client base, keeping a stable workforce was almost impossible. In time, I learned that only by improving the selection process and fostering a family-type atmosphere was the firm able to anchor our best folks. [Note: Certainly today, there are many organizations, experts, and tools available in careful hiring practices; however, the advice is still the same. Better to get the right person than just fill the spot with the wrong one.]

Bowie, even in the 1980s, was a community wherein women were already respected in their own right. We had a woman in Congress, Gladys Noon Spellman, whom I fortunately had the opportunity to work for on Capitol Hill. We had a woman mayor and several women delegates, as well as business owners. "Mothers," whether in the Boys & Girls Club or Girl Scouts, were clearly respected. I was coming home, and I bet on the community welcoming a woman trial lawyer. Luckily, I was right. [Note: Know your audience if you want to start out on your own or with partners, have some foundation underneath you that you can count on. Whatever the chosen field, don't go out on a limb until you know you have either a loyal following or an unshakeable group of referrals.]

The first six months were the hardest. Sleepless nights and days were spent finding people to teach me all that went into running a business. For computers, advertising, taxes, accounting, and human resources, you need good people you can trust. Do not forget that being a great lawyer is not enough; now you run a business. [Note: Keep excellent records and good business practices from the beginning.]

My letter to you has a very happy ending. After years of determination and hard work, my firm was very successful. Everyone has a different definition of success. My formula is a combination of exceeding monetary goals, being respected in my field, producing results for my clients, and always finding ways to "give back."

After 22 years, at age 50, I merged my law firm with Joseph, Greenwald & Laake, P.A. in Greenbelt, Maryland. Today, I am expanding my base, once again.

Best to all of you.

DEBORA FAJER-SMITH is of counsel to Joseph, Greenwald & Laake, P.A. in Greenbelt, Maryland, where she focuses on workers compensation and personal injury matters. She graduated from law school in 1984 and founded her own firm in 1988. *www.jgllaw.com*

- ELLEN A. PANSKY -

"Find some purely personal outlets for stress, preferably including physical activity. Do not worry if you decide to take time out to raise a family or try a different career. The law will always be here for you."

In 1989, when my late husband and I decided to quit our respective law firm affiliations and open our own office, it took a huge leap of faith. At that time, our children were ages one and four. Neither of us had a trust fund or family money, and we knew we would sink or swim on our own. We did have many resources, however. First, our initial relationship was as professional colleagues, and we were certain that we would work well together. We also had a rock solid marital relationship and were willing to be flexible in maintaining and sharing our homelife responsibilities. Very importantly, we had stable childcare, as well as my helpful parents. With the confidence that, in a worst-case scenario, we each would simply go out and find new jobs if this venture didn't work out, we entered the brave new world of small firm practice.

I had an advantage over many women lawyers who would start their own practices, in that I had a niche practice in an area where, at the time, few lawyers specialized: attorney discipline. My husband and I met as California State Bar prosecutors, and we each had many years of experience in that unique (and for most lawyers, very scary) venue. Additionally, I had been quite fortunate in that, while working for the state bar, I had already briefed and argued a half dozen supreme court appeals, and I had achieved a level of professional experience few of my colleagues in the discipline defense bar could claim. Also, both my husband and I had become associates at mid-size litigation firms when we left the bar prosecutor's office, and we recognized that we could apply large-firm civil litigation techniques to the administrative proceeding we knew so well.

At the outset, we did three things that contributed to our success. First, we made a business plan, in which we identified our preferred client base, which included not only solo and small firm practitioners, but also another market share—mid-size and larger law firms—that was not being targeted by our competitors. Second, we deliberately created a style of litigation that was patterned more after the "big law" litigation model, to appeal to larger firm practitioners. Third, we arranged for a credit line in order to manage cash flow pressures and to fund our day-to-day operations if necessary.

In keeping with our plan to market our practice to established lawyers and law firms, we leased office space in downtown Los Angeles, in an "A" class building, in order to be close to large downtown law firms, close to the courts, and close enough to home so that we could reduce our travel time and maximize the amount of time we could spend with our children. We also invested in high quality business stationery and placed a prominent ad in the monthly state bar magazine that was delivered to every member of the California State Bar. Compared to today's smartphones, our technological ability was a joke. Although I have never had much technological acumen, even 21 years ago, I understood that taking advantage of technology could allow even a tiny firm to compete with big law practitioners. We hired an experienced legal secretary who was an excellent word processor; we continued to invest in then state-of-the-art equipment, which allowed us to do desktop publishing of briefs and highly professional pleadings; and we brought our billing in-house.

We watched our bottom line very closely. "Lean and mean" was my motto. As the sole decision makers of our firm, my husband and I made quick decisions and conserved our resources. We did not skimp on essential expenses, like competent staff, new equipment, and effective advertising, but we also took on many office management tasks ourselves, in addition to actually practicing law, in order to maximize our profits. We tried to reduce waste and were quick to terminate staff whose performance was lacking. We made sacrifices of leisure time, and we both frequently brought work home to complete in the evening and nearly every weekend.

Our children were accustomed to coming to the office on weekends, where we had books, crayons, markers, and other art supplies, and the conference room table provided a fun "fort" to play in. To this day, I work a majority of weekends because I love practicing law, I feel a sense of accomplishment when I work, and I would prefer to enjoy the fruits of my labors by traveling and attending cultural events (and yes, shopping!) more than I value rest. My daughters are well-adjusted, well-rounded young adults, and each has had tremendous academic success. They both assure me that neither felt deprived as a result of not having had a stay-at-home mom. I don't feel even a twinge of guilt for having been both a mom and a full-time lawyer. I firmly believe that we must all make an individual choice whether to be a working parent, but I vehemently disagree with those who claim that "you can't have it all," and that a working mother necessarily deprives a child of a proper childhood.

I did make sure that my children had excellent childcare and a high quality pre-school education. A benefit of working with one's spouse is that the balancing of home and work responsibilities is personally experienced by both, and schedules can be coordinated. I was able to run home in the middle of the day if necessary, and my husband could leave work early to watch a Little League game. I often worked on a draft document while sitting in a softball stand. We often took our children with us on business trips, building family vacations around the business meetings.

As my children became older and were more self-sufficient, I began to become more active in bar association activities. Bar association activities provided me with important opportunities for professional development. By becoming affiliated with associations in my practice areas, I fulfilled my continuing education requirements with information that I actually used in practice and stretched my intellectual muscle with colleagues I might not have otherwise met. Speaking on CLE panels provided me a chance to volunteer for the benefit of the profession and simultaneously provided a mechanism to market my services to attendees of the CLE programs. I have formed numerous rewarding personal and professional relationships with lawyers I have met through bar association activities.

In 2002, my husband was diagnosed with pancreatic cancer, and he began a valiant struggle against the disease. During the period of his treatment, partial recovery, and ultimate death, I found the practice of law to be an escape, a comfort, and in a sense, my savior. Being able to practice together for the brief period after he returned to the office following his chemotherapy was a blessing for him, and for me. After he passed away, having a practice to run gave me purpose and strength, and having so many of Jerry's clients and fellow lawyers share with me their appreciation and love for him assisted me to survive the sorrow and grief over his loss. Together with my fierce love for my children, and the support of my family and friends, proving to myself that I could continue the law practice we started together permitted me to go on with my life.

To new woman lawyers, I have the following advice. Be true to your heart. Do not allow the judgment of others to dictate your choices. Always maintain a professional demeanor, even if your feelings are hurt and your emotions are high. Find some purely personal outlets for stress, preferably including physical activity. Do not worry if you decide to take time out to raise a family or try a different career. The law will always be here for you. Like hard work, the practice of law often is its own reward, and many other rewards will follow if you take advantage of all that the legal profession has to offer.

ELLEN A. PANSKY is a partner in the law firm of Pansky Markle Ham LLP in South Pasadena, California, where she focuses on professional liability litigation, state bar disciplinary defense, legal ethics consultations, and expert testimony. She graduated from law school in 1977 and founded her firm in 1989. *www.panskymarkle.com*

- FAY CLAYTON -

"[I brought along] the reproductive rights case,
NOW v. Scheidler, *which would stay active for over*
20 years, providing a host of joys and challenges. . . .
[S]ome things are more important than money."

I am writing in response to your request to share my experience—both joys and challenges—in creating a majority-women-owned firm, Robinson Curley & Clayton, P.C. (RCC). There was a time, back in the early '90s, when I was told we were the largest women-owned law firm in the state of Illinois. I'm glad that there are many more majority-women firms now, including a number that are larger than ours. I hope that our experience will encourage other women to found even more, because the rewards are great.

First, a few words about how we got started. RCC began in 1989, when I joined Ellen G. Robinson to establish a firm that would focus on complex litigation. Ellen and I had met while we were both partners at larger firms, where we were both working on different aspects of a complex fraud case. I was on the team that represented the plaintiff class, and Ellen led lawyers for the receiver of the insolvent insurance company where the fraud occurred. It was clear from my earliest meetings with Ellen that she was a strong and excellent lawyer, and we quickly became friends.

When I decided to leave my firm, Ellen and I discussed starting our own firm. But I had two children in college at the time, which made it too scary to take the financial risk just then. Ellen went ahead and opened her own doors with another colleague from her old firm, Phil Curley. Meanwhile, I accepted a partnership at another firm.

A few years down the line, Ellen called me up and asked me to help her with a case that was about to go to trial in federal court. She had been representing two plaintiffs, but a potential conflict had arisen, and they needed separate attorneys. Discovery had been completed. How could I turn down an offer like that?

That trial with Ellen was transformative. Not only did we win the case, but we had such fun working together that I decided it was time seriously to consider joining her and Phil in their budding practice; so we all got together to talk about it. I liked Phil instantly, and, to his great credit, he didn't seem to mind the prospect of being a minority member of a majority-women firm.

I remember Ellen's business plan, a handwritten list of the expected expenses: rent, books (we used actual books back in those days), word processors, insurance, a secretary, coffee, things like that. The plan looked realistic. Two of my daughters were about to graduate from college by this time, and my youngest had chosen New College. I was finally ready to take the financial plunge. I said yes, and RCC was formed.

Although I didn't expect to bring a paycheck home in the first year, as things turned out, we were profitable—although not wildly rich—within six months. I brought along several cases I'd been working on at prior firms, both commercial and pro bono. Among the latter was the reproductive rights case, *NOW v. Scheidler*, which would stay active for over 20 years, providing a host of joys and challenges, though no actual money. But some things are more important than money. In fact, it was clear to me that Ellen and Phil were solidly committed to public interest work. Over the following decades, when someone would present a new pro bono case for the firm's consideration, Ellen would often say, "Isn't this why we went to law school?" And so our pro bono work has spanned not only reproductive rights, but also fair housing, death penalty, LGBT, environmental and poverty issues, race relations, and of course, gender equality. Our niche has continued to be complex commercial litigation, including a number of extremely large cases with international aspects, but the public interest work—particularly the highly complex cases—has been an excellent counterpoint.

Soon after I joined Ellen and Phil, we realized we needed associates. We were fortunate that Phil's younger brother, Al Curley, agreed to leave his firm to join us. Through contacts at my law school, Chicago-Kent, we connected with Susan Valentine, who was thinking of leaving the top-notch criminal defense practice where she had worked for several years. Both proved to be stars—truly excellent lawyers—and I'm happy that both are shareholders today.

Our little firm rapidly grew to 12, then to 15 lawyers, a number that has always felt just right. This size gives us enough depth for the complex cases we thrive on, but it is still sufficiently intimate to feel almost like family. And most importantly, it lets us serve our clients efficiently.

The advantages of a majority-women firm include the fact that we rarely have to worry about sexism, although we do have to take care not to discriminate in a pro-woman way. Discrimination is bad no matter what its form, not to mention being illegal.

I'm not sure whether it's because we're a women-owned firm or not, but all of our lawyers have lives outside the office, whether it's a spouse, kids, civic activities, sports, the arts, or something else. We like it that our colleagues are well rounded. We work hard when we need to, and we work as long as necessary, but we try not to work around the clock (except, of course, when we're on trial). And we cultivate our young associates with the hope that each of them will become a shareholder in our firm someday.

In the 20-plus years that RCC has been in business, we haven't purposefully set out to hire women rather than men (that would be discriminatory and illegal), but somehow outstanding women seem to come our way—as well as outstanding, feminist men. Ellen retired a few years ago, but with other female partners who have stepped in to fill her shoes, we bring our clients the advantages of a majority-women firm. That has even turned out to be a good marketing tool, for we find many companies and government bodies want to retain highly capable but diverse legal services vendors, and we fill that bill. We are proud that the Fortune 500 companies and governmental clients that have retained us tell us that we are a great value.

Looking back, I am pleased I chose this path, first with Ellen, and then with other good women—and men—who have made this majority-women-owned firm thrive.

FAY CLAYTON is a founding partner of Robinson, Curley & Clayton, P.C. in Chicago, Illinois, where she focuses on complex litigation, general commercial litigation, and a broad variety of civil rights cases, especially those involving women's rights. She graduated from law school in 1978 and founded her firm in 1989. *www.robinsoncurley.com*

CHAPTER 3

1990–1994

Controlling Types of Clients and Practice Philosophy

"We emphasized to prospective clients that we could provide the same high-quality representation that they were getting at a large firm, but at a much lower rate. We were innovative in structuring fees, and matters were handled efficiently and without over-staffing."

— Roberta D. Liebenberg

Visionary reasons for starting firms run through this group of letters.

The 10 contributors in this chapter's five-year period include two who graduated in the 1970s and eight in the 1980s. With their experience in practice, they knew their economic power. They could see opportunities presented by the legal marketplace.

The most experienced practitioner in this group started the first women-owned firm in Philadelphia with two others in order to focus exclusively on commercial litigation. They benefitted from media attention to the novelty of their approach—women founding a commercial law firm—and established a strong practice representing major corporations.

In a different part of the nation, a writer was assessing the poor fit between herself and the firm, whose partners had discovered after hiring her that she was an assertive female. She founded a new firm with one of them and describes 17 years later how she has managed the firm and run cases worth several billions of dollars—obviously with grace and certainty.

In other examples, a writer as an associate had made an entrepreneurial and successful proposal to her firm that she lead the domestic relations practice. As her reputation spread, she was recruited to double her income by becoming a partner in another established firm. She decided that, with this level of economic power, she should split out her practice into her own firm instead. Another was recruited to go in-house after leading her own practice for six years, following a decade in a large law firm.

From this group emerges the theme that large-scale growth in law firms was generating unfortunate consequences. One writer, having worked in law for 15 years before law school, watched "in awe" as mass production hit the legal field in the '70s and '80s, and "attorneys began to use each other and their staffs as they would use disposable equipment." After entering practice with a traditional firm, she ultimately broke out in order to start a practice "that reflected my own needs and ethical responsibilities to my clients and my family."

These inspirational narratives and other letters filled with practical advice portray a maturing marketplace for women owning law practices.

---

*"My life, my family, and my work are now on equal grounds—
with each needing respect, attention, and love. Each can be
selfish, if allowed to do so. Therefore, it is my responsibility to
control the balance."*

- DIANE L. DRAIN -

The Adventures of a Young Woman from Designing Clothes for Barbie Dolls to Managing Her Own Law Firm

I was born in Tucson, the oldest of three children of a self-employed general contractor father and bookkeeper mother. From an early age we were all encouraged to use our imagination and to participate in the world of business. At the age of eight I designed, manufactured, and sold clothing for Barbie dolls. Some of my ventures were not financially profitable, but the experiences more than made up for financial losses. My parents did not save me from any financial disasters; instead they helped me to understand the reasons for my failures and made valuable suggestions for future endeavors.

When I was 11 my parents established a mechanical engineering firm in our rarely used front room. My mother was the bookkeeper/secretary and my brother and I were trained as draftsmen. Finances were tight, but everyone was committed. So, within a few years the business grew successful and moved out of our home. I moved on to start my own family; however, the lessons learned from my parents were never forgotten.

My early experiences taught me that an entire family can be actively involved in the management of a flourishing business. In addition, I learned that a business can be a success if everyone is willing to work. More importantly, I learned never to say "that's not my job" and that a job was not automatically done at 5:00 p.m. I learned to demand the best from myself and from those around me, but to accept that not everyone had my same priorities. I learned the importance of planning ahead, both for the current workload and for future business. I learned the importance of good communication skills and how to manage difficult clients. Lastly, I learned that in order to be really happy, you first must determine your personal definition of "success" and then be willing to commit 100 percent to achieve that success.

At age 19 I began working in the legal field as a secretary at the Maricopa County Public Defender's Office. From there I moved to many different positions at several private firms and eventually opened a temporary legal secretary/paralegal service. During this time I realized that a surprising number of law firm managers had little to no experience at the business of managing a successful law firm. I did not know it at that time, but having this opportunity to view the inside operation of several firms of varying sizes gave me a good understanding as to why law firms succeed or fail.

During this same 15-year period I observed a nationwide philosophical change regarding the employee-employer relationship. The age of mass production hit the legal field, and attorneys began to use each other and their staffs as they would use disposable equipment. I watched this phenomenon from a distance with awe that so many brilliant people could buy into such a destructive business practice.

An inviolate principle throughout my life has been to honor the golden rule: *Do unto others, as you would have others do unto you.* During my 40-year involvement in the legal profession I found that we rarely go wrong if decisions are based on what is morally and legally ethical. I teach everyone in my office to treat all clients as though they are dealing with their own grandmother and to treat each other with the highest level of respect.

A few years after law school, I decided to take on the role of a legal educator in addition to my role as a lawyer. One objective was to teach the lay person that law can be understandable and lawyers can be professional, practical, and approachable. A second objective was to help young lawyers understand that the time of the "bull-dog" lawyer is gone and that professionalism and ethics are more important than "winning at all costs."

Ultimately, I found that lawyering and teaching could complement each other. Each made me better at the other. Unfortunately, my commitment to being a teacher and mother and to staying active within my profession and community was a direct conflict with the hourly requirements of a large firm. Therefore, in 1991 I opened my own office and established a practice that reflected my own needs and ethical responsibilities to my clients and my family. I have never regretted that decision.

In what I thought would be a temporary situation, I decided to save overhead and put the office in our home. *Déjà vu*—talk about coming full circle back to my childhood. The guilt I felt in trying to fully separate my profession and my family was gone the moment we opened the office. A year later I decided that a home office worked for everyone—including my clients. The reduced overhead allowed me to offer lower fees to my clients. Therefore, my husband built a permanent office next door to our home. This proximity allowed us to incorporate our active family into our business. I made certain that the integrity and confidentiality of our clients were honored by all members of my family and that my clients and staff respected the privacy of our family. There were times when it was a challenge to accomplish the blending of both worlds, but in the long run everyone benefited.

My children are now grown, but they learned a good work ethic by being productive members of our staff. After all, how many 18-year-olds have résumés that include five years of experience in a law firm? More importantly, I was part of their lives by being physically and mentally available.

For years my husband has been my office manager, bookkeeper, and full-time paralegal. (Silly man thought he was going to retire.) My clients are warmed by my office's professional, yet congenial atmosphere. I benefited from the opportunity to customize my style of practice into an environment that reduced external stress.

I will be the first to admit that the combination of work and home is not for everyone. It works for us because our practice is limited to real estate and bankruptcy. I co-counsel other attorneys on many projects in order to provide my clients extended legal assistance. The referrals are such that I can pick and choose clients and the type of legal assistance offered.

I have continued my commitment to educating lawyers and the public, am a member of the state bar board of governors and several state bar sections, operate the bankruptcy court's Self-Help Center, received the Arizona State Bar's Member of the Year Award and President's Award, and the Governor's Commission on Service and Volunteerism Volunteer Service Award, and was featured in the *Arizona Business Gazette* and the *Arizona Attorney* magazine.

My life, my family, and my work are now on equal grounds—with each needing respect, attention, and love. Each can be selfish, if allowed to do so. Therefore, it is my responsibility to control the balance. I take pride in knowing that I have been a positive influence on each member of my family and that I have respected the needs and given faithfully to my profession and clients. Thus, when I am gone I can take pride in knowing that I did not compromise my ethical responsibilities in raising my family, assisting my clients, or in being a respected professional.

DIANE L. DRAIN is the founder of the Law Office of D.L. Drain, P.A. in Phoenix, Arizona, where she focuses on creditor and debtor rights and real property lien enforcement. She graduated from law school in 1985 and founded her firm in 1991. *www.dianedrain.com*

- Roberta D. Liebenberg -

"We established the first women-owned law firm in Philadelphia to focus exclusively on complex commercial litigation, including class actions in the areas of employment, securities, and antitrust."

In 1992, I left the security of a large law firm, where I had been an associate and then a partner for more than a decade, to embark on a challenging new venture with two other women attorneys. We established the first women-owned law firm in Philadelphia to focus exclusively on complex commercial litigation, including class actions in the areas of employment, securities, and antitrust. Although our decision to start our own firm was fraught with considerable risk, we were excited about the opportunity to work for ourselves, and we derived enormous professional and personal satisfaction from the firm we created. This experience taught me several valuable lessons that I would like to share:

1. Create Marketing Opportunities

We opened our firm in 1992, which was a very propitious time. That was a watershed year for women in national politics and was in fact dubbed the "Year of the Woman." There was a great deal of enthusiasm about women in politics, which carried over to women-owned businesses. Consequently, our new firm garnered a considerable amount of free publicity. We were interviewed by legal and business publications and asked to speak and write about our new firm, which was the first of its kind in the Philadelphia legal marketplace. Indeed, we had a unique brand.

We were also fortunate inasmuch as the creation of our new firm coincided with efforts by federal government agencies, such as the Federal Deposit Insurance Corporation and Resolution Trust Corporation, to secure representation by minority and women-owned law firms (MWOLFs) in connection with the recovery of money lost by those agencies in the savings and loan crisis.

Our firm qualified to participate in the MWOLF program. This participation ensured several significant fee-generating matters and thus gave us a running head start. Equally important, it facilitated our networking with other female and minority attorneys around the country, who were also working on similar cases. We also marketed our firm to corporations and nonprofits, who had growing numbers of women serving as in-house counsel and general counsel. Many of these women were anxious to help other women succeed, and they were a tremendous source of referrals.

2. Develop a Thoughtful Business Plan and Proceed Carefully

We began our practice at a time when many smaller banks were interested in helping to capitalize small law firms. The bank we used looked at us as an investment opportunity and was interested in creative financing arrangements. I think one of the smartest decisions we made when we started was to insist that we would not place our homes as collateral for our line of credit. While we were fortunate to have had individuals who co-signed our loan, we never had to worry that if we failed, we would lose our residences.

We started modestly by subleasing relatively inexpensive office space and hiring slowly. We also decided that we would have a mixture of both hourly and contingent cases, and this too proved to be a prudent financial decision.

Opening your own firm necessarily entails financial risk, but you can minimize that risk with careful planning and budgeting. For example, you need to evaluate your financial needs, including whether you need a line of credit and, if so, how much and how it will be secured. Prepare a monthly and yearly budget of your operational and administrative expenses, including salaries, rent, insurance, taxes, and other overhead.

We also evaluated the costs of leasing versus buying certain equipment, such as a copier. We also invested in a computer expert who helped us select computers and who was also able to provide technical support. After a year or so, we hired a web consultant who developed our website, which was critical to our marketing efforts.

In setting up your firm, you need to be organized and realistic. You can set ambitious goals, but you should proceed incrementally. It is important not to lose your confidence when you encounter the inevitable setbacks along the way and not to let yourself get overwhelmed by the myriad business decisions you will be forced to make. While starting your own firm will seem completely nerve racking at times, you will have a real sense of accomplishment once you are up and running.

3. Ask for Business and Use Creativity in Fee Structures
I can honestly say that it was not until I left a large law firm that I really honed my business development skills. There is nothing like the prospect of having to meet payroll each month to incentivize you to market aggressively.

We were fortunate that many of our previous clients followed us after we started our new firm. We were also careful to leave our prior law firms on good terms. This proved to be advantageous, because many of our referrals came from our prior firms, who often had conflict situations or smaller matters that we were well suited to handle.

In our marketing, we emphasized to prospective clients that we could provide the same high quality representation that they were getting at a large firm, but at a much lower rate. We were innovative in structuring fees, and matters were handled efficiently and without over-staffing. Clients knew how much their business meant to a new start-up firm. Excellent client service, creative billing arrangements, and outstanding results led to increased referrals, repeat business, and an expanding base of loyal clients.

4. Change IS Good
If you find yourself dissatisfied or frustrated in your current practice, you ought to consider leaving to create a new firm, either by yourself or with others. This is particularly true if you have already developed a client base of your own.

One of the best career decisions I ever made was to leave a large law firm and create my own firm. This provided me with the flexibility and autonomy to set my own schedule and to work on the types of cases that I wanted to handle.

While I truly enjoyed creating and working at my own firm, I decided after eight years that I was ready to make another career change. I became a partner in a prominent antitrust boutique, where I still practice. As before, this change created new challenges as well as new opportunities, and the insights I had gained from my prior firm proved invaluable. I am a strong believer that if the status quo is dissatisfying or unfulfilling, you should not hesitate to try something new. After all, change can be a good thing.

ROBERTA D. LIEBENBERG is a senior partner at Fine, Kaplan and Black, R.P.C. in Philadelphia, Pennsylvania, where she focuses on class actions, antitrust, and complex commercial litigation. She graduated from law school in 1975 and founded her women-owned firm in 1992. *www.finekaplan.com*

- PATRICIA NEMETH -

"Our firm is now in its 18th year, and we are continuously looking for new ways to improve our firm by reinvesting in its future."

I pondered over how to address this letter and realized that first and foremost if you are a woman lawyer and are thinking about opening your own firm, you must view your firm as a business. When I first opened my firm, the first two computer programs I learned to use were Timeslips for time entry and QuickBooks for accounting purposes. Since it was only me at that time, I wanted to make sure that I knew how to get the bills out and how to properly account for the money collected. Even before opening the firm, I scheduled a meeting with another woman lawyer who had been in business as a solo practitioner for over 10 years. She provided me with a lot of great information, but the best piece of advice that she gave me was to make sure I had a good accountant and a good corporate lawyer. I did that 18 years ago, and both are still my advisors today. Their wisdom and counsel over the years have been immeasurable. There have been a number of challenges as the firm has now grown to 15 attorneys and approximately 30 employees. My accountant and corporate counsel have walked me through, talked me through, and cajoled me through those difficult times.

For a business, you need to have a business plan. Everyone's business plan will be different. For me, my business plan was in pictures, rather than words, on an 8 × 11-inch piece of blank paper. I had a picture (stick figure caricature) of me in the middle with a number of lines drawn leading out to pictures of things that were needed: business cards, furniture, telephone, computer, office, money, and administrative support (phone answering/typing). Those were items that needed to be accomplished prior to the firm opening. I then worked through each of the pictures, accomplishing and providing more detail as I did. Back then, in 1992, there was no Internet to be concerned about. Things have definitely changed, and my picture would look different now to reflect those changes.

Today, before opening the firm, in addition to the accountant and lawyer, I would also make sure that there was a good IT person or company in place. You can waste so much time and money unless you have someone in place who is competent and trustworthy. One lesson that our firm learned was that our IT systems did not grow in sophistication at the same rate as our firm. We reached a point where we needed additional servers and experience in an IT company greater and broader than the company who had been servicing our firm. As a result, our system crashed, and we had a number of problems. Let's just say it was a long hot summer. We spent a significant amount on upgrading our IT area of the firm, changing the company who was then providing service, and implementing procedures so that we would not go through what we did again.

With respect to financing, initially I used my own money to finance the firm's opening and growth. I did not finance the firm through bank credit or other credit. I opened the firm with $500. I was able to do so because I purchased used furniture and subleased space, which included phone answering and mail processing. The sublease arrangement also allowed me to purchase secretarial usage on an hourly basis. I wanted to make sure that I was able to make my monthly rent payment, which led to me teaching employment classes at a business university for managers obtaining their masters degree in business. The teaching money was solely to pay the office rent. I taught for two years at night until I felt the firm was stable enough that I could pay the rent without teaching. As an added benefit, the people in class referred me business. There were also other attorneys subleasing space in the same suite who did not necessarily practice in the management labor and employment law area. They too referred me work.

I remember when I was subleasing space and talking to one of the other solo attorneys in the suite. He said he wanted to have a firm where he had employees and could provide them with health insurance, dental and vision insurance, and a 401(k). My response was, "Geez, I just want to pay the rent." Yet, now that is exactly what our firm is doing. It was a slow process built on a conservative growth strategy, targeting potential clients that did not primarily focus on the auto industry.

With the first expansion, the firm leased rather than subleased space. It was necessary for me to personally loan the firm money with interest being paid back to me over an eight-year period of time. As the firm continued to grow, it was imperative that we develop a good relationship with a bank. When we expanded and moved into new space for the second time, due to the costs involved, a loan was needed. Five years later (just after paying off the first loan), we needed to expand again, necessitating another bank loan. Luckily, we were able to obtain financing at a favorable rate prior to the limitations placed on financing. In addition, with the second expansion and associated costs of more employees, in order for our business to be on financially sound ground, we needed to have a line of credit in place. Wisely, our accountant advised us to have the line of credit in place prior to actually needing it. It was and continues to be imperative that we have a line of credit to draw upon when the need arises. We have also found that obtaining a secure enough line has been more difficult since the banks have tightened up on finances. As a result, even though we had worked with a bank for over a decade and paid all loans back on a timely basis, we were required to find a new bank to provide the line of credit we needed to feel secure in the running of our firm. The new bank worked with us to find the right amount for our line of credit and to modify language in bank documents to fit our needs.

Our firm is now in its 18th year, and we are continuously looking for new ways to improve our firm by reinvesting in its future. IT has become more and more a part of our business, and this year our IT projects include a new website and document management system. Next year we focus on our computers again. It's always something. It's always evolving and most of the time it's a lot of fun! Working for myself—with the flexibility it provides and the ability to choose the people with whom I work—was a great decision for me.

PATRICIA NEMETH is founder and president of Nemeth Burwell, P.C. in Detroit, Michigan, where she focuses solely on management-side labor and employment law. She graduated from law school in 1984 and founded her firm in 1992. *www.nemethburwell.com*

- A. HILLARY GROSBERG -

---

*"You need to be an experienced lawyer before you go it alone. . . .
You will have your hands full opening and running a business.
You will not have time to learn how to practice law."*

My name is A. Hillary Grosberg. My practice encompasses business litigation, real estate litigation, creditors rights, probate and trust administration, and litigation and selected family law cases.

I have been in practice in Los Angeles since 1981. Eleven and one-half years later, in 1993, I opened my own office. I have never looked back or in any way regretted my decision. It was not ever my intent to be a solo practitioner, but fate has its own journey. Why did I leave a firm, you ask? I did not fit well at the last firm where I was employed. I was miserable. I spent a year looking for a new firm to join, but with no book of business of my own and as an 11-year attorney, I was simply too expensive for a firm to hire. (The practice of law is a business, after all.) I had been saving as much as I could because I knew that at first I would not have clients and would need savings to pay the bills. One day there was a last straw, and I gave notice. I felt wonderful! Off I went with no clients or office. Can you say "leap of faith"?

First, I called a law school buddy and found a place to temporarily office. Clients would be helpful. I began calling lawyers I knew for overflow work or projects. I told all my friends. I looked for groups to join. Some were pure networking, and some were areas of interest outside the practice of law. I joined local bar associations and attended events of interest. I created a website and now avail myself of online networking avenues. Results are not immediate, but most of it brings business in time. Give each group six months to a year. If by then you see no progress, move on to find a better fit. I find most of my referrals come from other lawyers whose practices are different than mine. Ask all the people you know in business for themselves what worked best for them. You will be amazed at the useful information.

You need to be an experienced lawyer before you go it alone. Both the good and bad news is that you, and you alone, make all the business decisions and client strategy decisions. You will have your hands full opening and running a business. You will not have time to learn how to practice law. More importantly, other lawyers are not going to refer to you if you are not experienced because their reputations are on the line.

I am an extremely organized person. Some of the most valuable information I can share will be the practical considerations in opening your office taken for granted when you are part of a firm.

What office supplies will you need: From paper, to printer toner, fax and scanner, writing instruments, files, envelopes, postage, paper clips... I made a list of what I had in the firm where I was working. I actually perused the supply room and took a look around my office.

What will be in your library? Will you use books, online, or a combination? For me this has been the biggest expense, even more than my office rent. Will you need an attorney service—every day or only as needed? How will the telephone be answered? Directly, by a receptionist or voice mail or answering service? Will your telephone be connected to the suite or will it just come to your office? Furniture is always nice, and a computer is a must. Will you have an office at or away from home? Do you want your clients coming to your home? Do you have a practice that takes you to your clients' places of business instead of your office?

That was the glamorous part. Now comes running the business. You will need systems. You will need to record income and expenses both for each client and the business as a whole. (Uncle Sam will be most interested in your income and expenses, thus accuracy is key.) You should be able to put your hands on all financial records for a client at any time. I have had clients call needing information on fees and costs to date for their own business or personal reasons, such as loan applications, their own taxes, estate planning, or divorce proceedings in which you are not their attorney. How will you open files? Will there be a way to confirm that all files are opened the same way and that retainer letters are signed before any work is done? I made a file opening form and it includes the client information, opposing party information, and a list of other matters to do such as check for conflicts, prepare a costs sheet, enter the client and matter into my billing system, create a ledger, and (since I keep paper copies of my bills) create a notebook divider to insert in the notebooks where I keep my bill copies. Will you keep a client list? How will conflicts be checked? Will you keep your files by number or name? What happens when a file is closed? Will a letter go to the client to confirm the closing? Where will you keep your copy of the bills—in the billing software and/or saved elsewhere in your computer and/or paper copies (in each file or centrally located)?

I find forms very helpful. I have retainer agreements, file opening checklist, client costs, document and pleading indexes, client ledgers and client trust account ledgers (yes, I keep written ledgers), a client list, a closed case list, expense and income lists, mileage list, and the ever important time sheets, among others. The ledgers have been lifesavers! While everyone laughs at my handwritten ledgers (and it does take time at the end of the month), when my computer has crashed (yes, it will happen, and you are the IT person) I can simply check my client ledger sheets, and when I have an operating computer again, simply enter the current balance and move forward!

On the subject of billing, I have made it a practice to send my bills at regular intervals. For me, that is the last day of the month. Even if a matter is a flat fee case, I still record all time spent and send a no charge bill to the client. I find this a good way to let the client know what is being done all month for the money that has been paid.

OK, systems in place! Next, decide about software. The four main types are word processing, billing, calendaring, and financial. Word? WordPerfect? Both? (These days that's what I have. I prefer to work in WordPerfect, but many clients only have Word.) What type of calendaring software will you have? There are many available. You will need to decide whether you will do your own billing and have software or outsource your billing. There are many billing software sources and many companies that offer billing services. Unless you outsource your bookkeeping, you will need financial software (to use much like your checkbook). Talk to an accountant about what accounts to set up. This will make tax preparation a breeze instead of a nightmare.

Now, protect all your work and records. You will need some sort of backup system for your computer. There is online offsite (stored in space), accessible from any computer—that brief due in two days can actually get filed! There are external hard drives, flash drives (this is what I use for my data on a daily basis), and a plethora of other ways to save the data and programs so that when that computer crash occurs, you have not really lost it all.

Consider insurance (boring, but necessary). I talked to an agent experienced with lawyers' malpractice insurance to learn all the coverage variations. Employees? Workers' compensation insurance. You may also want to have general liability and contents insurance.

You are now armed with information. This may sound overwhelming, but if you set it up right, it runs like a well-oiled machine. The single best thing about being a solo practitioner is the power to decide who will be my clients. Exercise that power while running a great business! It is well worth your time, and what an accomplishment!

A. HILLARY GROSBERG is a solo practitioner in Encino, California, focusing on business, real property, bankruptcy, and probate and trust administration litigation. She graduated from law school in 1980 and founded her firm in 1993. *www.annhillary.com*

- JULIE I. FERSHTMAN -

"Jay warned me that I probably would starve. These words of wisdom, though much different in nature, came as a challenge to me and inspired me to make my plans come true."

I made the decision to start my own law firm in 1993. Back then, I envisioned creating a practice of my own that would focus, to a large extent, on the niche of equine/equestrian-related law and associated liability and transactional issues. I also wanted my practice to include personal injury defense, insurance coverage, and commercial litigation.

The clients I wanted to serve were primarily insurance companies. Clients of this type, I realized, could send me tort cases to defend that I found personally fascinating as well as coverage matters and would offer a steady income. This certainly was not a traditional practice for a solo practitioner and especially not typical for a female solo practitioner. Back then, I had already developed one major insurance company client that, fortunately, was willing to continue working with me when I broke off on my own.

By this time, I had been a lawyer for seven years. Having worked as an associate at Detroit-area firms during this time, I had worked closely with some excellent, experienced, and respected lawyers. Their guidance not only instilled in me effective writing techniques but also gave me valuable courtroom and trial advocacy skills.

I asked older, accomplished lawyers for advice on my business plans. The first, an accomplished trial lawyer whom I greatly respected, told me:

> You plan to ask major companies to take a chance on you. It's a gutsy request since these companies have only worked with large law firms, not young solo practitioners. And every one who hires you will be accountable if things don't work out. What you want is for the people who hire you to be absolutely certain that you were the right person for

the job to the exclusion of the large firm they'd used for years. That way, if, down the line, things don't work out, the client can tell his boss: 'She was the expert in that area of the law, and nobody else had her expertise. I had to give her a try.'

In 1993, when I attended an ABA convention, I approached the legendary marketing expert Jay Foonberg (author of the ABA book *How to Start and Build a Law Practice*) about my plans. Considering the geography alone—suburban Detroit, as opposed to states notorious for large horse populations—Jay warned me that I probably would starve.

These words of wisdom, though much different in nature, came as a challenge to me and inspired me to make my plans come true. I had to find a way to break through, get the attention of the persons from whom I wanted work, and demonstrate to them that I offered a level of service and expertise that they could not find elsewhere. I set out to develop credentials that prospective clients simply could not ignore. My goal was not to undercut other firms by offering cheaper rates. To the contrary, I wanted to convince them that I, as a specialist, should be paid more. And I made myself constantly visible to prospective clients through updates and articles that nobody else was sending them.

Back then, my client development efforts were anything but easy or cheap. This was before the Internet. As a solo targeting major corporate clients, I made sure that every communication I sent to an actual or prospective client looked exactly like it came from a large law firm. I invested in the same high quality raised-letter engraved stationery and cards that the big firms used. And I sent informational mailings to my growing list of business contacts, sometimes placing copies of my articles in expensive, engraved presentation folders just like the big firms used. As insurance companies began to take interest, some flew me out to speak to their claims and underwriting staffs. Sometimes, as some claims staff moved on to work at new insurance companies, they recommended me, and I added a new client.

I credit many of my marketing strategies to bar association involvement and publications. My favorite book on legal marketing is *Women Rainmakers' Best Marketing Tips*, written by Theda Snyder and published by the ABA.

I also credit much of who I am as a lawyer to many years of sustained involvement in bar association activities. In the late 1980s, not long out of law school, I decided on a whim to run for a position on the State Bar of Michigan Young Lawyers Section Executive Council. This group was composed of lawyers from throughout the state and organized projects serving the public and the bar. My intent at the time was to meet lawyers from around the state (I went to an out-of-state law school) and to relieve the isolation associated with being a hard-working young lawyer in a firm. This involvement grew, and I developed some close friendships. In the years that followed, I became chair of the group and had the unique opportunity to work side by side with some of the most articulate, caring, ethical, and accomplished lawyers in the state. As we worked together on many worthwhile service projects, these attorneys became my role models and mentors. Never would these opportunities have arisen had I stayed in my office.

As I write this letter, 17 years have passed since I began my solo practice. My mission has largely been accomplished. Several insurers now send me work on a variety of legal matters, equine and non-equine related. The volume of work has necessitated a full-time associate, whom I hired in 2007. And later this year, I will probably have merged my practice into a Detroit-area law firm, where I will become a partner, and my associate will join me.

The many marketing strategies I employed years ago to jump-start my practice—writing and speaking—have continued in full force, even as the years have passed. I have written hundreds of published articles and have had about 150 speaking engagements at conventions, CLE programs, and conferences in over 27 states. Many of my articles are now included in the two books I published, *Equine Law & Horse Sense* and *MORE Equine Law & Horse Sense*. And last year I coauthored a book for the ABA called *Litigating Animal Law Disputes*.

My involvement in the organized bar has continued in full force as well and has become a source of personal pride. In September 2011, I will be sworn in as the president of the State Bar of Michigan, only the fifth woman to hold this position in the bar's 77-year history. In the future, when I meet with women law students and lawyers, I hope my personal experiences will inspire them to achieve their own personal goals by dreaming big, working extremely hard, and staying steadfastly focused on becoming the lawyer they always wanted to be.

JULIE I. FERSHTMAN is a shareholder with the Farmington Hills, Michigan office of Foster, Swift, Collins & Smith, P.C., where she focuses on insurance defense, insurance coverage, commercial litigation, and equine law. She graduated from law school in 1986 and founded her firm in 1993. *www.fershtmanlaw.com*

- ROSEMARY EBNER POMEROY -

"Ask yourself honest questions: What areas of the law do I enjoy? What past practice experience will help me zero in on the areas of the law I would be best at?"

A Strategy for Success

Making the Decision to Start My Own Practice

In January of 1993, I was a young mother with a two-year-old and pregnant with a baby due that July. I started to realize that my cousin, who had had her own solo practice for many years, now a lawyer in Chicago, had the right idea: control your destiny, start your own practice. I remember it as if it were yesterday: I went into the partner I was working for at a mid-size law firm in Columbus, Ohio, and told him I was leaving the firm. He looked up, rather strangely at me and said why? I responded, I am expecting baby two and I am leaving before the balls I am juggling drop. He asked me what I planned to do, and I told him I wanted to start my own law practice. He proceeded to look at me, again with a blank stare, and asked me where my office was going to be. I responded, my dining room.

As I walked out of that partner's office, I thought to myself, you are completely crazy, Rose! And I guess I was. So on April 3, 1993, the Law Offices of Rosemary Ebner Pomeroy began. I had a phone line, a table, a file cabinet, and hope—hope that I could break even my first year and be in the black by my third year.

Previous Practice Experience

My Dad was a lawyer, one of my uncles was a lawyer, and I had cousins who were lawyers. The law and lawyers were all I ever knew. I worked for a title insurance company in high school and college and saw that the lawyers I worked for were genuinely happy in their chosen profession. After under-graduate education at Michigan State University, I was undecided about law school. After a short stint in bank management, I decided first to become a paralegal and went through a three-month certificate program at the Institute for Paralegal Education in Philadelphia, Pennsylvania. I landed a position at a suburban Detroit law firm. There, I was working on document management for complex litigation involving asbestos manufacturers. The longer I worked as a paralegal, the more I realized I should be a lawyer. So, I started in night law school, at Detroit College of Law, now Michigan State University School of Law, and completed my legal training in four years, while working as a paralegal full time.

During my paralegal years, I met and married my husband, Mark C. Pomeroy, who is a technology lawyer. We relocated to his hometown of Columbus, Ohio, as we both perceived that the central Ohio economy might be better for our future legal careers. I was hired as an associate at a mid-size union side labor firm and ended up doing personal injury litigation and some of the firm's general practice work. I determined that if I ever started my own practice, the general practice work I had done would create a skill set marketable for my own practice.

When I commenced my solo practice I did a little bit of everything, domestic relations, bankruptcy, probate, collections, and minor litigation matters. After about three years of solo practice I determined that I would confine my practice to the areas that were part of the probate court. Therefore, I made the decision to handle only probate, estate planning, guardianships, and adoptions.

Challenges of Starting My Firm and Challenges as My Practice Expanded

The main challenges in starting up a solo practice are devising a plan of action for your practice and developing a plan for the financial challenges that lie ahead. Any future solo practitioner needs to analyze what type of clients he or she wants and the areas of law that are going to make up the practice. Ask yourself honest questions: What areas of the law do I enjoy? What past practice experience will help me zero in on the areas of the law I would be best at? Do I have any apparent sources of business income?

Also, one needs to look at the practical aspects of developing a practice. The location of the office is important. Are you easily accessible to present and future clients? Determine what type of office furniture works with your work style. Do you really need or want a traditional mahogany desk? Technology is part and parcel of every successful law practice. What types of computer systems and accompanying software do I need? Question whether you need an assistant with secretarial skills or a fully trained paralegal. Who will serve your practice best? Borrowing funds to get one's practice off the ground may make sense. Do I need a trained financial professional to help me determine if I need to borrow funds to begin this endeavor? The foregoing issues are just a few of the things you need to consider when developing and starting your law practice.

What I Wish I Had Known Before I Jumped Out Into Solo Practice

I wish I had taken time to analyze the areas I really wanted to develop in my practice. I don't think a true general practice is possible in this economic climate, and I wish I had started working solely in the adoption, probate, and estate planning areas. I also don't think I would be so eager to get an actual physical office space today. Perhaps one is better served financially if one works from her home with a dedicated office space and utilizes an office suite system for client meetings, depositions, and conferences with fellow lawyers.

I also wish I had spent more time talking to other lawyers in the community to determine whether they had overflow work they could refer to me and to let other lawyers know what my practice areas were going to be so I could develop referral sources.

My View Backward

I try to not look back, but I often do. Starting my own practice let me continue some meaningful work as an attorney, while balancing my time as a wife and mother. I created a flexible schedule, which worked well with my children. My daughter Sarah is 19 now and my son Michael, 16. My practice has created flexibility to attend school functions, be a band booster parent, and attend all kinds of scholastic, music, and sports related events for my children.

I made less money in solo practice, but I also had time, time I would not have had if I were working in a large or mid-sized law firm. The flexibility has also enriched my husband's career immensely, and he and I both agree we probably would do it the same way if we had to do it all over again.

Looking Forward

In a short amount of time Mark and I will have both of our children in college. Though I love my practice and my many wonderful clients, I am at the point where I am starting to look at other opportunities. I threw my prover-bial hat in the ring for an open probate judge position in my county where I practice. I wasn't the governor's choice, but by putting my name out there, I let a lot of lawyers know that I was considering other options, now that some of my family obligations are near completion. I am also considering teaching opportunities and positions with nonprofits as a way to continue a new phase of my legal career.

The Law Offices of Rosemary Ebner Pomeroy is still in business. I'd like to think that whether I continue with it another five years, or move on to a new opportunity, my practice created a lot of good fortune and blessings in my legal career.

ROSEMARY EBNER POMEROY is the owner of Law Offices of Rosemary Ebner Pomeroy in Columbus, Ohio, where she focuses on adoption law, estate administration, and estate planning. She graduated from law school in 1986 and founded her firm in 1993. *www.columbuslawyerfinder.com/adoption-and-surrogacy/rosemary-ebner-pomeroy*

- GEORGIALEE LANG -

"To practice law is more exciting than I could have imagined, but to run your own business at the same time is career nirvana."

Opening my own law firm 17 years ago was a daunting challenge that began my journey as a businesswoman who happened to have a law degree. Like most law school graduates I believed that in order to really succeed in the legal profession, one needed to associate with a high-powered "blue chip" law firm, so that's what I did!

I began as an associate lawyer in a large business-focused law firm in 1989. The firm practiced over the spectrum of legal areas, with one exception. A year prior to the commencement of my employment, the firm's well-known family law lawyer left the firm.

I recognized an opening and approached the firm management suggesting that I reinitiate the firm's divorce practice while acting as a junior in the firm's wills and estates practice. The synergy between the two practice areas was a natural fit. Despite admonitions from senior management that a "white collar" corporate litigation practice was far superior to a "pink collar" divorce practice, we went ahead with my plan.

Within five years my practice was flourishing, and I had a junior lawyer and a paralegal working exclusively with me in my practice. But I really didn't realize how successful I was until year three, when a boutique family law firm headhunted me to join them as a partner in their firm.

I was startled when they advised me that my salary would immediately double. It was at that point that I began to realize that I might be able to start my own firm, but I knew I wasn't ready yet. I stayed with the blue-chip firm soaking up as much of their business savvy and systems as I could.

In year five of my career, I opened Georgialee Lang and Associates, leasing 1,600 square feet across from the courthouse in Vancouver and hiring two legal secretaries. I prepared a business plan that I presented to a bank to secure a line of credit to operate the business. The bank loaned me $75,000 on my signature, but incredibly, I never once drew from my credit line. The firm I left gave me their blessing, and I took about 100 clients with me to my new practice. Once I left the big firm they completely abandoned the family law practice area and treated my new law firm as the "branch" office down the street. Within three months I hired my first associate and over the years offered employment to dozens of young female lawyers, culminating in a firm with five lawyers working for me. I doubled my space and upgraded my offices and equipment to match the escalating revenues.

But to build a career and scale the pinnacle of your profession requires work—and lots of it. To build a business you need clients, great staff, excellent accounting advice, a firm manager, and congenial relationships with members of your practice bar. To build a reputation as a leading lawyer in your area, you need to achieve excellence and you need to find a way to let everyone know how good you really are!

So how do you sing your own praises without being labeled a megalomaniac? You need to get your name out there. Seventeen years ago lawyers didn't have access to the Internet, blogs, or social media. The steps required to earn a big reputation a decade or so ago are the same as they are today. The only difference is the method of conveying the message.

In the first 10 years of my practice I published prolifically for lawyers' magazines, legal periodicals, and continuing legal education. I also developed my public speaking skills, which grew as I became a more confident litigator. I was fortunate to develop several local media contacts (TV and radio) and began providing on-air commentary and off-air background information to media producers. From there I began accepting invitations to appear in public legal educational videos for a variety of audiences, from judges to self-represented litigants.

What was the hardest part? It wasn't practicing law, it was running a business with 10 employees. I had to learn how to manage people: how to be their friendly boss, but not their best friend; how to hire good people and when to fire them; how to manage workplace bullies and water-cooler gossips; and how to keep the overhead expenses in line with my net revenue goals. Two memorable anecdotes come to mind. In 22 years of practice I hired only four male lawyers (by happenstance, not by design). Lawyer #1 was a cocky, good-looking young man who failed to meet my expectations, and he apparently knew that. I asked him one day to provide me with case law on a particular family law legal topic. He presented a fistful of cases to me, which I took home with me to read that evening. In amongst the cases were five cases on wrongful dismissal! He was boning up on the law, no doubt. On another occasion I hired a very serious male lawyer who was several years older than me. On his first day on the job, when I was giving him instructions on his first assignment, he reminded me that I should not think I am such hot stuff, even though I had worked for one of Vancouver's leading law firms. I wanted to fire him on the spot, but the firm was so busy that I ignored his comment. During his tenure I changed his work hours to evenings and weekends only, when I was not there! He left shortly thereafter.

Has it worked out the way I hoped? To practice law is more exciting than I could have imagined, but to run your own business at the same time is career nirvana. Welcome to my world: financial freedom, intellectual discourse, collegial professional relationships, and the opportunity to give back: to young lawyers and to people who simply can't afford a lawyer.

GEORGIALEE LANG is president of Georgialee Lang & Associates in Vancouver, British Columbia, Canada, where she practices high net worth family law and focuses on both trial and appellate cases involving complex corporate, trust, tax, and business matters and international child abduction. She graduated from law school in 1988 and founded her firm in 1994. *www.georgialeelang.com*

- Monika Holzer Sacks -

"As a family law firm, we needed to balance our personal needs and those of our families with our professional need to deliver excellent service and support our community while making sufficient money to . . . pay our staff and shareholders a decent salary."

The best decision I ever made was to join a firm with three other women attorneys. Ours is a carefully planned firm. We were fortunate to have input from a business consultant who provided us an outline of important issues to discuss before we decided if we were a good fit for one another. We carefully considered our individual goals and our attitudes about serving clients, level of service delivery, treatment of staff and fellow attorneys, decision-making within the firm, manner of billing, sharing the income and expenses, community service, rainmaking, and collections.

After about four sessions, we decided that we were a good fit and were excited about embarking on this adventure as the first all-woman, family law firm in Ann Arbor. The community is known as being progressive, but we had our doubts that it was sufficiently progressive to accept this well-known and reputable, but still all-women, firm. Fortunately, we made the right decision. It has been a pleasure working in this supportive, service driven, intelligent, highly ethical environment.

As a family law firm, we determined that we needed to balance our personal needs and those of our families with our professional need to deliver excellent service to our clients and support our community while making sufficient money to keep our doors open and to pay our staff and shareholders a decent salary. In short, we strove to maintain balance. Our firm policies and manner of dealing with one another keep this as our core focus.

This is a firm that works! We govern by consensus. At times getting five shareholders to agree on a significant change can be trying. We feel this is important to avoid having factions within the firm. There is no politicking between three members to build a majority. As a result, when the decision is made, everyone supports it. It requires patience, respect, trust, and the courage to identify your real needs. At times, some very frank, difficult discussions have been needed to keep factions from developing.

It helps that we are all trained mediators and collaborative practitioners. We place a high value on continuing education to hone our skills. We apply our mediation/collaborative practice skills not only to our clients' cases, but to problem solving within the firm. When necessary, we have hired business consultants to assist us to work through particularly troubling issues.

We also systematize problem solving. We hold monthly staff meetings where everyone is expected to and does contribute. Our staff is encouraged to bring office environment, drafting, procedural, and workflow problems to the group. Our philosophy is, "if it's a problem for one person, it concerns everyone." Our shareholders meet once a month to review firm management, budget, and income, and any issues that require group review. Clients are asked to fill out evaluation forms at the end of our representation. Their suggestions of how we can improve our service delivery are valued. Drawing from these combined groups, we can address potential difficulties before they become major problems. As a group, we also amplify our strengths.

We have an excellent office manager who runs our firm seamlessly, while the attorneys are free to concentrate on what they do best: practice law. We began by sharing the office manager with another firm on our floor, since we could not afford to pay for her full time. We also shared the expenses of the office machines and common space, all of which the office manager coordinated. As we grew, the position changed to full time within our firm. The shareholders have principal areas of responsibility, such as human resources, marketing, finances, and building maintenance and serve as back-ups to our office manager.

We currently operate two offices: one in Ann Arbor and one in Brighton, in a contiguous county. Our goal is to encourage the use of humane problem resolution in family law cases that empowers our clients to make good decisions for their families and reduces conflict. Achieving this paradigm shift from the litigation model has been challenging, but tremendously rewarding.

Our firm has grown by design. Of the original four shareholders, three remain. One has retired and is still a strong supporter of our firm. Our plan is to add attorneys who possess values consistent with those of our firm and who are at different age levels to allow continuity. All of our attorneys have strong leadership abilities and commitment to serving the community. We count three county bar past presidents, two past chairs of the state bar family law section, three members of the American Academy of Matrimonial Lawyers, a past chair of the state bar representative assembly, and numerous other visible, demanding positions in our résumés. No one allows her ego and individual ambition to override the mission of the firm.

Internal policies for paying expenses and sharing income were also developed to discourage competition between individual attorneys. We share a portion of all the income that comes to the firm between the shareholders. As a result, when a client asks to work with one shareholder, but presents a case that is really better suited for another attorney in the firm, the client is encouraged to work with the best-suited attorney. Our attorneys share a common philosophy of empowering clients and avoiding hostility, so case sharing becomes easy, since the client is likely to receive similar advice from his or her regular attorney and from the substitute attorney who is covering while the regular attorney is on vacation. Yes, we all take vacations and days off to spend with our children, spouses, and significant others.

We are very proud of our well-run firm that meets the individual needs of our shareholders, associates, and staff and provides a great service to our community.

MONIKA HOLZER SACKS is a shareholder in Nichols, Sacks, Slank, Sendelbach & Buiteweg, P.C. in Ann Arbor and Brighton, Michigan, where she focuses on family law by mediation, collaborative practice, arbitration, and when necessary, litigation. She graduated from law school in 1978 and founded her firm in 1994. *www.nsssb.com*

- JUDY A. TOYER -

"My advice: Get comfortable with fair competition and develop a plan and the discipline to market your services honestly, confidently, and vigorously. This is easier said than done."

Hanging Your Own Shingle

I understand you may be contemplating forming your own law firm, a bold endeavor filled with many challenges and rewards. I did that over a decade ago. Although after six years of solo practice (1994–2000) I accepted an in-house counsel position, founding and operating my own law practice was one of the most important periods of my personal and professional life. I have no regrets, although I would do many things differently. I am writing to share with you some of my experiences and lessons learned. There are far too many to share in this letter. So, as I look back in the rearview mirror with the benefit of nearly 10 years as an in-house counsel who retains law firms, I have focused on some critical issues for success and contentment in building and managing your own law firm: planning and making your decision, strategically developing and maintaining relationships to get clients and keep them, selecting and training reliable staff devoted to excellent client service, and taking care of yourself.

The Decision to Hang Your Own Shingle

After clerking for a federal judge and working as an associate attorney in a large law firm and a small law firm, I thought I would try to create the practice setting that would allow me to achieve that elusive "work/life balance" in practicing law and being a wife and mom, to represent individuals and nonprofits as well as business clients, to combine litigation and transactional work—in a nutshell, to chart my own destiny. I considered potential partnerships and for various reasons rejected that idea. With my own savings, my husband's support, and books and information from some well-seasoned solo attorneys, I took the plunge and set about forming my own law firm in 1994, focusing on a corporate and employment defense practice primarily. In setting up a law firm I did many things right, and I did them well. I retained a lawyer and certified public accountant; leased and furnished beautiful office space; and purchased professional liability and other insurance, office equipment, law books, electronic legal research, word processing, payroll and other services. Then, I waited for clients, a big mistake.

I financed my own start-up; so, I worked from a "checklist" rather than a formal business plan. I highly recommend a business plan. Opening a law office is only the first critical step in creating a viable and successful law firm. Before you decide to form a law firm, prepare a business plan that addresses every aspect of creating and operating a law business, including monthly and annual budgets for revenue, expenses, and profit; cash flow analysis; marketing and client development goals; and certification as a woman-owned and/or minority-owned business. To obtain free assistance, contact the Small Business Administration (SBA), which has a wealth of information at its website, www.sba.gov. The business plan is a living road map for success. Preparation of a plan will force you to understand the magnitude of the undertaking and the need for discipline to reach your goals and objectives. SCORE (www.score. org) is another great resource for free and confidential advice on the business aspects of starting a law firm.

Getting and Keeping Clients

Although I had been practicing law for 10 years, at the time I opened my own firm, I was a novice at client and business development ("rainmaking"), one of the most important aspects of building and sustaining a successful law practice. I attended continuing legal education programs and networking events and read articles. Rainmaking was one of the most challenging aspects of managing my own law practice. To some extent, I thought that simply doing great work for current clients would generate more business. I also wrestled with overcoming discomfort with the "singing my own praises" and "tooting my own horn" syndromes.

In a very competitive legal marketplace, providing excellent service is foundational but has to be vigorously supplemented with strategic, intentional actions to get on the radar of prospective clients and to persuade them that you are the right attorney to handle their legal business. A colleague once shared that a client commented that many women do not know how to ask for business. My advice: Get comfortable with fair competition and develop a plan and the discipline to market your services honestly, confidently, and vigorously. I recommend working with mentors, a coach, or a marketing professional to build and hone your client development skills. Also, make strategic decisions about marketing activities (e.g., speeches/presentations, articles, newsletters) and about joining organizations for the purpose of client development. Success will come with planning, focused activities, discipline, learning, and patience.

Selecting and Training Staff

I enjoyed and wanted to continue representing clients in large, complex litigation, but this presented staffing challenges. Initially, I was the Jill-of-all-trades. I did everything solo. Later, I hired employees and used contract services. To address the staffing issue, I also partnered with other law firms in handling a couple of matters. However, eventually, staffing and its importance in getting and keeping clients were important factors in my decision to close my law firm and become an in-house counsel.

Understanding from the beginning what level and type of staffing you need to meet clients' expectations and to provide excellent service is extremely important. Plan to put in place and maintain not only a competitive staffing model, but also the right staff, who bring the same values and commitment to quality service to clients that you do. Poor or inappropriate staffing may prevent you from getting business, and it may cause you to lose business. Find creative and cost-effective ways to train and retain excellent staff. It is one of the best investments you will make.

Take Care of Yourself

My goal of achieving work/life balance in my own law firm was illusory. As an owner/manager, I spent more time handling client matters and managing a law practice than I had as an employee with billable hours requirements. In addition to the stress of handling client matters well and in a timely manner, there is responsibility for meeting all costs and other obligations associated with your business, particularly making payroll for your staff and yourself. Years before I started my own practice, I attended an awards ceremony for an outstanding local attorney, highly respected and very successful in representing his clients. I do not recall the details, but to the best of my recollection, at the ceremony he or someone else told a story about a bill collector calling his small law firm repeatedly for payment of an outstanding bill. After several collection calls, he said to the creditor, if he did not stop calling, the creditor's name would not be put in the hat that they used to draw the name of the creditor(s) that would be paid that month. This story evoked a lot of laughter from the audience, but I did not get the point or see the humor of the story. After starting my own law firm, I remembered the story and chuckled. I got it! In fact, it was reassuring to know that so great an attorney had challenges paying all the firm's bills and that the financial pressures of owning and operating a law firm could be spoken about publicly with humor. To meet the demands of running your own law firm, take care of yourself physically, mentally, emotionally, and spiritually: eat well, exercise, get enough sleep, spend time with family, friends, and other lawyers to keep the right perspective, laugh, and pray. I hope this helps. Best wishes.

JUDY A. TOYER is senior counsel with Eastman Kodak Company in Rochester, New York, where she advises businesses and staff organizations on personnel matters and manages employment litigation. She graduated from law school in 1983 and founded her former firm in 1994. *www.kodak.com*

- SHARLA J. FROST -

"Nothing in Evidence 101 class prepares you. . . for the indescribable feeling of satisfaction that comes from charting your own course or receiving that unexpected 'thank you' note from the young lawyer who thanks you for having helped her develop her own practice."

Even Cowgirls Get the Clients

Growing up on a cattle ranch prepared me for the practice of law in unanticipated ways. I learned that the cows must be fed whether you are making money or not, they must be fed no matter how bad the weather or how tired you are, and they must be treated and medicated no matter how inconvenient. In other words, it's like running a law firm and caring for one's clients and employees. Running a firm is the same 24-hours-a-day labor of love and inconvenience. I thought, however, that getting away from the "natural fertilizer" and bales of hay was going to lead to a more genteel way of life.

As it turns out, there is nothing genteel about the practice of law, but what I soon discovered was that living on the ranch had not prepared me for the difficulty of practicing law *while being female*. Who knew that the gender issue was going to make the business of being a lawyer so difficult?

The answer, I suppose, is that probably everyone reading this knew that. I, however, was a starry-eyed young lawyer trying to navigate the legal world. I expected to go to my first job and stay there forever, although that turned out to be wrong. In some ways, I was Goldilocks: the first firm was too big, the second too dysfunctional, the third too male-centric. It was the third firm that catapulted me into entrepreneurship.

They promised all the right things when they hired me: responsibility, partnership, training, experience. I even thought they meant it. Not until they got me, however, did I realize their hearts weren't in it. The firm was a small litigation boutique with no women partners, but the stated goal of finding one. Two partners interviewed me and expressed concern only about whether

I would be willing to learn how to handle firm management. They were happy to hire an experienced young trial lawyer who wanted to learn how to run a firm. I was happy to go to a small firm with young partners, a casual sensibility, and the prospect of meaningful partnership. Alas, it turned out they were looking for a less assertive female than they quickly found me to be. And, I discovered I was looking for a firm with a different outlook on life and the practice of law than the one they had.

Just before I started my job there, the firm had renovated their office space. Among the improvements, they built a partners' lounge with a security-coded door and, as it turned out, no women's facilities in what the associates referred to as the "Royal Potty." In keeping with the secured partners' lounge, each of the partners' doors had an automatic door closer with a red light on the outside of the door to indicate when the door was locked, and no one was permitted to ask for admittance. A female friend of mine always referred to it as the sexual harassment light, but she was wrong. It wasn't about harassment; it was about control, and it was clear to me I would never have any, despite their earnest representations to the contrary. Their commitment to women in the profession was demonstrated more by the red lights and the keypad than by anything they said.

I knew that the time had come to move on when I went in to visit with the managing partner to talk about attending an ABA Women Rainmakers session in New Orleans. He was lying down on his couch, shoes off. His secretary was at one end of the couch taking dictation; his female associate was at the other, taking directions for the case she was handling for him. (Both women had their shoes on, by the way). I made my case for the trip, which I could do with a free airline ticket and no need for an overnight stay. He patiently explained to me that my business development goals would be better served by staying in the office and billing more hours. I thanked him for his time and stepped out into the hallway.

I called my now partner from the freeway on my way to the airport. I figured someone should know where I was in case I got run over by a bus.

No one ever asked me where I had been or why I had not been in the office that next day. I have always assumed they lit a prayer candle in the Royal Potty, hoping for the day when I would go bother someone else. (My now partner later told me that they had lamented in the first two weeks after hiring me that I was a much stronger personality than they had expected. I have always attributed that misimpression to my good farm-girl background.)

Not long after the rainmaking incident, my now partner and I decided we could do better running a firm of our own. The business divorce with the prior firm was a model of civility and honest discourse. We sublet space from them; they gave us recommendations to the bank and helped us transition the clients we were taking with us. Though I later learned that they had been so magnanimous because they predicted we would go bankrupt in six months, I am still appreciative of their assistance in those early days. The smooth start we made meant that we could focus on the development of the firm and our practice. I went from obsessing about how to satisfy supervisors and employers to obsessing about how to find and satisfy clients.

I have always told people that my partner had clients and I had credit. We relied on my credit card to tide us over for the first few months before the accounts receivable starting trickling in. In those days, my partner was the trial draw; I was just an ingénue in the trial world. He tried cases week after week while I learned to read bank reports and get comfortable asking potential clients for business.

In time, the firm grew from three lawyers to 47 and then back down to 10 after tort reform reconfigured the legal business in our state. At each stage of the growth and contraction of the practice we have had growing pains and learning opportunities. I have fed and watered the firm at times when I was too tired and too distracted to keep moving. My clients have entrusted me with cases worth several billion dollars; bar organizations ask me to speak to them, and young lawyers ask me for advice on career development. I never expected any of that when I was calling to say that I was going absent without leave to an ABA meeting, but I knew that I needed a different environment and the chance to try supervising myself.

Being responsible for your own business involves a layer of complexity that the practice of law alone does not. Law school does not prepare you for negotiating with the bank, negotiating an office lease, training young lawyers, or supervising employees. I have spent endless hours reading business publications to understand the business aspects of firm management. There have been untold hours trying to figure out how best to train and retain the young lawyers we have hired, and additional hours spent figuring out how to part with lawyers who turned out not to be a fit for the firm or for whom we no longer had enough work. Nothing in Evidence 101 class prepares you for the difficulty of convincing a company to hire you to defend them in litigation, nor does it prepare you for the angst of supervising lawyers and other employees. It also doesn't prepare you for the indescribable feeling of satisfaction that comes from charting your own course or receiving that unexpected "thank you" note from the young lawyer who thanks you for having helped her develop her own practice.

If I had it to do all over again, I would still choose to be boss instead of being bossed. I highly recommend it for any woman who finds that she fits poorly in a traditional firm. My firm is in its 17th year. The guys at the third firm finally found a couple of female lawyers who were better suited to be their partners. I like to think that I was a learning experience for them as they were for me. As it turns out, sometimes, even cowgirls get the clients, whether they have permission to do so or not.

SHARLA J. FROST is the managing partner at Powers & Frost, L.L.P. in Houston, Texas, where she defends corporate defendants in products liability and commercial litigation trials throughout the United States. She graduated from law school in 1987 and founded her firm in 1994. *www.powersfrost.com*

CHAPTER 4

1995-1999

Creating
Work/Life Balance

"And if you were a woman, chances are you were told (or it otherwise became clear) that you had to make a choice between working as a professional and being a mom. You certainly would not make partner if you did not sacrifice family life for the long hours."

—Michele Ballard Miller

Letters from women who founded firms during the five years from 1995 through 1999 articulate work/life balance as the prime motivator.

In addition, this period marks the first spread of new firm founders across the age groups. Among the 17 writers in this chapter are seven who graduated in the 1980s and 10 who graduated in the 1990s. Largely, they are a group with significant experience in practice, making choices to take charge of the shape of their weeks and the productive use of their time.

As to the emergence of discussion about work/life balance, the subject was entering mainstream legal media in the late 1990s. Firms were broadly adopting part-time policies, and some were turning to alternative childcare programs. Many women lawyers saw the strain on their families created by increasing competition at the office around high billable hours. The bad fit between traditional firm practices on the one hand and the requirements of parenting or caregiving on the other had become commonly acknowledged.

Perhaps this context gave women "permission" to articulate work/life concerns publicly. Perhaps it helped parents to acknowledge the bad fit and to act to solve it. Whatever the cause, numerous writers in this chapter speak frankly about time to serve the family being a prime motivator for breaking out. Indeed, a group who founded one of the first "virtual law firms" explains that the genesis of their inventive business model was precisely to create a better fit between complex and interesting legal matters and the need to preserve the family. They transformed their practice environment.

Different mechanisms to achieve work/life balance appear here. The writers describe firms founded while their children were babies, firms that encourage flexible part-time schedules and impose 1,800 hours as a *maximum*, and firms founded by leaders who were impatient with working full time on part-time schedules and part-time compensation.

To be sure, not all writers in this chapter point to balance as their issue. Some point to new legal specialties, such as elder law and special education representation, as the driver for them to leave their firms and to differentiate their new firms. Others had come to recognize the pocketbook power of their grasp on practice, as did one family law practitioner who learned that clients were drawn to her old firm because of her work, rather than through the good offices of senior partners.

These writers highlight that women lawyers, with or without families, are businesswomen, are ambitious, are passionate about their careers, and will pursue practice methods that give their careers balance in the broadest sense.

- GENA TONER -

"Remember this Latin phrase that I first saw in a plaque over a judge's door: 'Illegitimus non carborundum est.' If you don't know what that means, you should look it up."

I started my own firm about a year after a period of major transition in my life. Within about two weeks' time in 1994, I became engaged, then suffered major personal injuries in an accident, then had my house burn down. If it hadn't been for all this, I might still be working for the state. The situation really made it the right time to go into private practice, and I was able to rely on my husband's salary and health insurance while I got the office up and running. When I started my practice, I was doing some contract work for the public defender's office. I was able to finish out my contract work while starting a law office, which gave me some income. That was a good thing, because it sure wasn't coming from the law office at first.

One thing I learned quickly is that clients don't just flock to your new office. I talked to my local judges, who gave me court-appointed work in guardianship and criminal cases. The first few months were pretty frustrating financially. What saved me was that I started my practice in a satellite office shared by several established firms. I had negotiated a set price per month and had the use of the conference room, waiting room, copier, and so forth. When the other lawyers came out to the office, I had someone to ask questions. Getting to know these folks was a good way to get referrals, which I still get today, 15 years later.

After a few years at the "little office," as I now call it, my husband and I were getting ready to have our first baby. I negotiated with the landlord of the center that my office was in and got him to agree to pay for a build out on an empty office space in the same building. By working with the walls that were already in place and making a few minor adjustments, a coat of paint and some carpentry work (supplied by the landlord) made the office like new, at least to me. I used a tiny room for a nursery, and soon I was toting a briefcase in one hand and a baby carrier in the other to go to hearings. Maybe it was because I practiced in a relatively small town, or because I knew the judges through my previous practice experience, but they all agreed that I could bring my baby to court with me. Amazingly enough, my clients also didn't object to a lawyer showing up with a baby. So for the first year and a half of Mia's life, she attended more court hearings than many lawyers do in a lifetime.

At this time I was also determined to establish myself as a heavy hitter in the legal community. My husband came into practice with me a few months after Mia was born, and he took over all the criminal defense. That left me focusing on family law, which was not what I set out wanting to do, but those were the cases I got. I had plenty of trial experience from my starting out years at the public defender's office, and I used that experience to establish myself as a top contender in the eyes of the other local lawyers. I had a great case of a man who wanted custody of his four kids, and I knew with some hard work I could beat the legal aid attorney handling the wife's case. I don't think the judge had ever awarded custody to a man before, and winning that trial was sweet. Then I wanted to win a trial against a private attorney. Another case came my way of a man who wanted custody of his son in his divorce. I worked hard on that case, writing direct examination questions on the weekends and having numerous meetings with my client, his parents, and witnesses. I got a private investigator to do some great work on the case for me. When I won that case against a respected local lawyer, I felt competent, confident, and successful. I was also nine months pregnant. I had to finish the trial in a maternity sweat suit outfit and sneakers. I asked to meet with the judge in chambers prior to court and apologized but explained it was the only thing that fit.

Then I had a newborn and a toddler at the office every day. I am so glad I had them with me during that time. After a while, it became apparent that the best thing to do for them was to let them be at home and not stuck in an office all day. Eventually we moved to within walking distance of the office. That was great to balance out my work and home life. We soon built a house and were a few miles away from the office. At the end of my neighborhood was an empty lot, and every time I would drive by it I would think, what a great place it would be for my office. One day, a for sale sign appeared, and I told my husband we were buying the lot and putting up a building. Always one to agree to my ideas, he went along with it. The day my son Riley started kindergarten, construction began on the "new office." We were able to design and build a space that met our needs and those of our kids. They have their own room with a couch and a TV, where they can go when they get off the school bus. Almost everyone who comes in compliments us on the interior, often mentioning how the sage green walls are such a soothing color. I always laugh inwardly, because when that color went on the walls, there was no carpet or white woodwork to balance it out, just total greenness. I had begged my husband in the middle of the night to go look at the color and tell me if it was hideous or not. The saint he is, Steve went up to the office with a flashlight and came back and reported that the color was fine.

Now we have been in our building for four years. We rented a separate office unit in our building to another law firm, which helps pay the mortgage. Our practice is still the two of us and two support staff, which includes my secretary-paralegal Judy, who has been my right hand and confidante for 13 years. In the midst of all this my husband and I both became board certified by the Florida Bar, Steve in criminal trial law and I in marital and family law. The same year (2001) that I became certified in marital and family law, I got my certification as a family law mediator. I have been involved in pro bono work, professional organizations, and bar committees as time permits.

It has been a very eventful but not especially easy road. As with any working mom, it is hard to do it all. I have been blessed in having my own firm with the ability to take off work for events at my children's school or to have time for long weekend trips and memorable vacations. It is a great help to have a wonderful caring husband to literally work by my side.

As some sage advice for women starting their practices, I say retain who you are as a woman. You don't need to be abrasive with other lawyers to try to make an impression as to your professional aggressiveness. Keep your ethics above all, because if you don't, word will get around with the other lawyers and judges, and it will be detrimental to you and your clients. Remember, this law stuff is a business. You may feel bad for the potential client sitting across the desk with the tale of woe, but most likely you are doing this to make a living for yourself and your loved ones. So don't undercharge for your work or take a case for payments that you'll never really see. Don't be afraid to withdraw from representation if your client won't pay. Remember what is important to you, whether it is your family, your hobbies, your spiritual beliefs, or whatever, and keep that thing in its place of importance in your life. Try not to let the office intrude on that. And perhaps most importantly, remember this Latin phrase that I first saw in a plaque over a judge's door and now is inscribed on a paperweight on my desk: "Illegitimus non carborundum est." If you don't know what that means, you should look it up.

GENA TONER is the president of Toner Law in Spring Hill, Florida, where she is a Florida Bar board certified lawyer specializing in marital and family law. She graduated from law school in 1986 and founded her firm in 1995. *www.tonerlaw.com*

- BARBARA WALSH MOSER -

"Business development for your own business is so much easier than when you work for someone else. . . . I eat, sleep, and breathe my business."

I urge you to take the plunge and start your own law firm! It's not only scary and challenging, I can promise that it's fun, it's exhilarating, it's liberating, and it's rewarding, both professionally and financially.

My partner, Susan E. Kaye, and I worked together in the tax department of one of the oldest and largest law firms in San Francisco, California. We are two very different women, but in the fall of 1994, just after I had my second child in 16 months, we decided it was time to strike out on our own. We started our firm (Kaye·Moser, now Kaye·Moser·Hierbaum LLP) on May 2, 1995, with $5,000 each, three computers, two offices, and a secretary station with no secretary! By the end of the first month, we were in the black, and we have never looked back. Fifteen years later, we are now a well-known family law and trusts and estates boutique law firm with five attorneys and two staff members.

The decision to leave big firm life was both easy and hard. It was scary. We earned great money at our firm and had amazing benefits. However, even in the 1990s, life at a big firm was no picnic for women. I had gone to law school to become a family lawyer, and this was the most elite practice in town. I loved working there actually, but after having two babies in 16 months, it was clear that I needed to move on and take control of my life (or alternatively, to be sure I could have a life). I was lucky to have a fellow associate who also wanted to move on. So, two "girls" from different backgrounds with a shared vision made a plan. The firm is 15 years old today, with five attorneys and gross revenues of well over $1 million! Sometimes we have to pinch ourselves to know if it's real or a dream.

I have several pieces of advice at several phases of the game:

I. Plan Ahead! Planning and Implementation

Where to house your new practice? We opted for subleasing space from a big firm. We have now done that in various places for all 15 years. The pros outweigh the cons for us: We receive hundreds of referrals from the other lawyers at the firms we have sublet from (firms will only let you sublease if they don't offer your practice area), which now includes all of the firms those folks have moved to; we have bigger and better space than we could get as a small firm; we utilize their conference rooms and their receptionist (one less employee for us!), as well as their fancy copiers, postage meters, and the like. In most of the subleases, we did not need our own furniture. It's like buying a house in move-in condition, furnished!

Don't burn bridges at the former firm. We took clients with us, but we kept in touch with former colleagues, and they, too, refer us business. You can check with your local bar to find out the ethical rules about informing clients of your departure (and hope they come with you!).

Take other practitioners in your field to lunch. We did this before we left our old firm, with anyone who would have us. Our colleagues did not yet see us as competition, so they gave us advice, showed us their financials, told us who they used for messenger service, professional liability insurance, and billing, and dispensed other practical advice.

Send out announcements about your new firm. We never put anything in our local legal newspaper, as many do, because we found that sending out announcements and brochures is more effective and more personal.

Do your research before you start. Do your research about things you will need like computers, supplies, printers, faxes, telephone lines, etc. before you are in business. Then you can be ready to work as soon as you get set up.

II. Where's The Business Going to Come From?

Opportunities are everywhere. Business development is my favorite part of the business! Business development for your own business is so much easier than when you work for someone else. I like to say I eat, sleep, and breathe my business. I am fascinated by being a businesswoman and fascinated that people are interested in my business. Wherever I go and wherever I perceive there could be a referral source, I work what I do into the conversation. For example, early on, when I was touring preschools for my sons, I would strike up conversations with the other young mothers. I remember one of my first clients came from a preschool tour. I always carry cards with me, and now I even carry our beautiful and glossy brochures in my purse. When everyone else passes out their cards, I give people my brochure, with bios and all—it turns people's heads! Recently, I was sitting at a sports game at my son's private school with someone who was telling me that her wealthy friend had just died—of course, I'm thinking business (my partner does probate and trust administration). This person doesn't really know me. So, I say casually, "You know, if you need help, let me know. My partner does that. Here's my brochure." She had no idea who I was before that. Her friend is now a client of ours. All of my physicians refer cases to me, and everyone at my children's schools (we've given talks about estate planning to them) and at my law school refers cases to me. If you belong to a church or synagogue, a gym, or anywhere you are, you can talk up your business! Again, I eat, sleep, and breathe it, and for me, it's a challenge and a very fun part of my job.

Referrals are potential referrers. Also, anyone who calls me about a referral or who calls me for my services is a potential future referral source. I speak with potential clients and screen my own calls. This way, (a) I can tell if a case or client is appropriate for me, and (b) people feel very taken care of either way—very important for future referrals. I often say, the people I refer away refer me the most cases!

Thank your referral sources. Ask your client who referred them, and send a thank you letter. That, in and of itself, is business development. They may have given your name out months before. Now you've reminded them about your services again. Another great thing that I learned from a really smart businesswoman in Los Angeles was to send a gift around the holidays to those who have referred you business. She did this once, and I never forgot it. I do this every year to those who gave me a good case or to those whom I'd like more referrals from. It's a few thousand dollars to generate hundreds of thousands of dollars worth of business.

In Summary
I would say the following, looking back: starting your own firm is exhausting, but it gives you the ultimate power, the ultimate control over your life, and it

is a great feeling owning your own business. As a mother of two, I have felt I could be with my children whenever I needed to be but also have an amazing and rewarding career. It was good for my marriage, good for my health, good for my well-being, and in the end, good for my kids.

BARBARA WALSH MOSER is the founding partner of Kaye·Moser·Hierbaum LLP in San Francisco, California, a boutique family law and estate planning firm serving high net worth individuals with complex matters. She graduated from law school in 1990 and founded her firm in 1995. *www.kayemoser.com*

- SUSAN CARTIER LIEBEL -

"It just couldn't be that hard. Every new client, every retainer agreement, every client victory was testament to my new ability to make our three-lawyer firm succeed. It felt so good."

When Duty whispers low, Thou must, The youth replies, I can!
—Ralph Waldo Emerson

This is the first quotation to enter my mind when I reflect back upon my journey from entering law school as a nontraditional student in 1992 to creating Solo Practice University in 2009, the #1 web-based educational and professional networking site for lawyers and law students. But this journey began because I had a desire to be an entrepreneur, the captain of my own ship, long before I went to law school 10 years after graduating college. Ironically, I saw law school as the ultimate entrepreneurial adventure, both a noble profession and an opportunity to be in business for myself. It had all the necessary ingredients: high portability, minimal overhead, one self-contained package—me. After all, I am the product, the service provider, the marketer, the accountant, and the technology guru. This combination made me unstoppable. Except, law school (and the profession itself) wanted to stop me. From the moment I entered law school, if I mentioned solo practice as the ultimate goal, the true measure of my success, the cherry on the sundae, the pinnacle of legal practice—I was mocked, disparaged, made to feel not only lesser than, but "insane." I felt like Alice falling down the rabbit hole. I was in an alternate universe where black was white and wrong was right.

Now, if you knew me well you'd understand this: the very fact I received little to no assistance from my law school and the profession turned the desire to become a successful solo practitioner into the ultimate challenge. It was X-Games for the over-30 crowd as I entered law school at 32. I was going to prove the naysayers wrong by becoming wildly successful. And therein lies the rub. What was success? What was my definition of success? The traditional journey on the cattle car to the Big Law dairy farm to be milked daily in my billable hour stall? Never. Yet I had to know what success meant to me both professionally and personally before I could move forward. Without knowing both there would always be friction, imbalance, and inevitable competition between the two. And when there is friction and unwanted competition, there is misery. When there is misery, one questions why she ever opted for solo practice, sometimes even questioning her choice of the law itself. I knew with every fiber of my being that working in a large law firm was simply not an option. I could never work for another.

Success defined by me is freedom to choose. Freedom of time and space. Unlimited sky above. It is this simple. It is this complicated. I knew I wanted to one day be married, have children, have a steady income from my law practice, or a business of my creation, which would allow me to contribute to the growth of my family if I was blessed to have one. I wanted to contribute in a meaningful way to our financial comfort while contributing in my own unique way to the world. I absolutely knew in my heart I didn't require an employer to provide a paycheck. Quite frankly, I have always found the limitations of a paycheck inhibiting, not freeing. I wanted to be paid commensurate with my performance. I have always been willing to fly or die on my own steam. I knew I could make this work.

While in law school I met two kindred spirits, and upon passing the bar we opened our practice. We started out working from our homes long before it was chic, turning home visits with clients into a positive experience for all of us. We then negotiated office space, bartering legal services for paint, carpeting, and more. We found mentors and challenged ourselves through each process, knowing in our hearts we could figure it out or find someone who would help. It just couldn't be that hard. Every new client, every retainer agreement, every client victory was a testament to my ability to make our three-lawyer firm succeed. It felt so good. And then I knew. I knew I had to teach others how to do it, how to believe in themselves, how to become a legal entrepreneur, the solo practitioner, because it was not only not fair, it was dishonest not to teach this very real and very viable option to law students. In January, 2001, I became an adjunct professor at Quinnipiac University School of Law helping students bridge the gap between law school and starting their own business, a course I wish they had taught when I attended. I taught this wait-listed class for eight years. Then, after five years of a small firm partnership, I became a true solo practitioner while continuing to teach. I finally addressed the other part of my definition of "success." I got married and became a mom. It was during this transition to wife and mother that I realized my true passion lies in helping others fulfill their dreams of solo practice. This epiphany dovetailed nicely with my desire to be home to raise my son. Eventually, I closed my solo practice and opened my consultancy full-time. One thing led to another, and as my son blossomed, so did my dream to create Solo Practice University, where more than 40 faculty provide online nuts and bolts education to law students and lawyers on how to be solo practitioners.

I have no patience for people telling me what I can't do. This profession is sadly full of those who would quash your desires and dreams, imposing their fears upon you. Listen to yourself and your significant other as your choices directly impact their definition of success, too. Shut out those who will tell you your ideas are folly. Define success based upon your professional and personal wants and needs. This can be owning the largest law firm in your state, working out of your home office next to your child's nursery just three hours a day, three days a week, or writing books on law. Your law license gives you the freedom to choose. While your degree was costly, buying into someone else's idea of how you should use it is far costlier to your mental and physical health and to those who love and need you most. Your degree should not handcuff you to an image of what a lawyer should be. It should free you to redefine that image as well as how law is practiced. It should allow you to shape your life in a way that is immensely fulfilling, which could also mean practicing law is just part of the journey toward your real destination.

The golden thread present through all my life's experiences, the purpose of my law degree, was to experience this journey before you, to learn how to define success on my own terms, and to find fulfillment in creating an environment to teach others how to do so as well. I work from my home. I'm here for my son and husband the way I want and need to be. I'm in charge of my own paycheck. I capitalized upon technology, social media, and my personal experiences to create a thriving business catering to the solo practitioner while giving back to the legal community in a way that satisfies my personal and professional definition of success. There is no tension or competition between my personal and professional goals. To do it any other way would be to cheat myself. For you to do it any other way than what is right for you would be to cheat yourself. There is nothing more rewarding than being in charge of yourself and your time, owning your choices and taking pride in the end result.

SUSAN CARTIER LIEBEL is the founder of Solo Practice University, an online educational and professional networking community for lawyers and law students headquartered in Connecticut. She graduated from law school in 1994 and founded her first firm in 1995 and her company in 2009. *http://solopracticeuniversity.com*

- MADELEINE WELDON-LINNE -

"Keeping the client by providing superior legal services has been our responsibility. Today about 20 percent of our firm's cases are assigned by clients who gave our firm a chance because of our WBE status."

The decision to leave an established defense firm and start my defense firm was based on the fact that my practice was self-sustaining and self-contained. My clients were brought to the firm or developed by me for over 13 years. My clients had no relationship with the firm's equity partners. They hired me to do their work and assigned cases to me. Unlike the male equity partners, my clients were not concerned with the amount of time I physically spent in the office. They knew that I was immediately responsive and available to them. I kept one to two associates busy full time assisting me on my cases. I had not been assigned a case by a partner in 12 years. All case assignments came directly to me.

My relationship with the firm was not healthy. I was less than the male second class or non-equity partners. I was a non-equity partner/mother who worked 12-hour days in the office three to four days a week. I agreed to minimally bill 1,500 hours per year (4/5 of the 2,000 hour requirement) at 3/5 salary. My trial schedule drove my billable hours. At my last annual partnership meeting, I learned that when I billed 2,000 hours in the previous two years it was more hours than two of the equity partners. All of the partners, including the other non-equity partners, received a large bonus, but I was excluded from the bonuses because I was part-time—even though I billed full-time hours. I decided that I could never overcome the stigma of organizing my successful practice differently than the other partners (all men or women without children) to accommodate my family.

Even if my clients decided to stay with the previous firm, I knew I could earn other clients. I had everything I needed professionally to control my practice. It made no sense that the partners controlled my compensation and devalued my contributions.

I did not initially intend to form a Women's Business Enterprise (WBE) law firm. I decided to form a partnership with a male non-equity partner in my previous firm because I trusted him and respected his legal abilities. I had more experience and a larger client base than he did, so it was understood that I would be the majority partner in our new firm. We initially brought two associates with us.

At first, we had fewer cases to work on. I had a six-week trial scheduled the first month of our firm's existence, and that case provided the majority of our firm's revenue for the first six months as a law firm. We developed new clients, and more cases were assigned from the clients who came with us to our firm.

Because I was the majority owner of the firm, our firm was eligible for WBE status. I was certified by every state, private, and municipal entity as a WBE law firm. I recertified every year. The paperwork was voluminous, tedious, and the violation of my privacy (all assets and W-2s provided) was concerning. I wrote RFPs. I was sometimes interviewed. I was sometimes selected as panel counsel. Our WBE firm was listed on dozens of websites as approved panel counsel, but we were not assigned a case due to WBE status for almost 10 years. It seemed the work was always awarded to larger firms. The RFP winners were not WBE or MBE law firms. It was disheartening. Certification seemed like a sham. Why get certified? Was it just an exercise? Why was our firm on the approved panel if we were not assigned cases?

My attitude toward the WBE certification process changed when I associated with the National Association of Minority & Women Owned Law Firms (NAMWOLF). I learned that NAMWOLF's affiliation with similar law firms and an enthusiastic collaboration toward the goal of providing opportunities to WBE/MBE law firms were the key to securing work from clients who would not otherwise consider a 10-person WBE or Minority Business Enterprise (MBE) firm. Keeping the client by providing superior legal services has been our responsibility. Today about 20 percent of our firm's cases are assigned by clients who gave our firm a chance because of our WBE status.

Our business model was to simplify the large firm bureaucracy and distill it down to the basic elements of communication and collaboration with the client. We did not stress structure of the individual lawyer's practice but demanded an excellent work product from every lawyer.

Our biggest challenge has been the retention of loyal and driven associates willing to provide the firm and our clients with more than is asked of them and more than what is expected. Associates who remain a firm expense after a reasonable ramp up period (six months) do not further the firm's mission and are not a resource valued by our clients. Valued associates are wooed by bigger firms. We have never lost an associate to an MBE or WBE.

MADELEINE WELDON-LINNE is the founding partner at Weldon-Linne & Vogt in Chicago, Illinois, where she focuses on complex negligence litigation, including medical malpractice defense. She graduated from law school in 1981 and founded her firm in 1996. *www.wlv-online.com*

- SANDRA P. GREENBLATT -

"My next goal is to identify a talented young lawyer to join me, so that I can nominate her as my 'heiress apparent' to continue our firm if I ever want to slow down or retire."

I was a cheerleader—not in high school for sports teams, but for the major Florida and national law firms that employed me as an associate and later a partner. I never intended to have my own law firm. My parents were working class people, and I had never considered being an entrepreneur. It was only after my first large law firm employer dissolved and several later unpleasant experiences with male partners in large law firms that I exited my comfort zone. In desperation, I called a good friend who has her own solo law firm, knowing I couldn't take it one more day. Having no business experience and no idea how to start a law office, by reaching out to friends I quickly learned that help is available. For not much money and lots of moral support, my friend recommended a wonderful consultant who helped me locate shared office space with other solo practitioners, including a former big firm colleague, buy computers, and comply with the Florida Bar requirements and notices to get started.

As one who spends more hours at work than at home most days, I suggest not skimping on your surroundings and location. I had feared, needlessly, that I would be all alone in a small lonely office off a deserted hallway. I advise others not to go that route but to find a synergistic, friendly, and professional office environment in which to establish your firm. It made the transition much easier. In hindsight, however, my biggest mistake was selecting a location out of the mainstream. Over the next few years, this proved to be somewhat of a barrier to developing major clients. When I established my own firm a second time (after accepting an offer from a big firm that was too good to refuse but should have been), I located my firm in the heart of the downtown in "A" space, subleasing from lawyers who were better positioned to refer me clients and vice versa, with much better results. While I sometimes missed having other associates and partners to consult with on legal questions, I soon created a network of other quality solo practitioners who were more than willing to brainstorm and consult on matters in exchange for my returning the favor.

In addition to finding a kind and effective consultant to help establish my first solo office, the best advice I received was to establish a personal relationship with a senior bank officer. Before this, I had always banked at Citibank and other large banks where I almost never interacted with anyone but a bank teller. In starting my law firm, my accountant introduced me to a manager at a smaller bank known for service, who helped me establish appropriate operating and trust accounts, as well as a line of credit. Inevitably, especially in the beginning, I made errors in my banking and QuickBooks, from which I was rescued by the personal attention and service of this bank manager. Over the years, I have fostered such banking relationships and found them invaluable.

The economic reality of solo practice was pleasantly surprising. If you keep your overhead reasonable, you need far less revenue (i.e., billable hours) to earn the same income or even more than in a larger law firm, due to their high overhead and compensation formulas. At first, I missed law firm "perks," like going to seminars for free. I soon realized that, although now I had to pay for the seminars, I no longer needed to ask permission to attend! Priceless! It took me several years, but I also learned the importance of not undervaluing my services. I think women find this a greater challenge than male lawyers. Check the going rates in your specialty and geographic area, and set a fair rate for your services. Remember to increase rates as you become busier, if the market allows. Another benefit of being independent is that you have the ability to be more flexible in charging clients for your work—for example, on an hourly or per project basis—that you may not enjoy in a larger law firm. Telling clients that they will have your personal attention and experience and not be delegated to junior associates is an excellent selling point and one for which clients are willing to pay.

Significantly, I now believe that solo practice enables me to best serve my clients. As a health law specialist, my clients occasionally require tax or securities legal advice, or litigation, none of which I provide. In a big firm, I was taught always to tell clients that the firm could handle whatever they needed. Keeping the business within the firm did not always serve the best interests of the client. Now, as a solo practitioner, I have the freedom and flexibility to select and refer my clients to lawyers with the necessary specific expertise who will serve the best interests of the client. Those attorneys appreciate my referrals and treat the clients as their own, which they are for the specific engagement. Meeting clients' needs in that fashion also has the benefit of creating new sources of client referrals back from those other lawyers.

Large firms generally have large marketing budgets and even professional personnel for that purpose. As a solo or small law firm, both the expense and the responsibility of marketing generally are yours. You may be the best lawyer in town, but if no one knows it, your phone won't ring. It is very important to build a reputation and promote your special expertise. Give speeches, write articles, and advertise in applicable trade journals, if possible. If networking at cocktail parties and chambers of commerce is not your strong point, try selecting a charity or community organization in which to become active. Marketing takes many forms but is essential to growing a law practice. I was terrified when asked to give my first speech. Now, I actually enjoy speaking, and my presentations have generated significant business and helped establish my reputation as a leading transactional health lawyer. And ladies, don't be afraid to *ask* for referrals and for work from potential clients and colleagues! Don't assume that just because they know you, they will think of you when they need legal services unless you have made it very clear to them (in a professional manner, of course).

Well, I've now run my own firm for a total of 12 years. I get regular calls from head hunters seeking a health lawyer for a large law firm. I used to be tempted, but when they talk about billable hours, origination credit, blah blah blah, I smile and honestly tell them I'm not interested. I love the independence and flexibility I have being my own boss. I am accountable only to my clients and not to other partners or employers. However, "be careful what you wish for" is true at times. I am thankful I have a steady flow of work from quality clients. My challenge today is managing that success. For now, my home life during the week takes a back seat, but I am fortunate to have a supportive husband and kids who are grown and on their own. I feel at the top of my game, and I intend to enjoy it for as long as possible. My next goal is to identify a talented young lawyer to join me, so that I can nominate her as my "heiress apparent" to continue our firm if I ever want to slow down or retire.

SANDRA P. GREENBLATT is president of Sandra Greenblatt, P.A. in Miami, Florida, where she represents health care professionals, facilities, and payors in their regulatory, corporate, and contractual matters. She graduated from law school in 1984 and founded her firm in 1996. *www.flhealthlawyer.com*

- SHERYL L. RANDAZZO -

"Keep it simple. Your clients . . . don't care if you have mahogany trim in your office. . . . Get so good at what you do that people will be happy to pay for your time and advice."

Anyone who knows me has heard me say that I was probably the least likely person from my law school graduating class to start her own practice, but that's exactly what I did. And it didn't happen after many years of working for others or because I felt I had no other option. It came from self-knowledge, respect for my clients, and recognition of my ability to learn everything I need to know or to seek out assistance when necessary.

I went to and through law school wanting to practice elder law, and I had exemplary clinical and internship experience with the elderly, as well as significant, albeit not lawyer, employment experience with senior citizens. But the legal community in Suffolk County, Long Island where I wanted to live and work is made up of primarily small and solo practitioners, most of whom were not in a position to hire another full-time attorney, so opportunities were scarce.

After significant pavement pounding, I was hired by a defense litigation firm, being candid about my intentions to practice elder law while promising to work hard and apply myself fully during my time with them. The partners appreciated my candor, and they didn't have to pay me much. Simultaneously, I joined two different county bar associations and the New York State Bar Association and became a member of their respective elder law and surrogates court related committees. I took every then non-mandatory continuing legal education course even remotely related to elder law and estate planning. I also shared my enthusiasm for eventually practicing elder law with everyone I met.

Approximately two years in, when I was getting frustrated for not being able to practice elder law yet, two different associate positions were made known to me, not through the *Law Journal* or other formal employment listings but directly by partners of two different firms, based solely upon my evident commitment to the practice of elder law although I was practicing elsewhere. Quite unexpectedly, both positions were offered to me, with as close to a bidding war as I could imagine ensuing. I chose the one I believed was the right fit and would have the most potential for me.

It did not take long to see that the position was not a right fit, and I initially wondered if I had made the correct choice of firms. This is when self-knowledge came into play. With much soul searching, particularly about why I personally wanted to practice elder law, I realized that working in either position would not enable me to be true to myself. Through my experience to that point in time, I learned that there are two basic reasons attorneys practice elder law. The first is based upon a business decision and recognition of the ever-increasing number of people who will need legal services as they age, which will result in a growing pool of potential clients. The second reason to practice elder law is based upon a call to service for this very special group of people and a genuine respect and appreciation for their legal needs.

As I implied initially, I do not view myself as a businessperson, but I do know I love my clients, want to help them, and personally benefit by doing so. (I often refer to my clients as my "CliffsNotes" to life, because given sufficient time, my clients generously share their most valuable life lessons with me, and I benefit tremendously.) So, although not a businessperson per se, I started my own business as an attorney with a practice limited to elder law, estate planning, and estate administration.

Before actually hanging out my shingle, I spoke with family, friends, and respected colleagues to garner their support and request practical advice. I made a particular point of speaking with a few attorneys, male and female, who appeared to be satisfied in their practices, balanced in their demeanors, and happy in their lives. After all, isn't that what we all want? The advice I received was invaluable.

Keep it simple. Your clients want you to return their phone calls. They don't care if you have mahogany trim in your office. You are one person, why do you need 15 phone lines? Get so good at what you do that people will be happy to pay for your time and advice. Make good use of your downtime. If you treat people right, you won't have much of it for very long. I could go on indefinitely

That was 1996. I practiced on my own until 1999, when my brother came to work with me, and we then formed our partnership in 2000. There has not been a day I regret doing so. Why? Because I love what I do and that I get to decide how I do it. I continue to enjoy my clients, and I genuinely feel that I am able to make a difference in their lives. I have the best partner I could hope for, who wears my name proudly, has similar values, and is entirely trustworthy. Professionally, I am able to be active in my local bar association, and I enjoy being surrounded by and collaborating with colleagues who are hardworking, kind, positive, and want to give back to the community.

My referral sources are primarily my prior clients and attorneys who don't do what I do. Many are people I met along the way who consistently heard me say I looked forward to practicing elder law and knew it was my genuine passion. People, both attorneys and laypersons, appreciate working with people who love what they do. Business is good, and I recognize how fortunate I am in every aspect of my life.

SHERYL L. RANDAZZO is a partner at Randazzo & Randazzo, LLP in Huntington and Manhattan, New York, where she focuses on elder law, estate planning, and estate administration. She graduated from law school in 1992 and founded her firm in 1996. *www.randazzoandrandazzo.com*

- Johnna Goodmark -
&
- Amy Hillman -

"While virtual law firms are now haute couture, *our particular firm model was born over 15 years ago. More than anything else, its genesis was necessity."*

We understand that you may be at a crossroads. You are thinking about starting a law practice—perhaps with others or perhaps on your own. To be sure, it is a big decision. As you study your options, we thought you might benefit from our experience.

First, you may want to know a little about us. We are partners in a small, women-owned, virtual law firm. While virtual law firms are now *haute couture*, our particular firm model was born over 15 years ago. More than anything else, its genesis was necessity. At that time, there were very few options for women attorneys with families wanting flexibility and control of their time and advancement to partnership. The traditional firm model seemed to demand an "either/or" choice. The road for women attorneys was to either continue on the legal autobahn without making allowances for family or find the exit ramp. The concept of a work/life balance was a goal, but not a reality. We needed a firm that allowed each of us to take control of our career, provide for our families, and work on complex and interesting matters—all without sacrificing our relationships with our families.

You may wonder how our firm works. For us (and for our clients) the allure is in the simplicity. We have no central office, no employees, and no associates. We are partner-level attorneys glued together by personal relationships, a common work ethic, and technology. We meet monthly to discuss firm business and other important matters. We share expenses and duties related to firm administration. We each have our own clients. We refer clients to each other and often work together on matters. We are there for each other to provide a second opinion and support when someone is out of the office or on vacation. The limited overhead of our firm model translates into cost savings that we pass along to our clients. When a face-to-face client meeting or negotiation is required, we travel to our clients' offices, meet at a mutually convenient location, or utilize conference room facilities.

Each of our partners spent several years working in large, traditional law firms developing her knowledge base, leadership skills, and potential to generate business. Though varied in our experiences, we share a collective philosophy with respect to work product and client service. We never sought to change who we were as lawyers or reinvent ourselves. We sought only to reinvent the environment in which we practiced. From a financial perspective, the start-up costs of our firm model are relatively small. However, you do have to be prepared to incur expenses and go with little to no income for several months. From an emotional and professional perspective, it is helpful to have supportive spouses and professional mentors to ease the transition. Training, support, and being financially prepared are integral to success.

Running any business has its challenges, and a law firm is no exception. You must accept that the buck stops with you. With flexibility and authority comes responsibility. It can seem daunting, but if you have self-discipline and desire, you will succeed. Always remember that whether you have a virtual office or a panoramic view from the tallest building downtown, you must develop your core competencies and bring value to the matter at hand in order to attract and serve clients.

One very obvious challenge that anyone with a virtual office must confront is maintaining the self-discipline to essentially practice law "from home." For some this may mean putting pen to paper, and for others it means being sufficiently disciplined to turn off the office lights and call it a day. Make no mistake—it is not for the faint of heart or easily distracted practitioner. The quality of work must be top notch. You will not be graded on a curve by your clients or colleagues because you are a woman or because you practice in an unconventional firm. In fact, you will find yourself working harder than your traditional firm counterparts because of those factors. Rest assured, the rewards are worth it. We can honestly say that each of us loves our firm and our practice. Yes, there are challenges, but as with most things in life, hard work and a positive attitude will carry you far.

Billing and client management can present challenges for the newly indepen-dent practitioner. With respect to billing, do not over-sell yourself. Your abil-ity to contain costs should be reflected in the rates you establish. Lower rates will make you more competitive in the marketplace. Of course, don't under-sell yourself either. Be sure to factor in administrative and other nonbillable time that will be spent managing your matters. Remember that since you probably will not have the same level of administrative help that you enjoyed at your previous firm, you should expect to spend more time on nonbillable tasks than you did in the past. Send your bills out promptly, and make sure that each bill represents excellent value for services rendered.

With respect to client management, you need to find a way to become an integral part of the client's service team. You do that not only by adding value, but also by being reliable, diligent, and professional. Know your subject matter, complete your work on time, deliver error-free e-mails and documents, return phone calls and e-mails promptly, and do not waste the time of your colleagues and clients. Care about your work, and you will build an excellent reputation.

With respect to practice and caseload growth, our experience is that as the size of the firm and the volume of work expand, periodic reexaminations of firm objectives and cohesiveness are crucial. It is our philosophy that growth should be managed and deliberate. When we look to add a partner to our firm, we examine not only our needs in terms of servicing existing and po-tential clients, but also whether or not the particular person and her practice area is a good fit. A quick word on workload management—remember that "No" is a very powerful and liberating word. You cannot and should not take every matter that walks through your door. Listen to your inner voice.

We recommend that you join professional organizations that can provide net-working opportunities, leadership opportunities, and support. However, you should know that your gender will not make it any easier for you to develop your business and practice. Clients ultimately hire an attorney based on her skill, responsiveness, work ethic, and personal relationships. The fact that you have a women- or minority-owned business may help you get your foot in the door, but from that point forward, it is entirely about what you bring to the table, not your gender.

As we look forward and back upon our experience, we realize that our career paths are limited only by our vision. By cultivating creativity and ingenuity you expand your ability to see. As part of drafting this letter to you, each partner of our firm considered whether or not she would have done anything differently. Not one partner answered in the affirmative. Each of us is in exactly the place where she wants to be.

Coco Chanel is attributed with saying "Don't spend time beating on a wall, hoping to transform it into a door." Rather than beat the walls that existed in the traditional law firms from where we all started our legal careers, we chose to build a new door. The door that we envisioned and ultimately created is not only sturdy and strong but enabled us to walk away from the confines of those original walls onto a path of career satisfaction, camaraderie, and work/life balance that never before existed for us. We challenge you to build your own door. You will be amazed at where it will lead.

JOHNNA GOODMARK and AMY HILLMAN are partners at Tatum Hillman Hickerson & Powell LLP ("THP") in Atlanta, Georgia, where they practice in the area of commercial real estate law. They graduated from law school in 1995 and 1998, respectively, and later joined and helped to further develop the virtual law firm model of an existing practice, which some of their partners had helped to start in the mid-1990s. Ms. Goodmark and Ms. Hillman are founding partners of THP, which was established in 2009. THP co-founders MICHELLE HICKERSON, CATHERINE POWELL, and ELIZABETH TATUM and partner SUSAN KOLODKIN provided invaluable content and editorial contributions to this letter. *www.thplawfirm.com*

- THERESE G. FRANZÉN -

"I've never regretted for one moment the day I walked into Loretta's office over 14 years ago and said, 'I think I'm going to open a law firm. Want to join me?'"

My best advice to someone considering starting a firm is to be true to yourself. When Loretta Salzano and I founded our firm, we started by discussing our values and goals for the firm. (As I tell people, a partnership is like a marriage, but without some of the added benefits!)

We hoped to achieve a balance of work, family, community service, and professional development. Loretta and I both were married, I had three children, and Loretta hoped for children. We both were active in our communities and in professional organizations and wanted to continue those activities. We both believe it is imperative to provide pro bono service.

We have been able to achieve this goal, while building a profitable firm with a loyal staff. We now have seven lawyers and continue our niche practice of consumer financial services, representing the industry in regulatory compliance, regulatory enforcement, litigation, employment, and corporate matters. We also represent auto dealers in these same areas of practice.

Our philosophy of work/family/community balance is reflected in our firm's culture. We have a low billable hour requirement of 1,500 hours annually. We incent our professional staff to bill up to a maximum of 1,800 hours per year. Currently, all of our lawyers are women, four of whom work a flexible part-time schedule. Our lawyers' professionalism and commitment to our clients allow this flexibility to work well for everyone.

We try to make our firm a nice place to work. Since the beginning, we have taken all our staff and their spouses (or significant others) on a weekend resort trip to celebrate the firm's anniversary. We have monthly firm lunches and an annual holiday party, again including everyone, not just the lawyers.

We have excellent benefits and encourage all our attorneys to attend one out of state conference annually. We incent pro bono work by "counting" those hours in the annual billable requirement.

We have always been intentional in marketing the firm and its lawyers. We encourage the lawyers to speak at various seminars, to publish, and to become leaders in their chosen area of practice. We regularly evaluate whether participating in a particular organization has attracted clients to the firm or provided professional growth for the participant.

We encourage our lawyers to develop their own clients by paying an annual bonus based upon new clients or matters brought to the firm. We believe that the benefits of early involvement in rainmaking far outweigh any perceived disadvantage of the potential to "steal" clients and leave the firm. Our experience has certainly supported this belief as our lawyers have been with the firm for many years.

Along the way, we definitely had some challenges. When we started the firm, I was completing treatment for breast cancer. Unfortunately, five years later, breast cancer reared its ugly head again. Loretta and others at the firm were my strength and support as I had surgeries and chemotherapy. Then, Loretta got pregnant! So, I was able to repay her a little by keeping her practice going as she enjoyed new motherhood.

Another challenge that we had was when we made one of our associates an equity partner at the firm. After three years, we decided to part ways, which necessitated a layoff of professional staff at the firm and a reduction in hours for our support staff. This was extremely painful for everyone involved. I have spent many nights wondering why this partnership was unsuccessful. In retrospect, I think we were more concerned with the nuts and bolts of negotiating our membership agreement than we were in exploring whether our new partner (a long-time associate at the firm) shared our values and goals for the firm.

Having your own firm provides joy and worry daily. You have the freedom to develop a fulfilling practice but worry that the phone will not ring! You have the pleasure of working with those whom you enjoy but are concerned about feeding their families! At our firm, the advantages have definitely outweighed the disadvantages. I've never regretted for one moment the day I walked into Loretta's office over 14 years ago and said, "I think I'm going to open a law firm. Want to join me?"

THERESE G. FRANZÉN is a partner at Franzén and Salzano, P.C. in Norcross, Georgia, where she focuses on consumer financial services litigation and regulatory, compliance, and employment law matters. She graduated from law school in 1980 and founded her firm in 1997. *www.franzen-salzano.com*

- MARTHA JP MCQUADE -

"Budget for the worst-case scenario. Better to spend less and be surprised. . . . Plan for the best-case scenario. You want to be lean but look sharp."

I can still hear his strong, confident voice as he did an absolutely insane thing. "Don't be afraid, Ma'am!" shouted the wonderful New York redcap as he hoisted my Mom, in her wheelchair, over the space between the train and the station platform. Would I have asked him to do it? No way. Would I have okayed the plan had I been asked in advance? Probably not. Had the conductor not neglected to call ahead for the bridge plate, the transfer would have been far easier and less fraught with anxiety. But the urgency of getting her off the train before it left the station made drastic measures a necessity. So the redcap did what he had to do—without hesitation and with great results. But then he'd obviously done it before.

Going into business for yourself can be much like that—except that you haven't done it before. Sometimes staying where you are has more downsides than the risks of getting off the train. Happily, going into business for yourself can also be much like taking your mom to a place she's never been and has always wanted to go. Believe me, you don't want to miss it. But you do have to plan for it, be ready for it, and then, when there are unexpected issues, be able to get the right help and continue going forward.

So how do you plan for your own business? As carefully and as thoughtfully as you can. How do you make sure you're being justifiably confident instead of foolhardy? Here are some suggestions:

First, take a hard look at your client base. I hesitated to start my own business for years because I honestly thought most of my clients came through senior partners at the "big" firm. When I started tracking, however, that turned out not to be the case. Stay or go, this is good information to have.

While you consider a possible move, try to secure an AV rating with Martin-dale-Hubbell. Although most lawyers (including me) are surprised to be noti-fied one day that they've achieved this through random peer ratings, there are ways for you to speed up the process and/or control who rates you. Call Martindale-Hubbell to find out. Whether you start your own business or not, an AV rating can only help your career.

While those two tasks are underway, think about starting your own firm as you would with any important decision: Make a list of the pros and cons. If the con list includes "I don't make enough money," you may want to posi-tion yourself for a raise or look for another job before going on your own. At a minimum, you'll want to do more investigation. Associates often only see how much they are bringing in for their firm and not how much it's going to cost to pay for their own office space, computers, clerical and other help, the additional "employer pays" part of your own paycheck as well as your em-ployees, malpractice insurance, health insurance, retirement (you do want to retire someday, right?), not to mention pens, paper, and paper clips. You cer-tainly can make a lot of money, even from the beginning. But chances are you won't, at least not for a while. One wonderful thing about being on your own, though, is that you can control your spending (which is seldom possible in a big firm), and you can decide how hard you are willing to work to make more money. If the pro side includes "I only want to take cases/clients that interest me," you might want to consider how realistic you're being. I strongly suggest (especially if you're going into solo practice) that you limit yourself to cases in fields of law you know, are good at, and care about. Still, not every case is going to fuel your passion; there is grind work even in areas we love, and you can't always tell from the beginning which clients are going to be good or bad. Some wonderful things about being on your own, though, are that you can turn down clients you know you shouldn't take, you can (yes, you can!) fire clients who are costing you more stomach lining than their case requires, and no one will force you to take a case in an area of law you don't want to learn.

Next, gather information. Talk (discretely—confidentiality being asked for, and agreed to, before the conversation begins) with several successful people who have already taken the plunge into their own practice. They don't all have to be people you know well or on a social level—but you must respect them all and trust them to give you honest answers. Ask as many questions as you can, in as detailed a way as you can. How much does office space cost? How long do you work in an average week? What insurance carriers do you use? What were the resources you found most helpful in setting up your practice? (Don't forget the ABA Commission on Women in the Profession in this respect.) How many and what kinds of employees did you have in the beginning? Anything you would change about that? Do you have a payroll service? What timekeeping software do you use?

If, by that point, the idea of starting your own firm has begun to have real possibility, budget for the worst-case scenario. When I decided to start my own firm, my potential partner and I went through our billing records, cut our average billable hours in half (in case we didn't have much business at the beginning), multiplied by a lower hourly rate (which we'd decided to charge to entice existing clients to stay with us), and then cut that in half again (in case our collections ran slow—now I require an all evergreen advance, which means I always get paid and upfront, but I'm much better known now and far more confident than I was back then). The numbers were far lower than we would have liked, but that's the number we used to plan our budget. Better to spend less and be surprised at how much you bring in than the other way around.

Be prepared to make sacrifices, but be careful in choosing the kinds of sacrifices you can live with. While you are still employed by someone else, take out a line of credit. But don't use it if you can help it. We agreed not to take a salary at all until we had built a certain amount in reserves for the firm. That was tough, but it made us both save for the venture and invest in making it a success, and it gave us an incredible high when we hit that mark and got our first paychecks. Plus, in part because of the reserves, we never missed a paycheck after that. If you have a bad month, it's so much wiser to realize it, use reserves to get past it, and immediately work harder to remedy the situation. I've known too many lawyers who worked hard but didn't pay attention to how much was coming in (because the line of credit made sure they got a paycheck regardless) and didn't know until it was overwhelming how much debt they'd taken on. Choosing the sacrifices you are willing to make in the beginning can pay off handsomely in the end—not only in terms of the money you need to save before you make that move, but also in terms of how many nights you lie awake worrying about not getting a paycheck or the debt piling up.

Plan for the best-case scenario. You don't have to have 5,000 square feet of prime real estate to be a successful solo practitioner. But very few successful lawyers practice from their kitchen table either. You want to be lean but look sharp. Your office needs to be professional, well organized, and well staffed. But you might be willing to do with less space and less help than you'd like—until you can afford more. Again, consider the sacrifices you're willing to make. We chose to have less space and only one full-time staff member. In retrospect, I would have added more staff sooner.

Don't forget to advertise your new status. It's not necessary to put an ad in pricey publications or send formal notices to every lawyer in your state. It is essential that you notify every lawyer you even casually call a friend, every judge you've appeared in front of or know otherwise, and every personal friend and relative you know in the jurisdiction where you'll be setting up practice. Remember: Many of them were in the same boat back when, and all of them want you to succeed. The referrals you get, and the letters and calls of encouragement, will boost your morale and provide even more resources for gathering information and getting help as the problems you didn't foresee arise.

Enjoy, enjoy, enjoy. I have been in my own practice for 13 years, have achieved great success, and have been named a Best Lawyer in America. More importantly, while not every day has been easy, I can honestly say I have never looked back.

MARTHA JP McQUADE is a partner at McQuade Byrum PLLC in Alexandria, Virginia, where she practices exclusively in the field of family law. She graduated from law school in 1984 and founded her own firm in 1997. *www.mcquadebyrum.com*

- KATHLEEN H. PAUKERT -

"Like most small business owners, you will likely experience busy times and slow times. No matter how busy you are and how well you are doing, have a safety net."

Starting Your Own Law Practice

I graduated from law school in 1990. After graduation I joined a small Spokane law firm and was trained as an insurance defense attorney. There I received excellent training from three outstanding lawyers, all with different styles. I remained with that firm until 1997.

For some reason unknown to me to this day, I decided to start my own law practice. I was the mother of two children, ages three and one. I did not know if I would have a caseload. I had no training in law firm management. But I decided to do it anyway.

I started my own firm in 1997 with another attorney who had recently left her job. Fortunately, I was able to bring 12 cases with me. I am forever grateful to the attorneys who trained me and permitted me to bring those 12 cases with me.

With a young family, failure was not an option. Although I had those 12 cases, I didn't have sufficient money in savings to purchase the equipment and supplies needed to operate a law firm. Fortunately, I found a banker who was willing to loan me $10,000 to get started.

We found a decent but small office space in downtown Spokane. We purchased desks, computers, a conference table, client and reception chairs, and supplies. The telephone system set us back more than we could have ever imagined. We kept within our budget and started our own law firm. Now we had to make it work.

The first task was to hire a quality receptionist/legal assistant. I knew the importance of having quality help, having been raised by parents who ran their own small businesses. They drilled into my head that someone must be available to help customers during every minute of every business hour. I feel as strongly about that today as I did back then. To compete against larger firms a small firm must excel at customer service. Obviously, providing expert legal advice is a must, but it's the little things that count. I do everything possible to return telephone calls within 24 hours. If I cannot personally return the call in 24 hours, my paralegal does. Keeping the client informed is a must. We do this through the use of monthly or quarterly status reports to the client. As a result, we have more than enough work.

I know successful lawyers who don't use a receptionist. Those who are succeeding are the ones who either answer the phone when it rings or call back in a very reasonable timeframe. A new trend is the use of the "virtual office," where a group of independent attorneys hire a reception service to answer calls and do other clerical work. Telephone calls are forwarded to the attorney's cell phone or landline. This allows the attorney to work from any location that is equipped with a phone. Some work at home. Others rent small office spaces. Some of the reception services have their own conference rooms and office space available for client meetings.

I know one lawyer who pays his paralegal to use her home phone and address as his office. The paralegal transfers calls to him and scans and e-mails important documents to him. That way he can work when he wants. I also know a lawyer who has his office set up in his home on the lake. He has divided the space very well, and clients meet him at his house. There are many ways to set up a small firm. But whatever form you choose, never forget that you are in the service industry.

Like most small business owners, you will likely experience busy times and slow times. No matter how busy you are and how well you are doing, have a safety net. Build a savings account to carry you through the slow times. Admittedly, I was much better at this when I first started my own practice. It came in very handy when a large plaintiff's case came my way. I had enough in the firm savings account that I was able to front the costs and cover business expenses during a period of low cash flow. There has been more than one occasion when I have had to go without a paycheck or dip into the law firm savings account to pay the costs for a large case.

Cash flow is always a challenge, particularly when you first start out on your own. While it helps to have a book of business when you start, it can be done with none at all. The very first case that came into the firm was a request to recover possession of a mule in Idaho. While not the sexiest case in the world, it helped pay for that new phone system. We took a $2,000 retainer, and my partner successfully recovered that mule. We learned two important lessons from that first case. The first was to take any case that comes in the door, provided that the client can pay and you are capable of doing the work. The second lesson learned was to never underestimate how important referrals from other lawyers are in the development of your practice. In my experience, if you tell other lawyers you are in need of work, they will help you out if they can, particularly when you are starting your own practice.

It's very important to network with other lawyers. In the past, I have been active in Washington Women Lawyers, local and state bar associations, and trial lawyer organizations. My biggest case came on a referral from a lawyer I met in a state young lawyers group.

Don't be afraid to tell people that you are an attorney. You never know what may come your way. My second largest case came to me during a poolside conversation at my kids' swimming lesson. There my client explained how another lawyer had turned down her case. Thankfully, I took the time to listen to her story, a story I would never have heard had I not told her I was an attorney.

I never pass up the opportunity to tell people I am a lawyer. Consequently, I get a lot of referrals. As the mother of three very active kids, I currently don't have a lot of time to get involved with bar association activities, but that doesn't stop me from marketing. Whether I'm at a soccer game, school carnival, basketball game, lunch duty, football game, field trip, or any number of activities that mothers "volunteer" for, I never pass up an opportunity to let people know what I do and to see if I can help them.

The Internet is a valuable marketing tool. We have a website. It is fairly small and inexpensive. We do get business from it. However, I now practice with three other lawyers, and we all agree referrals are the best source for marketing. While others may disagree, in my experience the phone book is not helpful for personal injury referrals, unless you have a full-page ad.

My advice is to only start your own practice if you are absolutely passionate about doing it. I have seen people do it not because they wanted to, but because they just didn't think they had other options. Those people generally are not successful. You must truly want to run your own business. It is not easy, but it is very rewarding. I look forward to the future of running my practice. I would like my firm to stay small.

I was given advice by someone who had opened her own firm and went out of her way to help me. Thank you, Jacqueline Newcomb. I am happy to give advice to anyone who wants it. There always seem to be little details that come up, and I am happy to help. Good luck, and have fun!

KATHLEEN H. PAUKERT is a partner at Paukert & Troppmann, PLLC in Spokane, Washington, where she focuses on Washington and Idaho litigation of personal injury and medical and psychiatric malpractice cases and also handles insurance defense matters. She graduated from law school in 1990 and founded her firm in 1997. *www.paukertlawgroup.com*

- MARISA A. DEFRANCO -

"If you are not excited to talk about what you do every time you walk in the room, then get out of law and find something else less competitive to do, like becoming a movie star or a talk show host."

Declaring Independence: No Fear, No Excuses, No Apologies

When I started my practice 13 years ago, I charged forward without hesitation. No businessperson, woman or man, can be successful if she second-guesses herself. Objective review, yes, but don't confuse analysis with fear. My first and foremost insight is don't start a practice if you can't stand behind your own decisions. Self-employment is not for people given to self-doubt. Have a commanding presence and a firm handshake. If you act weak, people will perceive you as weak. An annoying trend is that women end all sentences with an interrogatory inflection. I call it the lost decade of the declaratory sentence. State a sentence as a sentence, a question as a question. That inflection shows weakness and uncertainty.

If you are ready, your greatest assets will be knowledge and confidence in your skills. Make yourself an expert in your field: I know what I'm talking about and I know it cold. People respond positively to me because I can answer their questions plus 20 others they didn't even know they had. Clients come to you to solve problems, often putting their lives and livelihoods in your hands; you must be strong and instill confidence in them. I cannot abide other lawyers who dictate to clients without explaining the case to them. Clients who come to me for a second opinion have no idea what their case is about because the lawyer did an intake, not a consultation—the difference therein is the key to your success. My consultations run one and a half hours, or longer, because I want the client to leave knowing the potential benefits and risks—they retain me because they know I will take their case as seriously as if it were my own.

Now that you know what you are doing and are ready to be taken seriously, here are some tips on how to build your practice and how not to waste your time. *Website, have one.* Don't be afraid to put your prices and picture there. Many clients tell me that they made the first call because I had the personal touch of a picture, and I was up front about my fees. I am well aware that the legal field scoffs at posting fees, but the days of lawyers being mysterious about their fees are over. The public is savvy, so why waste their time and yours by being coy about money? You respect your potential clients by giving them knowledge. In addition, put substance on your site. Give people something that differentiates you from the pack.

On networking, my motto is "Not the *Nanny Diaries.*" Do you do pro bono? How many times have I heard that question? Too many. Note to women on networking—we are not there to solicit free work. Once, a woman started telling me about her friend who needed immigration help. I was interested in the prospect of a new client—if that feeling of excitement doesn't come to you when you hear about a new case, then the law is not for you. Well, she goes on to say that her friend's nanny has an expiring visa, and could I take the case pro bono? Now, think about that proposal for a moment—a woman who can afford to pay a nanny wants legal services for free? Rude. I simply said, "No, I'm at my pro bono limit, but here's my card for a consult. I do charge." Pro bono? *No* for someone who can afford a nanny. *Yes* for the nanny abused by her boss.

A permutation of this scenario is the friend who has money and asks you to meet with her friend with legal issues. Well, if she is so interested in helping her friend, why must I be the one who is out financially for her good deed? If she wants to help her friend, and if she is truly your friend, she would instead say to you, "I have a friend who can't pay; I'll pay her fee." As for free consultations, do not do them. People who come for free consultations rarely call to retain you. They come only to pick your brain, then try to file their case, i.e., make a mess. You are not a legal services organization; legal services get government and private funding for the exact reason of providing services to low/no income people. They have income intake for a reason—people must qualify for those services.

Free services are for people who *cannot* afford them, not for people who are too cheap to recognize the value of your services. You want clients who respect that your time is valuable. Now, as a newer attorney, you can certainly charge lower fees to be competitive, but once you are established, you charge the market rate per your expertise. When you do find good pro bono cases, take them, but don't be a martyr; set a limit and stick to it. Banks do not take martyr payments in lieu of mortgage payments.

Back to networking. It should be an ongoing component of your practice. The number one rule of networking (besides *not* asking people to do free work for you) is *say something*. *Say something* about yourself and your work. If you are not interested enough in your work to discuss it, no one else will be. Forget shy, demure, accommodating, and all of those dirty words. If you are not excited to talk about what you do every time you walk in the room, then get out of law and find something else less competitive to do, like becoming a movie star or a talk show host.

Say something when someone makes a misogynistic, homophobic, racist, or other such remark. There is a knack to reproaching people who are inappropriate—a firm retort with a blend of humor is always effective. Perhaps the offender might not like you, but people around you will take notice—I can't count the times people have said, "Oh, I wanted to say something. I'm so glad you did!" I can hear many of you out there worrying, "But people will think I'm not nice."

Nice, let's talk about that word. I am nice and firm at the same time. Nice does not mean pushover. As a woman, when you are firm, you are automatically viewed as "not nice" no matter how professional your tone and even your demeanor. People conflate the substance of what you say with the way you say it—if they don't like *what* you say, they tag you as not nice, no matter your delivery. You will not win that battle, so do not try. Good people will respect and like you when you are straightforward. Jerks won't, so why waste any time trying to please them? Move on to good people. Finally, say *"thank you."* When you ask someone for advice, and she e-mails you a response, e-mail a thank you; it's basic manners. Many don't—so crass.

My last note, a plea to women bar associations and networking groups— please stop with the fashion nights, clothing advice seminars, life coaches, and marketing pitches from people who are only out to get business for themselves, not for those of us who attend. Lately, many women's groups are only doing fluff, offering very few real business development programs and networking opportunities. Women lawyers should know how to dress as there is only one rule: if you are whip smart, you don't need clothes to draw attention to yourself—all the action is above the neck, baby. Give us real events, we can take it.

I am still in business: 12½ years on my own, six months as in-house counsel, one and a half years at a large firm. From all experiences, I can say that starting my own practice has more benefits than I can list, but at the top are being the master of your own life and the incredible satisfaction that comes from clients who put their trust in you and the successes you produce. I have never regretted being strong and determined; voicing my opinion has only served to increase my business connections and client base and earned me positions of leadership. My main message to women, to anyone who wants to start her or his own firm, is be an expert and an exhaustive researcher. Be matter-of-fact about fees, and respect yourself enough to get paid. You are a professional. Take the hard cases and differentiate yourself, and waste no time on the naysayers. The future is bright for the women and men who believe in themselves and the law.

MARISA A. DeFRANCO is the owner of the DeFranco Law Group in Salem, Massachusetts, where she focuses on immigration and nationality law. She graduated from law school in 1996 and founded her firm in 1997. *www.yourimmigrationcenter.com*

- MICHELE BALLARD MILLER -

"The accepted mantra of the time was that you could not be a part-time litigator. Nor could you represent business in anything but a large, multi-office firm. . . . I rejected the wisdom of the times. I have never looked back."

The Woman Advantage

We all remember how hard we had to work to earn our law degrees, wherever we went to law school. And then there were the long, sometimes thankless, hours as associate attorneys on the partnership track, honing our craft and earning valuable experience. But at some point along the way, many women lawyers come to a crossroads marked by the desire to start and care for a family and the drive to have a thriving law practice and professional career. Is it really possible to start and care for a family, without getting derailed from the practice of law or marginalized within a firm's ranks?

In the firms at which I practiced, as at most law firms even today, management was dominated by men, along with old-fashioned views of family and work. Firm goals were and often still are focused on money—hours billed, revenue generated, and what work an attorney can bring in. You had to dedicate yourself to putting in the hours. And if you were a woman, chances are you were told (or it otherwise became clear) that you had to make a choice between working as a professional and being a mom. You certainly would not make partner if you did not sacrifice family life for the long hours. Many women lawyers believe they have to make this choice, and withdraw from the profession, sometimes for 10 to 20 years, and then find it difficult to return to the practice of law after so much time.

After 15 years as an associate and then as a partner at large, national law firms, I came to the career/family crossroads. I had two young children and little time to enjoy them. And, while I adored my children, I also enjoyed my career. I thought long and hard about which path to take. I did not want to leave the practice of law, but I was not interested in the mommy track.

To further complicate matters, my specialty was representing business in employment law and related litigation. The accepted mantra of the time was that you could not be a part-time litigator. Nor could you represent business in anything but a large, multi-office firm. I was told in no uncertain terms that I would be crazy to start my own firm. Colleagues predicted I would be seduced by the dark side and end up representing plaintiffs. I was also told that I should simply accept fate, becoming one of the numerous women who left large firms to see their practice shrink to only employment counseling and advice. Litigation was simply not an option, so I was told.

I rejected the wisdom of the times, believing that one could litigate and still maintain some balance. Granted, there would be days when court-imposed deadlines would dictate long hours, even into the early morning hours. However, there would also be days when the press of work was not extreme, and I could enjoy my family and friends. I took the plunge, forming my own firm. I have never looked back.

My decision was driven not only by the twin goals of creating a work/life balance for myself and my colleagues and creating and building a successful practice that emphasized the strengths and values of women. In addition, I was determined that a focus on these core goals would give me an advantage—what I call the "Woman Advantage" in building a business.

The Woman Advantage is the opportunity to create and build a firm culture and environment that emphasizes the strengths and values of women. The Woman Advantage is a culture that encourages collaboration and teamwork, open and trusting communication. It is a vision that takes a longer-term perspective, providing superior service to clients while managing reasonable and sustainable financial goals and objectives. All of these qualities are, of course, important for most businesses—but as women we are, in particular, drawn to a culture that provides a balance of financial, professional, and family objectives. Successful companies are adept at balancing short- and long-term objectives; women are all about balance, and this is our advantage.

In retrospect, the decision to start my own firm was one of the most important decisions in my life. Now, more than 12 years later, my women shareholders and I have a thriving and financially successful law practice that emphasizes quality legal work and offers lawyers—women and men—a work/life equilibrium. My oldest is heading off to college, and I am proud to have raised a confident young woman while never losing focus on my career. And in the last four years, my firm has had a compounded growth rate of over 40 percent. The Woman Advantage means we can have it all.

The keys to a law firm's success and individual financial benefit are basic: The firm must attract and retain good people, and the firm must keep its clients happy. We have succeeded at both.

Our firm's environment and culture founded on women's values help us to attract and retain the best and the brightest, women and men. Our attorneys come from some of the largest national law firms and the most prestigious law schools in the United States, excited about the unique opportunity to do high-level legal work for interesting companies at competitive salaries, without sacrificing personal opportunities. Our attorneys can take the time to coach their kids' soccer teams (as I did for over 10 years), a few hours here and there to volunteer in the classroom, or even extended family trips over the summer. And it's not unusual to see kids in the office; in fact, they are welcome. We have a bright and fun kids room for use when mom or dad needs to finish up a brief or attend a client meeting, but the children have time off from school or maybe have a runny nose and the parent wants to keep them close by.

Keeping clients happy has to be the number one goal of any professional firm. At Miller Law Group we take a woman-based approach to our work and client relations, emphasizing understanding, collaboration, communication, and balance. We make the extra effort to understand our clients' needs and their goals and objectives before taking on a case, whether the client is a small start-up, a mid-size business, or a Fortune 500 company. We work with our clients early in the litigation process to resolve cases in a timely and efficient manner. We are good communicators, which means we write effective summary judgment motions and get cases dismissed. We collaborate with each other, relying on the strengths that each lawyer can bring to a case or legal issue. The end result is happy clients, leading to long-term client relationships, and professional and financial success for our lawyers.

Women do not have to make the choice between a legal career or a family that so many firms force them into. Attorneys at our firm are able to have it all: a family/personal life, a thriving legal career, and financial rewards.

MICHELE BALLARD MILLER is president and shareholder of Miller Law Group in San Francisco, California, where she focuses on employment law and related litigation. She graduated from law school in 1982 and founded her firm in 1998. *www.millerlawgroup.com*

- MARY B. GALARDI -

"I have found over the years that if I follow [the consultant's] advice and raise my rate for the year, not only do clients pay it, but I also get new and better clients each year."

The Power of Connections

Connections are an amazing thing. Had I not talked with a court reporter about looking for a change in law firms, I don't know how long it would have taken me to hear about the Georgia Association for Women Lawyers (GAWL). She knew the president at the time and suggested that I call her. I did and ended up joining and finding a new job (all through the connection with the court reporter).

Once I had the new job, working for a solo practitioner with one big client doing defense work, I continued to attend GAWL meetings. After about two years of defending slip and falls, false arrest, and malicious prosecution and being tied to a trial calendar, I decided I needed to expand my horizons, but I didn't know quite what I wanted to do.

GAWL had a training session consisting of a panel with other women talking about rainmaking. One of the lawyers mentioned that she had a potluck at her home for women lawyers only and offered to invite the attendees. I went to the next dinner. There I met another woman lawyer who had just opened her own office. Being very interested in her fortitude, I really wanted to hear about how she did it. She suggested that I call her for lunch, which I did. She shared everything she had done, such as marketing, getting office space, and buying a computer. Shortly thereafter, I decided to open my own office. I thought, if she can do it, so can I. I have now been practicing estate planning and business law for 12 years as a solo practitioner, and I trace it back to that connection with the court reporter and joining GAWL.

Kiss a Lot of Frogs

Because of the nature of my practice (estate planning), I have the need for a continuous stream of new clients. As a result, marketing is a very important part of what I do every day. The best advice I have received about marketing was that I would have to meet a lot of people to find a few that I would want to market to and meet on a consistent basis. I found that I needed to market to people I liked so they would send me clients I liked, because like attracts like. I can trace difficult clients to a referral source of whom I'm not very fond. For the most part, I enjoy all of my clients who have been referred to me by people I like.

Bill Like a Lawyer, Not a Social Worker

I have used a marketing consultant once a year for the past 12 years since my practice has been open. I call him specifically so that I can ask him what my hourly rate should be for the year. The consultant will tell me to raise it to a certain amount, and each year, I say, no, my clients won't pay that. However, I have found over the years that if I follow his advice and raise my rate for the year, not only do clients pay it, but I also get new and better clients each year.

MARY B. GALARDI is the solo owner of Galardi Law in Atlanta, Georgia, where she focuses on estate planning, probate, and business law. She graduated from law school in 1993 and founded her firm in 1998. *www.galardilaw.com*

- PAIGE GOLD -

"None of the large firms would even interview a new lawyer who was already middle-aged. While the knowledge and experience . . . went unappreciated by these traditional firms, it has proven useful in running my own practice."

I've run my own Los Angeles-based solo practice for a dozen years, representing small business owners, independent filmmakers, and other media-related companies. I fell into this area of practice after discovering that none of the large firms would even interview a new lawyer who was already middle-aged. While the knowledge and experience I'd picked up in my previous careers went unappreciated by these traditional firms, it has proven useful in running my own practice.

Since I've always been fairly independent and self-motivated, it was perhaps inevitable that I would start my own firm. I had held many nonlegal jobs in a wide variety of fields (business, politics, entertainment) prior to law school and had earned an MBA, both of which came in useful. The former may have been more useful than the latter; observing how others operated their businesses, both large and small, gave me an education in how (and how not) to run a business. This is not to say that anyone starting their own practice needs to have held a lot of jobs or earned an MBA, but they do need to have someone they can call on who has had significant day-to-day experience running a business.

Though I hadn't practiced law for long when I started my own firm, I had the benefit of having a large network of acquaintances who already knew and trusted me, and who were willing to refer clients to me. Having begun my legal career with a firm that defends lawyers against state bar disciplinary charges, I was extremely careful not to take on cases I knew to be beyond my ability to get up to speed on. For example, early on, I turned down a couple of medical malpractice cases I was asked to handle because I did not know any lawyers who could mentor me in this area, and I sensed that the workload would be too much for a one-person firm. On the other hand, I willingly took on a complicated international wrongful termination lawsuit that seemed like a long shot because I had access to lawyers who were knowledgeable about the many different areas of law the case entailed. (The case settled quite successfully, although it took two years to do so.)

After spending a decade litigating against insurance-defense firms, discovering in the process that all too often, big-firm lawyers are more focused on adding to their billable hours than efficiently resolving their clients' legal problems, I decided I'd had enough of litigation and began to focus on transactions. The entertainment industries have been profoundly affected by new media, and many independent producers neither need, nor have the money for, a law firm whose boilerplate contracts are designed for traditional, multimillion-dollar productions. I've found it interesting and challenging to devise workable contracts that fit my clients' production needs and budgets. I doubt this type of creativity would be encouraged were I working in a traditional large or mid-sized firm.

What I most enjoy about working for myself is having the freedom to only work with clients I feel comfortable working with and conversely, to end the relationship if I can tell that the client is not going to be satisfied, regardless of what I do. I also value the flexibility of determining my own work schedule and the absence of the minimum-billable-hour environment, where the quality of work is less important than the quantity.

The primary drawback of working for myself is that business and income tend to ebb and flow, depending on client needs. I compensate for this by occasionally taking on contract research and writing jobs with a couple of other firms.

Working for myself, I also miss having regular daily opportunities to discuss my cases with fellow lawyers in the same field. To compensate for this, I try to regularly get together with other lawyers I've met through voluntary bar groups, especially Women Lawyers of Los Angeles.

If asked to offer advice to someone contemplating opening her own practice, here is what I would say:

- Don't go out on your own unless you have a couple of steady paying clients to begin with, to help pay the start-up costs.
- Remember the importance of continual networking. It's crucial to getting new clients.

- Look out for red flags when interviewing potential new clients. For example, a client who has gone through one or more previous lawyers in the same matter, or who becomes inappropriately emotional at the initial interview, or seems to disagree with your approach or style from the very start, is a sign of things to come, and not worth the possible trouble ahead—no matter how much up-front money he or she may have to offer.

PAIGE GOLD is the owner of the Law Office of Paige Gold in Los Angeles, California, and Washington, DC, where she practices media and entertainment law. She graduated from law school in 1997 and founded her firm in 1998.

- JANICE P. BROWN -

"Starting Brown Law Group for me meant rejecting the safety of the status quo and trusting my instincts."

Starting Brown Law Group meant rejecting the safety of the status quo and trusting my instincts. This is an ongoing learning process that empowers me to accept that my core beliefs in personal and business integrity, ethics, and advocacy will lead me (and my firm) to the desired results. I wanted to be happier in my practice, and recognizing these qualities in me has made me so.

Each position in my career prior to Brown Law Group has provided me with important tools to step out on my own as an entrepreneur. I have learned that I accept and even relish challenge. The level of difficulty I'm faced with motivates me to work harder, smarter, and to succeed. For example, I wasn't a tax lawyer. Tax law, I was told, is difficult, but I learned tax law. Big firm life was a challenge, but I learned from some of the best lawyers how to provide the highest standards of excellence for the clients I represented. I thrive on business development, recognizing the work and personal commitment it entails. My vision leads me to success. I believe this, and that confidence seeps into other areas of my life.

I believe in the concept of team, the ideals of mediation, and the power that comes through empowering others. These core beliefs had made it challenging to accept the term boss, though I embrace leadership. Now, though, I recognize that terminology doesn't make the person. I enjoy calling my own shots. Once, I winced when my team would introduce me to others as their boss. But one day, recently in fact, I recognized that I needed to embrace that title and accept the responsibility of holding people accountable to their best selves.

Business development for me is an every workday, measurable habit. Like every aspect of my business, I must seek ways to attract new business and expand the practice. I strongly recommend Jeffrey Fox's book *How to Become a Rainmaker* as a guide. Developing business as a woman-owned firm is the same as developing business in a majority-owned firm. You must be highly motivated, focused, and intuitive. I believe that being a woman blessed with intuition gives me a huge advantage in creating and maintaining relationships.

Today Brown Law Group has seven lawyers. Currently, I do not have a growth strategy for this year. Instead, this year I have an excellence strategy, a policy strategy, a systems strategy. Next year, on the other hand, I will apply my energy, vision, and intuition into growing the firm. In life, I believe you are either growing or dying. But before we grow, we need to have every element of our business fine-tuned. The legal business has changed, and we as lawyers have to adapt to continue on a successful path. At Brown Law Group, we are implementing policies, identifying stricter standards of excellence, and building better systems so we can deliver our extraordinary legal product more efficiently with more strategic wisdom for the benefit of our clients.

There are several books to help you with the nuts and bolts of running a law practice. Jay Foonberg's books are very good. Certainly understanding the nuts and bolts is essential, but these do not create passion, and this business is too hard unless you remain passionate. (Isn't that true about everything?) In that regard, I recommend two books: one of my favorite books, *A Return to Love* by Marianne Williamson, and Michael Gerber's *The E-Myth*. In Marianne Williamson's book is a poem that relates to our calling for work. Our deepest fear is not that we are inadequate. Our deepest fear is that we are powerful beyond measure, and holding that vision is the real nut and bolt of any business, especially the law business, if you want to have fun while practicing law. Gerber's book tells us that owning a business is much different than the practice of law. As a lawyer, you may be great at achieving a positive legal outcome. But delivering legal product is just one component of running a law firm. You must learn to enjoy all the other aspects of running a firm. Gerber's book explains the difference between being a successful entrepreneur and being a successful lawyer.

My passion is helping other lawyers, particularly women lawyers, realize their power. I have been working on several models of how best to spread this message but have not yet found the right delivery system. But it is coming. I feel it. So stay tuned. Lawyers are important to our society. And many of us are run by fear or fake confidence. This is not an authentic representation of who we really are. My goal is to find ways to help lawyers develop tools and a vision for the practice and life, to approach the law holistically and authentically, to inspire, to develop business abundantly, and to leave a legacy of power beyond measure. This opportunity to contribute to this book is but one such tool.

Warm regards.

JANICE P. BROWN is the founder of Brown Law Group, ALC in San Diego, California, where she focuses on employment law and business litigation. She graduated from law school in 1983 and founded her own firm in 1999. *www.brownlawgroup.com*

- LANA L. TRAYNOR -

"[You] are not alone, you can do this, and you will find your path.
Your path may zigzag and be crooked, but it's your path."

Open my own law firm? No way. Special education law? Never heard of it. For the past 11 years, I have been doing just that, practicing special education and disability rights law as a solo practitioner in Oregon, Washington, and California. Unlike you, I did not have *The Road to Independence: 101 Women's Journeys to Starting Their Own Law Firms* to assist me. For the last 10 years, I struggled with self-doubt and second-guessing, constantly feeling as if I wasn't running my solo law practice the right way. The ABA Commission on Women in the Profession's request to write a letter for its new book stirred something in me, made me reflect on my journey. There is no right way to open or operate a solo law practice. My abbreviated list of lessons learned, as reflected in this letter, will show you that you are not alone, you can do this, and you will find your path. Your path may zigzag and be crooked, but it's your path.

In July 1999, I established my law firm out of sheer desperation and necessity. From 1997 thru May 1999, our family lived in Hong Kong, China, for my husband's job. In spring 1999, one of our three young sons was diagnosed with a disability. Our family returned to Portland, Oregon, in search of appropriate English-speaking special education services for our son. I was confident in my ability to navigate the unique and technical special education laws because, after all, I had worked at the Oregon Supreme Court in my pre-Hong Kong life. My arrogance quickly turned to fear and despair. I did not understand the myriad federal and state laws, but I had to learn fast! I opened my law practice in July 1999 to serve my toddler son, my first client.

Business Model

I do not have a formal business model, but two principles guide me every day: my passion for special education law and a willingness to seek honest, constructive feedback. First, my passion for special education law is nearly primal because I experienced firsthand the fear and pain associated with navigating the complex special education laws during a moment of crisis. Second, I seek open and brutally honest feedback from clients, staff, and opposing counsel. That feedback serves as a springboard for change and improved client relations. Lessons learned: One: Practice in an area of law that you believe in and love. Anything less is unfair to you and your client. Two: Solicit feedback about your communication style, office management, and client relations. Hire an outside, third party to conduct a confidential survey of current and former clients (after gaining appropriate consent) if you are uncomfortable tackling this project.

Integrity

My area of practice is emotionally charged and involves children and young adults. I have been blackmailed, stalked, and threatened by former clients. Each one of those cases had one thing in common: I refused to succumb to a client's demand that I engage in unethical or illegal conduct. As a woman from a small farming town where a person's word and integrity define her character, I refuse to submit to pressure from anyone—client, lawyer, or judge. I will not compromise my ethics or integrity for anyone or any amount of money. No exceptions. Lesson learned: Be mindful of ethical rules, but seek assistance. Call your local bar counsel, other attorneys practicing in your area, or the local authorities, when appropriate. If necessary, hire an ethics attorney to advise you. It will be worth every penny that you spend.

Time/Case Management

As soon as I opened my law practice, time and case management challenges surfaced. For 10 years, I worked seven days per week and gave my cell phone number to every client just in case. When I took a rare vacation, I filled my carry-on luggage with client files to review. Clients complimented me, and paid me, for that dedication. My health, family, and friends suffered, but I refused to change. Six months ago, I ended my extramarital relationship (addiction to computer and e-mail) cold turkey. My laptop remains at work, and I turn off my cell phone as soon as I leave the office. Lesson learned: Set realistic boundaries for yourself, and ask a trusted person to monitor your progress. Warn this person, in advance, that you may say inappropriate things when confronted during a relapse. However, you promise to calm down, analyze her comments, make necessary changes, and thank her. Expect the process to commence again when you falter.

Pro Bono Work/Delinquent Accounts

A very wise practice management advisor from the Oregon Professional Liability Fund recently told me that the attorney chooses pro bono cases, not the other way around. Clients who ignore an unpaid bill and continue to incur legal fees, she explained, become pro bono cases. By allowing that to occur, the client—not me—has chosen which cases become part of my pro bono caseload. Lesson learned: Review your accounts receivable every month and contact delinquent clients, no matter how uncomfortable that is for you. If a client is unable to make payment arrangements or refuses to pay, then review your legal services agreement and withdraw as legal counsel if/when it is appropriate to do so.

Mentor

I come from a humble and poor background where "ma'am" and "sir" are expected, children do not call adults by their first names, and all are treated equally, regardless of stature. In May 1999, scared and desperate for knowledge, I cold-called every attorney (both school district and parent attorneys) in Oregon and southwest Washington. To this day, I can name the attorneys who talked to me, encouraged me, and told me which laws to research. I also remember the attorneys who hung up on me or refused to take my call. To them, I was a nobody or potential competition, I suppose. Some attorneys' refusals to help a fellow member of the local bar stunned me. Lesson learned: Never, ever forget that encouraging words or an informational interview is the right thing to do for you and the person seeking assistance. Take time to help that new attorney. Who knows, she may send you a thank you note 10 years later and tell you how your kindness impacted her life.

Upon reflection, I never wanted to open my own law practice. But, guess what? I'm glad that I did. I love what I do, and I'm good at it. I play Legos and color with children, help families thirsting for knowledge, and maintain an ethical, successful, multijurisdictional law practice. You have this ABA book to assist you. Use it. If you're like me, though, you may read each chapter and say, I would never get myself into that particular problem, then turn around and get yourself into that particular problem. That's okay. That's how I learn. There is no right or wrong way to hang that shingle, just choose your path, crooked or otherwise, and have faith in yourself.

LANA L. TRAYNOR is the principal of Lana L. Traynor, LLC in Portland, Oregon, where she focuses on special education law in Oregon, Washington, and California. She graduated from law school in 1993 and founded her firm in 1999. *www.traynorlawfirm.com*

- YVONNE BARNES MONTGOMERY -

"You must break away from the societal stereotype of the quiet woman. Seek out people who have done what you are looking to do and ask for advice."

On the Road to Independence:
So You Think You Want to Be Your Own Boss

I have tried to live by the philosophy of not allowing others' expectations of me define my expectations of myself. For me, the road to becoming my own boss was not a direct route. Throughout my career, I found that embracing change and opportunity paved the way for success. Fresh out of law school, I wanted to be a prosecutor. The only problem: the office where I wanted to practice had never hired an African American female. Undaunted by what appeared to be a roadblock, I applied for and became a prosecutor. I initially thought that I would end my career practicing criminal law. I prosecuted for four years. At that time, the idea of going into private practice was the farthest thing from my mind. I enjoyed doing what I did.

From my perspective, there are two general pathways that lead people to start their own firms. There are a small percentage of lawyers who had their path to success completely mapped out by the time they entered law school. These are the "Alpha-A" types who simply check off boxes as they accomplish each predetermined goal. These are the people who in law school sat in the very first row in class, outlined every case, answered every question the professor uttered, made law review, interned at a white-shoe *American Lawyer* Top 100 law firm during law school, clerked for a federal judge after graduation, made partner at an international law firm, then made the transition into forming their own firm with connections, contacts, and clients already in place. Then there are the majority of us who came upon an opportunity or made the choice to pursue the idea of independence. This letter is for those of you whose path to independence, like mine, was a more circuitous journey.

As all young lawyers are prone to do, I tracked my progress with my "class." I took note of what my colleagues in private practice were doing in their careers. I considered a lot of factors, including job satisfaction, work/life balance, and compensation. I spoke to mentors and asked for advice. I was told that if I wanted to make a transition away from being a prosecutor, the fourth or fifth year of practice was the time to do it; otherwise it would be harder to leave. It was at this time that I read an article in a legal newspaper about a former colleague who was making a name for herself in private practice as a medical malpractice defense attorney. I reconnected with her. I decided to make the leap, for better or worse, into private practice working in a small medical malpractice litigation boutique. I knew that even though the practice of criminal law was not exactly in tandem with medical malpractice defense work, there were skill sets that I had developed as a prosecutor that would translate well as a litigator. I determined to learn as much as I could and hone my civil practice skills.

But I was restless. There was a part of me that craved the idea of deciding whom I would represent instead of being told whom I represent. Once again, I reached out to my friends. I shared my desire to do something more, although I could not fully articulate what that "more" was. A sorority sister put me in touch with her friend, another attorney, Joe H. Tucker Jr., who was contemplating hanging out his own shingle, too. I set an appointment to meet with Joe, to hear his ideas, goals, and aspirations. We connected. He had a similar mindset. His areas of practice included employment discrimination litigation and personal injury litigation, as well as general commercial litigation. He represented plaintiffs as well as defendants. I made another leap, from a small litigation boutique to working with Joe in a two-person law firm.

Now, I have been practicing with Joe for over 10 years and am a shareholder in Tucker Law Group, LLC. The firm has grown from the two of us to where we now have 19 employees. I've also grown in that time; I got married, I have two kids, and I have taken up marathon running as a way to decompress. Along the way, I have accumulated a few thoughts as to how you can help achieve your goal of starting your practice.

Do Not Underestimate the Value of Human Capital

You know people. Everyone knows someone. Even if you do not believe you have the "right" connections, you have connections—use them. If you are a member of any club, society, or organization, then you are in a position to make connections with people who may prove beneficial to your career development. I found that sometimes the most surprising opportunities came in the least expected ways. Engage everyone in conversation, and listen to what is being said. Your hairstylist may know another individual who needs legal assistance. There are former colleagues who may be in a position to, if not offer you a job, give you a glowing recommendation or a referral. Do not limit your involvement to legal organizations. Volunteer for a nonprofit organization or join a book club with other women. At the end of the day, the first step to making a name for yourself boils down to getting people to know you exist.

Articulate Your Needs

Sometimes, as women, we believe that we must be quiet and persevere. More than likely, however, you will not receive help and advice if you fail to ask for assistance. You must break away from the societal stereotype of the quiet woman. Seek out people who have done what you are looking to do and ask for advice. More often than not, they asked the same questions you are asking, have done the research, and know what tools, opportunities, or assistance is available in your local market area. There is no need to reinvent the wheel.

Even now, as a partner in a law firm, with two young kids, I have to remind myself of this rule. Now, I balance delegating responsibility at work while asking for assistance from family members at home. The notion of being a Superwoman, doing everything without assistance, is a myth. Often, the biggest hindrance to asking for help is ignoring the voice in your head telling you not to appear lazy by refusing to take on that extra project or missing a late night client dinner for homework time with your child. No one wants to disappoint anyone or be perceived as not pulling her weight. It took me a while to realize that *no* is not a four-letter word and to become more comfortable with setting boundaries on the responsibilities I take on at the office.

Flexibility in All Aspects of Your Practice Is a Must

Unless you are well settled in your practice area prior to starting your firm, you must be open to varying areas of practice. This will serve several purposes. First, it will pay the bills. You cannot forget that you are essentially a small business owner and must generate revenue. Second, it allows you to explore areas of the law that you might not have previously considered.

Maintain flexibility in your rate structure. As your own boss, you know exactly what your profit margin is, and therefore, you can set rates accordingly. You can utilize nontraditional fee schedules providing clients with fees based upon outcome, blended rates, and contingent fees. You can research rates of other lawyers by checking fee petitions filed with courts. This allows you to know what rates are acceptable in the market, and more importantly, you can set your rates to be competitive with your contemporaries.

Your journey to success may be circuitous. It is not instantaneous or absent of upsets and setbacks. Rather, it is the amalgamation of your education, experiences, and opportunities. Likewise, building a law firm requires tenacity, endurance, and embracing change. You may begin your career, as did I, in a prosecutor's office but ultimately transition to being a partner in a litigation boutique. Regardless, if there is one constant in life, it is change; learn to embrace it and success will follow.

YVONNE BARNES MONTGOMERY is a partner at The Tucker Law Group, LLC in Philadelphia, Pennsylvania, where she focuses on employment, higher education, and personal injury litigation. She graduated from law school in 1993 and founded her firm in 1999. *www.tlgattorneys.com*

CHAPTER 5

2000–2004

Responding to Tighter Constraints in the Large Firm Model

"The business model of the firm essentially involved the very senior partners bringing in business and everyone else working on it. . . . I decided that was who I wanted to be and that I couldn't become the senior partner with my own business from where I was sitting (in my office doing everyone else's work)."

—Melanie Damian

The 2000s opened up vast expansions in traditional firms. With media choosing profits-per-partner as a measure of firms' competitiveness, the practice evolved into more constrained costs and more exhaustive service demands. Against this backdrop, 20 of our founders fall into the first five years of this decade. That rate is nearly 50 percent more than among our 1990s founders and five times that of the 1980s founders. The writers' reasons to found a practice mirror the consequences of large firm expansion and compression of partner compensation:

Retaining a fair share of profits: Frequently repeated is a sense of unfairness or lack of access to a chance for a fair share of large firm profits. Writers seize upon their ability to profit more strongly outside the framework of large firms. For example, a writer, considering an offer from a large New York firm eight years after starting her own, was unwilling to exchange 75 percent of her earnings for the partnership deal. Two lawyers started their own practice upon learning that the client whose matters they covered was taking its work to a minority-owned firm; they believed they could serve such clients and control the business more effectively on their own. In a third example, a founder pulled her sophisticated practice out of an established specialty firm because of "origination credit" schemes, large billable hours, and traditional firm politics.

Freedom and support to establish strong new practice areas: Other writers pursued better ways to manage a law firm. One writes, "The entire legal industry was the most backward place I had ever seen, billing for time, valuing inefficiency." She strategically succeeded with her woman-owned intellectual property boutique serving the

---

largest companies. Other writers describe wanting to develop chosen practice areas without being stifled by partners who did not embrace their vision, acting on their creative insight into how to change the practice or wanting to be equity owners while developing new specialties. In the international milieu, one writer, who had secured her law license in India in 1984, earned her LL.M. in the United States after her children were older and founded a visionary practice in India that boasted commercial lawyers who also had U.S. bar admissions.

Achieving balance: Balance remains a theme in the writers' weighing of their best, most profitable, business forms. Here, balance strongly includes many factors besides the stereotypical pull of maternal obligations. For example, one writer, upon watching the World Trade Center collapse, confronted the importance of "getting on with her dream of her own firm" in order to secure balance, even amid incredibly hard work. Others focused on freedom, without having to ask permission, to manage both the legal work and other aspects of their professional obligations and lives.

Making a solo practice work: Unique professional circumstances became opportunities for some writers. A solo patent lawyer serves clients worldwide from Montana, using tools such as electronic publishing, frequent trips, and exceptional practices such as not billing clients for travel.

These women are embracing, not running from, private practice. And they are acting on their courage to make law practice what they believe it should be.

- JULIA SYLVA -

---

*"A business plan is a process—an evolutionary process.
Keep your vision alive and in writing."*

Making the Decision

On June 1, 2000, the Law Offices of Julia Sylva, ALC, was formed—not by
intentional plan—but by default. Since 1983, I had worked in downtown Los
Angeles at small, medium, and large law firms, as an associate and as a partner.
Though my professional career was taking off, I faced challenges in balancing
work and family.

In June 1999, my husband and I decided that I would take the summer months off
and then start "looking" for a new position in the fall. A couple of weeks into my
hiatus, I began receiving telephone calls from my former clients who asked, "Where
are you?" As a skilled and able professional, I pride myself on my excellent attorney/
client relationships, but I always considered the clients I represented as clients of
the firm. I was pleasantly surprised that these clients wanted *me* to continue to
serve as their lawyer—even though I was no longer a partner of the firm. Because
the clients sought me out, there was never an issue of "bringing" clients with me
from my former firm. Even if there had been an issue, it is important to note that
ultimately, it is the client who decides which lawyer to hire.

The Law Offices of Julia Sylva evolved—slowly. After about one year, I formed a
law corporation and hired an eager young woman as my part-time employee who
served numerous roles: receptionist, assistant, secretary, and paralegal. For the
first year, I worked from my home office, but I now have a separate law office in
addition to my home office.

Previous Practice Experience

Certainly, my prior law firm experience remains invaluable in my becoming
a strong lawyer. Actually, all prior *life* experience and knowledge are relevant
and helpful. Specifically, some law firms have effective systems in place for
training young associates—take advantage of these programs. From previous

work at various law firms, I learned technical skills such as client billing, on-line research, analysis, and legal document drafting. I learned how to super-vise and work with support staff effectively while developing a strong work ethic and organizational skills. I also joined partners in client development meetings. These are skills that can only be learned on the job. Inevitably, true professionals develop these valuable skills—over time. However, I believe that my law firm experience helped me learn these skills a bit more quickly.

Lessons Learned

There is an old adage that one needs "finders, grinders, and minders" to run a law firm. These words of wisdom are equally applicable to solo practice.

Finders. Go ahead—print glossy marketing materials, design a website, join profes-sional and business organizations, and conduct seminars to promote yourself and your law firm. There is still no substitute for *personal* networking for marketing your law firm. Law practice entails a close working relationship consisting of mutu-al trust and respect between attorney and client. You are your best marketing tool! RESOURCE TIP: *How to Get and Keep Good Clients*, by Jay G. Foonberg.

Grinders: You must always produce excellent work product—there are no excuses. Utilize online resources for legal research and technical information from rel-evant industry organizations and regulatory agencies. RESOURCE TIP: *Persuasive Legal Writing* by Daniel U. Smith and the ever-trustworthy *The Elements of Style*, by William Strunk Jr. and E.B. White.

Minders. Law firm administration is more time-consuming than you will ever imagine. Remember: you are an entrepreneur *first*, a lawyer *second*. You must have adequate support staff and accurate record keeping. Purchase state-of-the-art computers and law firm billing and small business accounting software. To this day, I still employ my one jill-of-all-trades. Similarly, my CPA has remained constant from day one. I have expanded my team; it now includes a network of independent contractors who are available, as needed: associates, paralegals, bookkeepers, pro-cess servers, and filing clerks. RESOURCE TIP: *The California Guide to Opening and Managing a Law Firm*, published by the State Bar of California.

Feelings and Concerns

Any woman forming her own law firm will face a scary question: Will paying clients continue to retain me? Fortunately, I have been able to overcome this fear. The best piece of advice here is: Keep overhead low!

There are many options for hanging out a shingle. You don't need that corner office. Consider working from your home office with virtual office support or sharing an office with other legal professionals.

Also, explore all options for start-up financing, including business credit cards, lines of credit, and SBA loans. Maintain a strong credit rating to help build your business/finance portfolio and your practice.

Business Plan

Yes, you should write one. Once you write a business plan, even if it's an outline, you should refer to it—regularly. A business plan is a process—an evolutionary process. Keep your vision alive and in writing. Visit *www.sba.gov* for guidance in drafting a business plan.

Challenges

Balancing Family and Work and Time for Self. Having your own law firm is continually demanding; I have to remind myself that it is not a 24/7 job. To make time for myself and for my family, I have learned to turn the computer and cell phone off. I make it a priority to go to the gym, walk the dog, and/or meditate at least one hour per day. With my own law practice, I am now better able to balance these activities.

Meeting Deadlines. In an effort to prevent calendar conflicts, I maintain three calendars. My BlackBerry is synchronized daily with my (1) law office and (2) secretary's desktop, while I manually insert deadlines into (3) a FranklinCovey calendar that I keep in my possession at all times. Also, I have an established network of attorneys who make special appearances for me, when necessary.

Technology. Don't underestimate the power of being technologically savvy. You must know how to fix the scanner and the printer; learn basic computer networking and troubleshooting skills. Of course, you also should have technical support at your disposal—these days, it is easier than ever with remote technician access. However, you must still have basic technology and troubleshooting skills at your *immediate* disposal.

Benefits/Advantages

Executive Decisions. You are solely responsible for all decisions. Being a type A-plus personality, I actually enjoy this aspect of owning my law firm.

Billing Rates. Owning your own law firm means that you can set your own billing rates, which, for me, remain competitive with large law firms. When appropriate, I am able to give discounts to loyal and consistent clients. Meanwhile, I don't have to account for every minute of the day as I did when I worked for law firms.

Control of Calendar. I can more readily juggle my calendar now. I no longer have to attend partner meetings that I always found to be unproductive. Instead, I spend more quality time with my family, friends, and clients. In my spare time, I conduct seminars and write articles to promote my law firm.

My View Backward

My plan as a young lawyer was to be an equity partner of a large firm. I believe that this is a vision instilled upon us by society. My family is most important for me; being a wife, mom, and daughter requires ample time and effort. Owning my own law firm has allowed me to meet family needs while practicing law full time.

My View Forward

Recently, I opened an office in downtown Los Angeles–near L.A. LIVE. I will be among many long-term personal and business friends. This will be a great environment for me with much synergy and opportunities for more business development. With my own law practice, I am professionally challenged and fulfilled —every day, and I look forward to this new and exciting venture in my career path.

JULIA SYLVA is the president/CEO of the Law Offices of Julia Sylva, A Law Corporation, with offices in downtown Los Angeles and the greater Long Beach area in California, where she focuses on public law, land use, real estate, business, and corporate law, including the representation of nonprofit organizations and estate planning. She graduated from law school in 1983 and founded her firm in 2000. *www.sylvalawcorp.com*

- JAYNE GOLDSTEIN -

"Female professionals truly understand the intense struggle balancing work and home. We understand that we beat ourselves up and are harder on ourselves than any outsider ever could be."

My professional journey to forming a women-owned law firm had a unique inception. Only through the development of strong female friendships was I given the opportunity, not only to have equity in a firm, but to change the concentration of my legal practice to an entirely different practice area. After moving out of the state in which I lived and worked my entire life, I had occasion to go back to visit dear friends who were already in business doing complex litigation. As I was sitting in my friends' living room, the idea came to me that I could open an office for them in the state in which I was now living. Of course, this meant that I would not only have to learn an entirely new area of the law, but also deal with all of the demanding decisions involved in opening and owning a new firm. Although 10 years later I am of counsel to a different firm, the many beneficial lessons learned along the road have proved to be invaluable. Had I not been given the opportunity to change my career path, I would not be prosecuting class action cases today.

No matter what type of prior relationship, if any, you have with your partners, make sure you understand that you are all embarking on a business venture together. As such, treat the process with the respect that it deserves and make decisions intelligently and rationally and try to avoid emotional decisions. Even though you are an attorney, spend the money to hire the proper legal and accounting professionals to steer you on the proper course—it is money well spent. One of the first decisions that you have to make is the type of entity you wish to become. With your professionals assisting you, try to envision what your law firm will look like two, five, and 10 years down the road. Discuss and determine whether you plan on changing equity configurations and the frequency of such changes. This is an important step in determining if you want to become a professional corporation, limited liability company, or a limited liability partnership. Make sure the professionals you hire have experience servicing law firms. Even though these decisions can be changed if you are unhappy with the structure, it will save time and money making the correct choice first. Take the time and spend the money to have proper agreements drafted to address everything from division of equity to what would happen in the event of dissolution. It is much easier to have these discussions in advance prior to any problems developing. Make sure you thoroughly understand the ramifications of your written agreements. When experiencing the excitement of the prospect of ownership, it is difficult to envision problems down the road, but you must nevertheless focus on any potential future misunderstandings. Speak to your accountant to gain an understanding of the various tax issues involved with your practice. If your area of expertise is not business law, make sure you learn how your capital accounts work and the result to your capital accounts if you decide to take draws. Make sure you find out about various local tax ramifications concerning the location of your office. In some locations these ramifications can be significant. Have open and frank discussions as to what each partner expects of the other regarding each partner's contributions to the partnership both in respect to time devoted and client development. Be sure to address how many hours each expects to bill, whether or not to take draws, and how much time off each partner plans to take.

Although it sounds clichéd, a law partnership is like a marriage, and communication is key. Be direct, and make sure you express your ideas, opinions, and concerns. Don't let a problem fester, but express yourself as soon as an issue arises. However, if you really do not have a strong opinion, for example, as to whether or not to advertise in a law journal, then defer to your partner if she does have a strong preference. If you have a nagging worry about an issue, make sure you attack it head on. Discussions should take place when emotions are under control. Make sure you keep your conversations private and not allow staff to become involved in a matter that should remain between or among the partners. Nurture communication in the partnership even if you were not personal friends prior to your business relationship. You do not necessarily have to socialize outside of the office, but by continuing to share your successes, aspirations, and hopes for the growth of the partnership together, you stand a better chance of continuing to "row in the same direction."

Never underestimate the value of the powerful connections that women are able to make. Although I have solid friendships with some of my male colleagues, they do not compare to the bonds I share with my fellow female attorneys. Female professionals truly understand the intense struggle balancing work and home. We understand that we beat ourselves up and are harder on ourselves than any outsider could ever be. Only another woman understands how after a deposition we dissect and analyze every question we asked. And only a fellow female can celebrate and enjoy the triumphs of success along with you because she truly understands how hard it was to get there. Make sure you develop and maintain your relationships. Utilize your female connections to build a strong referral base, and continue to network with them because you never know where the path will lead. I wish you well in all of your future endeavors.

Jayne Goldstein is of counsel at Shepherd Finkelman Miller and Shah, LLP in its Weston, Florida, office, where she focuses on class actions and complex litigation. She graduated from law school in 1986 and co-founded her firm in 2000. *www.sfmslaw.com*

- LISA BONNER -

"I calculated my overhead and risks, and I didn't see the need nor the benefit of joining another firm."

Starting my own firm almost 10 years ago was, without question, one of the best career decisions of my life. I started my law firm in September 2000, with two other lawyers who worked with me at an Internet start-up company. I was the third lawyer hired of 30. Our legal affairs department had grown rapidly with the Internet start-up. When the company began to contract just as quickly as it had expanded, I saw the impending layoff writing on the wall. I headed to my boss's office and volunteered my head on the chopping block. Armed with a $15,000 severance package, four years of lawyering, and a built-in client base, the first iteration of Bonner Law, PC was born.

I did not make my decision to start my law practice on a whim; quite the contrary. I searched for other opportunities while I was working out my severance package, yet nothing thrilled me. I recognized I was at a crossroads, a crucial time in my career, so the next move was an important one. My soon-to-be-former co-worker (let's call her Kris) and I were discussing our next steps over lunch (she opted for the severance as well) when she suggested that we start a law practice. I almost choked on my tea! When we began to outline the pros and cons on paper, I clearly recognized that this was a tenable option.

There are a few cardinal rules to adhere to before starting your own practice. First and foremost, in my opinion, is to be sure that you are adequately trained. Many people think starting your own practice is as simple as hanging out your own shingle and finding the right stationery and business cards. Quite the contrary, you should know the ins and outs of your field of law; never use clients as guinea pigs. Clients are paying for legitimate legal advice and should not be subjected to your learning curve. By the time we tossed around the idea of starting our own firm, I had experience as a litigator and several years of experience in my current field as a transactional lawyer. Most importantly, while at the Internet production start-up, we hired an outside law firm and kept them on retainer. I'd spent endless hours learning from the firm's partners and assisted them in creating our production templates. Once we embarked on our new mission, we'd garnered the firm's support and had the production company's support firmly behind us.

Second, it is important to have a client base. Kris and I clearly had this. We embarked on our own practice at a time when Internet and e-commerce law were both in their infancy, and few, if any, other lawyers understood production work as it related to the Internet. Kris and I helped craft agreements with the Screen Actors Guild (SAG) that allowed SAG actors to appear in Internet productions. Prior to this, SAG's new media agreement only allowed its actors to appear in video games, and SAG had been resistant to expanding its scope. With this feat behind us and our other professional accomplishments in Internet production, we'd made a positive name for ourselves. This translated into a built-in client base: referrals from other lawyers and requests for our legal services from some of our former staff producers who were once again freelance producers. Each knew and trusted our legal acumen.

Third, it is important to have a well thought out business plan. While it is true that the best laid plans often go awry, that does not negate the fact that you need a clear road map of where you intend to go and how you intend to get there. This road map should include information about your field of law: what makes you and your practice special and how you can differentiate yourself from the sea of lawyers who inevitably offer similar services? What are your start-up costs and where will this capital come from? Define your needs: if you are a litigator, your needs will be vastly different from those of a transactional lawyer. Do you need an office or can you work from home? If you need an office, will a virtual office with conference room and receptionist coverage suffice, or do you need a traditional office with four walls and room for staff? How will you pay yourself and your employees? Many people are shocked to discover the hidden costs of simply paying themselves. As an employer, you must pay employer taxes (Social Security, Medicare, federal and state unemployment taxes) even when paying yourself, which can potentially double the amount of money you need to simply write yourself a check. Be clear about the start-up costs; this is no time for surprises. Have enough money not only to cover your start-up costs, but to carry you through the inevitable ebb months. And remember to stash and invest money during those flow months.

Flexibility, as a rule of thumb, is a must; be open to change. Kris and I eventually amicably parted ways, and I found it easier and more desirable to go it alone. I birthed Bonner Law, A Professional Corporation using the same thought process: Kris took her clients, and I took mine. I had referrals, money in the bank, and a solid business plan. This was nine years ago, and Bonner Law, PC is still going strong. Since then, I have been courted by firms large and small and always keep an open mind.

In 2008 I'd been looking to move back to New York from Los Angeles and had what seemed like an incredible opportunity. I was offered a partnership at a Park Avenue law firm, heading its film and television department. This seemed like a perfect opportunity for me, as the firm also had offices in Los Angeles. I packed my bags, my assistant packed my office, and I headed back east.

Eleven months to the day after I started at the firm, its sole equity partner was indicted on various charges, and the firm imploded in less than 72 hours. The partners were besieged with calls from headhunters, and many wondered where their next check was coming from. I, on the other hand, ordered a car, packed up my office, threw my client files in my spare bedroom, and set up office from home while I figured out my next move. I went on several interviews with firms and continued to service my clients and collect checks for my legal work moving forward. Ultimately, I didn't like what I was being offered: partnerships in exchange for firms taking 60–75 percent of my earnings (my last firm was salary with bonus). Thanks, but no thanks! I calculated my overhead and risks, and I saw neither the need nor the benefit of joining another firm. While searching for office space, I was courted by an international corporate firm, which had offered me a partnership prior to my last firm. They understood my reluctance to join another firm, and we worked out an arrangement: I have my firm and my clients and handle their entertainment clients. My mantra remains: I don't work for someone because I can't—I don't work for someone because I can!

LISA BONNER is the managing partner and founder of Bonner Law, PC in New York, New York, where she counsels large media companies, film distribution companies, music artists and producers, and independent television and film clients (producers, artists, and writers). She graduated from law school in 1997 and founded her firm in 2000. *www.bonnerlawpc.net*

- Jennifer C. Wolfe -

"At the core [of our business model] is a value of efficient delivery of the highest quality service with predictable costs . . . while providing a dynamic and life-friendly environment to our team."

Diversity Only Means Something If Companies Stand Behind It When It's Inconvenient

My law firm story begins with the conviction of a few visionary lawyers inside America's largest corporations, who believed enough in my firm to give us an opportunity when it would have been much easier to follow the status quo. I started my law firm 10 years ago with a belief that there was a better way to manage a law firm.

It is because of a few lawyers willing to stand behind their company's mission to provide opportunities to women-owned law firms that I can share this story. I must admit, the opening line is not my own. I borrowed it from one of my favorite movies, *The Contender*. In the movie, the lead is a woman nominated to be the vice president of the United States. When evidence emerges to clear her name from a scandal, she profoundly states that it is not right for the questions to be asked of a woman if they would not be asked of a man and that principles only mean something if you stand behind them when it is inconvenient. I have had the pleasure and good fortune to find lawyers who, likewise, believe that diversity only means something if you actually support it even if it's inconvenient.

I realize the purpose of this book is to tell the stories of women who have started and built their own law firms to serve as inspiration and guidance to the women who follow. But it is important to understand the role of our clients as a central driving force of any law firm. And for me, that force was in-house lawyers of Fortune 500 companies. I'll get to my strategy and how I got there in a moment, but in these first few paragraphs let me offer a re-sounding "Thank You" to those companies and lawyers who determined that it was important to support women-owned law firms.

Today, the solo practice I started at age 28 has offices in Cincinnati and New York City, with more to come, and serves some of the top companies in the world. So, how and why did I get started?

Before law school, I worked as the marketing & public relations director of a regional advertising company. Seeing the founders create jobs and opportunities for others, I knew then I wanted to own my own business. Clinging tightly to my entrepreneurial dream, when I graduated from law school I was not sure what to do. With law school loans to repay, a job was in order. I found a boutique litigation firm with a talented group of partners. While I didn't think I wanted to be a lawyer for long, this seemed like a good opportunity to experience what it was to be a lawyer. And I quickly learned the entire legal industry was the most backward place I had ever seen, billing for time, valuing inefficiency. It was so contrary to common sense. There was no incentive to do it better.

I knew I had to find my own way. So I reached back out to my contacts from my prior career and built my own book of business. I handled contracts, franchise agreements, license agreements, general counsel, dispute resolution, and trademarks. I started attending networking events and got involved in the local venture capital association. My unique blend of public relations, business thinking, and law differentiated me and meant new clients.

Over the Memorial Day weekend of 2000, I made the decision. I would start my own advisory firm. I would charge lower rates than my competitors and offer more value. I built a thriving practice over the next couple of years. But after getting married and deciding to have a baby, I found myself on bed rest with complications in the last trimester of my pregnancy. The clients had to go elsewhere until I returned, questioning if I would return. Was it true that women were simply not made for this? Do we have to choose between a business and a baby?

I knew then I needed to build something so that the business could function even if I could not. So, while forced to bed rest, I researched and wrote my business plan. Over the next few years, I built a full-service law firm providing divorce, estate planning, real estate, litigation, IP, and business, primarily to privately-held companies and individuals in Cincinnati. While tackling problem after problem, I realized I still did not have a sustainable business. So I threw out the plan and started over. I studied the legal marketplace carefully, understanding what was in demand, where there was less supply, trends, and how we might be able to do something better than our competitors.

I realized that there was a demand growing for intellectual property boutique firms and that there was, at least publicly, a demand for women-owned firms in IP from the largest companies in the world. I knew for us to have sustainability, we needed big clients with budgets that could spend recurring dollars with us. And so, taking an enormous risk, I phased out the areas of practice that didn't fit the plan and solidified a team of lawyers and staff who were committed to the vision of a law firm that operated as a successful scalable business.

We invested in the best team, technology, and infrastructure. We built our values and our culture from the ground up. We evaluated our processes and became a certified Six Sigma Black Belt in process improvement. I co-authored a book on the connection of IP with innovation and branding (*Brand Rewired: Connecting Branding, Creativity, and Intellectual Property Strategy* published by John Wiley & Sons, Inc. in July of 2010). I wrote articles in trade publications focusing on our unique approach. We sent our lawyers to Harvard to be trained in negotiation. We invested in sponsoring, speaking at, and attending national conferences. I went to more lunches than you can possibly imagine. I never gave up. Nothing would discourage me. I would always offer to give us a try for free—we'll show you what we can do, just give us a try, I would say. Eventually, it worked. They did give us a try. And, success leads to more success. The more work we got from Fortune 100 companies, the easier and easier it was to get work from other Fortune 100 companies. This is what diversity programs are all about. Give us a try, let us shine, we will grow and prosper, and eventually, a woman-owned firm may be one of the most prominent firms in the country.

My firm grows because we stay focused on a few core principles. We believe in teamwork, efficiency, and delivering value. We have no origination fees and no compensation tied to billable hours. We set measurable team-oriented goals and share profits at the end of the year. We use technology to deliver better, more efficient service to our clients. While there is so much more behind our business model, at the core is a value of efficient delivery of the highest quality service with predictable costs for our clients while providing a dynamic and life-friendly environment to our team.

JENNIFER C. WOLFE is the founder and managing partner of Wolfe, LPA in Cincinnati, Ohio and New York, New York, where she focuses on providing Fortune 500 companies with intellectual property strategy and negotiation of licensing and technology transactions. She graduated from law school in 1999 and founded her firm in 2000. *www.consultwolfe.com*

- ANDREA M. BUFORD -

"Many clients say, 'We do not hire firms, we hire attorneys.'
That belief, if adhered to, works for small firms. Do not be afraid of
going after work because you believe you are not big enough."

I am the owner of a firm that specializes in tort, employment, and commercial defense litigation. We also perform in-depth, confidential internal investigations. I am African American, and I am female. My remarks will be colored by who I am and what I do.

I decided to go to law school to "keep up with the Joneses." I needed an advance degree, and at the time, I thought law would be helpful both professionally and personally. I did not intend to actually practice law but ended up at a firm that was Chicago's largest, predominantly minority-owned firm. After four years, I became a partner at that firm. I have always been a self-starter, a natural leader with an entrepreneurial spirit, and when the firm dissolved I made the decision to start my own firm. I was lucky and/or I was very good at what I did. As a partner at the dissolved firm I learned the management aspects of running a law firm. I learned how to attract and keep clients, how to accurately bill clients, how to manage HR issues, and the like. I was also lucky in that many of the clients of the old firm made a decision to remain with my new firm.

OK, so here I am, I have attorneys I trust, staff I know, and clients to get me started. It sounds like I had it all. However, I still needed financing. I had to have an office, pay staff, get insurance, and obtain the appropriate licenses and credentials. It is still so clear in my head. The first step was to the bank for financing. My first lease was in the building located at 111 W. Washington, Chicago. The landlord required security and the bank required security. I had to allow the bank to place a lien on my home. I had to learn to prepare a business plan, I had to estimate income and expenses, and I had to delve into the financial issues of starting a new business. Had I not had excellent personal credit (and existing clients) I do not think it would have been possible. So now, I had financing, I had a lease, I had clients, and I had to keep it all.

It is not easy. You have to develop systems. You have to have quality control. You have to instill confidence in your firm with your clients. I have always believed that attorneys are basically equal when we first start in the practice. We all sit in class side by side and learn from the same textbooks. We learn the same basic law, no matter what school we attend. It is what you do with that knowledge, how you build upon it, that will set you apart from your peers.

When you first start, you have to answer questions. What form will the business take? Will it be a partnership, an LLC, or a corporation? Consult with a tax professional. Establish a relationship with a bank. Do not forget your client trust account. Your tax professional is an important part of your business. The bank, certifying agencies, and some clients will require you to provide annual financial statements. You will need a federal employment identification number (EIN). You will need a payroll service. Make sure you are properly licensed, and do not forget to register with the state supreme court. You are operating a business. In addition to malpractice insurance, which will be required by your clients, you will need liability insurance, workmen's compensation, and possibly employee health coverage. If you are a minority- or women-owned business you should obtain the appropriate cer-tifications from the city, county, and state, as well as a national certification. You will need a billing program for billing clients and an accounting program to keep track of your accounts.

Something else I did that I am extremely happy about is that I purchased an office condo. I don't feel that I am throwing away money on an exorbitant downtown commercial rent. My office belongs to me. It is ideally located between the federal and state courts and it even has an outdoor balcony area. It is suited for late night and weekend work, as you will not be afraid of being in a large commercial building.

That is the business side of the business. But how does one attract and retain clients? I advise you to join bar associations and networking groups. Person-ally, I belong to many bar associations. I served as president of the Cook County Bar Association. These organizations, along with NAMWOLF (the National Association of Minority and Women Owned Law Firms) and DRI, offer opportunities for members to meet with representatives of corporate America who have expressed a commitment to hiring women- and minority-owned firms. Register online with government agencies that will notify you of the existence of potential opportunities. Get to know the owners of similar size firms that practice in your practice area. Once you have a client, nurture and work on retaining the client. You cannot make a mistake, you cannot have a misspelling in a motion, and you cannot not follow the client's guidelines. You must return all calls in a timely manner, and you must perform beyond what is expected. You will note that I have not dwelled upon the technical aspects of the work that you do. All of my remarks are premised upon the belief that you are technically good at the work you do but may need some fine tuning in letting the client know.

Whenever a client hires a new firm, the person who recommends your firm is putting his or her reputation on the line, and you have to do all that you can do to make sure that person looks good. You cannot expect to meet a client and come home from that meeting with new files. A client has to get to know and trust you. Many clients say, "We do not hire firms, we hire attorneys." That belief, if adhered to, works for small firms. Do not be afraid of going after the work because you believe you are not big enough. The work you are doing does not require multiple attorneys, paralegals, and other staff. In fact, most corporations (strongly) caution against the use of multiple attorneys to accomplish tasks on a file. Sell yourself and document your successes.

My advice, if you intend to someday start your own firm, is to work in a small or medium-size firm that allows you an opportunity to learn the business side of the practice of law and that allows you to learn the technical aspects of your area of law. If you are an associate in a large firm that has a marketing department, an accounting department, and a management team, it is not likely that you will learn how to manage a firm. Likewise, it is unlikely that you will have an opportunity to "cradle to grave" a case, to have actual in-court time, to develop case strategy, or to consult with clients.

To own one's own law firm can be a rewarding and satisfying experience. It is challenging, and it can be scary. Not only are you responsible for your own income, but you must pay the salaries of other attorneys and a staff. You cannot miss a payroll, a rent payment, or other expenses. You will have some sleepless nights. At times you will feel like you have the weight of the world on your shoulders. You will question your decision to strike out on your own, but in the end, it will be worth it.

ANDREA M. BUFORD is the managing member for Buford Law Office, LLC in Chicago, Illinois, where her firm focuses on tort, commercial, and employment defense litigation, as well as internal investigations. Ms. Buford graduated from law school in 1986 and started her firm in 2001. *www.bufordlaw.net*

- CHARLENE L. USHER -

---

*"I sought to build a law firm from infancy to maturity in a
way that ensured quality of life, encouraged excellence,
embraced community service, and promoted women and attorneys
of color into the pipeline of future attorneys."*

I made the decision to start my own firm after working for a very large insurance company, a large "white shoe" law firm, a mid-size firm, and ultimately, a three-person small firm in an effort to seek my own niche. I sought to build a law firm from infancy to maturity in a way that ensured quality of life, encouraged excellence, embraced community service, and promoted women and attorneys of color into the pipeline of future attorneys.

I truly enjoy the business side of the law, including marketing and business development, strategic planning, adjusting to market conditions, and dealing with people, both internally (employees) and externally (clients, vendors, etc.). Having my own law practice allowed me the freedom to develop in these areas without being stifled by bosses or partners who could not embrace my vision. I enjoy it because every day is like an executive MBA program, where each decision I make has an immediate, direct, and also long-term impact on people's lives. I also enjoy encouraging others to pursue their dreams by pursuing my own.

The greatest challenge was growing from being the only attorney to having employees and managing their issues, all while striving to provide the same quality service expected from large firms. I also continue to find it challenging to convince potential clients that they can gain excellent service while achieving economies of scale by using a small, capable firm.

Looking back, I think starting my own firm was the best decision for me because this position has led to unparalleled opportunities to represent women and women of color in the business world and as a role model in a variety of arenas. I do not think I would have evolved as much as I have without this experience.

My business model has changed over time as I have begun to really see myself as a businessperson developing products and services to meet the needs of the market, rather than sticking with one practice area for a lifetime. I believe because of changing times, with more women and attorneys of color ascending into positions of power as CEOs and general counsel, it is easier for attorneys of my generation who are women or attorneys of color to have a shot at their business in the corporate world.

At the same time, I am old enough to be trusted by individuals who are making decisions about their assets and legacy. Our firm is now poised to service many more clients in multiple areas, which will also allow us to provide internships and work experience to students and new attorneys. It's an incredible blessing to wake up every day knowing I put food on families' tables while working as a team to deliver quality.

What I wish I knew then that I know now is that I can do this! I am much more confident because of the mistakes and missteps, as well as the triumphs. I know I can recover and succeed. I am fortunate to have a wonderful team that believes in our mission and strives to meet that vision every day.

I recommend that anyone considering starting his or her own law firm spend time examining the business side of his or her current law firm or employer to see how billing and collections work, to see how business development and employee development work, and to see more of the day-to-day from the big picture perspective. My many different experiences allowed me to see more of the big picture than staying at the large law firm would have allowed. It is a pleasure to be the president and CEO!

CHARLENE L. USHER is the founder and managing attorney at Usher Law Group, P.C. in southern California, where she focuses on legacy and estate planning. She graduated from law school in 1996 and founded her firm in 2001. *www.usherlawgroup.com*

- KATHERINE FRYE -

"Thinking back, it seems plain stupid to do what we did.
At that time, I didn't have any responsibilities. . . . With almost
10 years of practice under my belt (and a small child under my feet),
I know I made the right choice for me."

Thinking back, it seems plain stupid to do what we did. At that time, I didn't have any responsibilities except a student loan payment, and I was pretty sure I could delay my payments for a while. I was already used to eating ramen noodles and enjoying cheap forms of entertainment. So why not . . . just go ahead and bite the bullet and learn to practice law on my own. It's called the practice of law for a reason, right?

I specifically remember telling my parents my plan:

Me: Remember my internship this summer?

Them: Oh yeah, the established law firm you worked for. Did they offer you a job?

Me: Um, no, but, well, I hated working for someone else, so I've decided I should just start my own law firm.

Them: Hmm, well, do you have a plan?

Me: Well, not yet, but I'm going to have a law license, and that's all that matters.

The stark naïvety of my statements now makes me chuckle. Fortunately for me, I have some wonderful parents and subsequently a wonderful husband, who just smiled and encouraged me. I had my support, so what was next?

Having a law license is critical to being able to start your own law firm, but it is similar to your receiving your driver's permit in that it gives you a false sense of confidence that you know what you're doing. The reality is you know the law better than most other attorneys, but you know nothing about the practice of law. In this letter, I'll try to bullet point the most important things I learned along my journey about the practice of law:

1. *Fake it until you make it.*

Our office looked like a lawyer's should, and we had a license to practice. Who knew we had been practicing less than a month and that we did not know a thing about how to accomplish anything practically. I learned quickly that it did not matter. If I provided good customer service and I worked hard on their case, clients believed in me. A client's confidence will radiate from the confidence you provide, and that confidence will help you retain that client and will bring new ones to you.

2. *Ask for help.*

As I mentioned above, confidence is a powerful tool, but be sure to keep it in check. Consider everyone at the courthouse or everyone you speak with as a potential person to help you either now or in the future. Courthouse personnel will help you, other attorneys will help you, and even on occasion a judge will help you. In every situation but the last, you should be happy to ask. You will never know it all, and trust me, the longer you practice the more questions you have. In fact, someone recently said that the more they practice the less they know, and I would agree with that statement. Uncertainty is something I am comfortable with now, based on my experience that court is uncertain. Asking for help can save you time and money, and the reality is that the best attorneys in your area ask for help every day.

3. *Find several mentors (preferably busy ones) and several professional friends (preferably smart ones).*

My initial plan was to have lunch/coffee with the top attorneys in the county in my field. I planned to woo them with my wide-eyed respect and optimism. What I didn't plan was that these attorneys would be a referral source for me. Any client who could not afford them or whom they did not have time to deal with was promptly sent to that new attorney with whom they just had lunch. Of course, these clients rarely had much money, but they provided experience. They also built confidence in my referral sources; I started receiving more referrals because I had done a good job.

Along the way, I met people, now friends, who turned out to be smart and helpful. At the time, they were just new attorneys or new court personnel whom I happened to befriend. Now, they are the people I turn to for help with problems, and generally, they are in an excellent position to help. The day you start may be the same day someone starts in the clerk's office, and then 15 years later, that same person may be the head clerk, a powerful friend from whom to seek help when you need it.

4. Luck has something to do with it or maybe you make your own luck?
I was lucky because I went to a law school where they valued graduating attorneys who could walk out of the school and start practicing. We actually had a mandatory course on law firm management, and we were offered a course on how to start your own firm. These resources are likely there at any law school, and if not, look online. You can find similar resources.

I was lucky that I worked (is it called work when you are not paid?) for the same judges that I would be appearing in front of once I started practicing. I had insider knowledge and an informal education on what to do and not to do. I didn't plan it this way, but it just worked out well in the end. Think ahead of ways that you can position yourself to succeed when you open your own office.

I was lucky to discover that I had surrounded myself, and continue to do so, with the best people in each field (insurance, CPA, banks, etc.). At first, we just followed the referrals of one person, but all of these people turned out to be exceptional. Having the best around me meant I could relax that other things were being done well. Remember, you are running a business as well as practicing law, and having experts on running your business is just as important as having experts in your field of law.

5. It begins and ends with you.
You only get one reputation. Be mindful of that fact. Do not shade the truth, and answer the questions honestly even if the answer is not going to help your client. You are an officer of the court first. Understand that mistakes will happen, but it is how you handle them that will determine your reputation.

With almost 10 years of practice under my belt (and a small child under my feet), I know I made the right choice for me. I now have the freedom to practice law and live my life my way. I make the call on when I work and for whom I work. One week I may want to be super-attorney, and the next week, I may want to be a stay-at-home mom. I've earned that right and that freedom, and I didn't have to ask anyone's permission along the way.

KATHERINE FRYE is the owner of Frye Law Offices, P.A. in Raleigh, North Carolina, where she focuses on family law matters. She graduated from law school in 2001 and founded her firm in 2001. *www.fryelawoffices.com*

- Jean Murrell Adams -

"Don't just think of your practice as the next step in your professional career—fully leverage your law license and use it as a platform to do really big things."

Building ADAMS ESQ, a special education law firm, has been an exhilarating and liberating experience, and I truly appreciate the opportunity to share my roller-coaster ride with those of you who have started or are thinking of starting your own practice. What follows is advice that I wish I had received nearly a decade ago when I first made the decision to strike out on my own.

1. Dream Really, Really Big!
You've already received your undergraduate degree, endured law school, passed at least one bar exam, and have probably apprenticed at a law firm or public agency. You're already successful. Don't just think of your practice as the next step in your professional career—fully leverage your law license and use it as a platform to do really big things.

ADAMS ESQ predominantly represents low-income students with disabilities and assists them in obtaining much-needed assessments, services, and access to appropriate academic placement. Prior to founding the firm, I ran the litigation department of a major movie studio. It was an incredible, high-profile position and both financially and intellectually rewarding. However, nothing that I ever accomplished at the studio compared with my joy in helping my very first client—an autistic little boy—gain access to a private school and support services that he desperately needed but otherwise had no hope of getting. Since then, ADAMS ESQ has grown to four locations and has similarly helped over 2,000 children representing a wide range of disabilities.

A decade ago, I could not and did not imagine how much of an impact a small firm could make. This is your opportunity to dream big—really, really big.

2. Plan Well.

Dreaming big is fine, but to make your dream a reality, you need a solid business plan, sufficient capital, and at least a general understanding of concepts like "break-even," "balance sheet," and "cash-flow." I also suggest developing an exit strategy—in the event of the unexpected, you may need to take a break and try again later.

When I first imagined ADAMS ESQ, I envisioned a firm with a financially sustainable business model that allowed flexibility, so that I could work from home and be near my children, and did not involve huge start-up costs. To realize that goal, I knew I needed a solid plan. I set my alarm for 4:30 a.m. and worked on my business plan for several hours each weekday until it was time to leave for work. (My weekends were reserved for family.) I also maxed out my 401(k) and IRA contributions, took advantage of our studio's health care and child care savings plans, and saved as much of my salary as I could in order to build capital. Once my savings were in place, I went to a local bank and obtained a small business line of credit designed for women-owned businesses.

At its core, a law practice is still a business, and it needs to be run like one. It needs to generate sufficient revenues to pay you (hopefully quite handsomely) as well as your associates and staff and meet overhead costs. Bill your time at an appropriate hourly rate. *Never undervalue yourself or allow someone else to undervalue you.* Invest in a good debt collection service to accelerate your accounts receivable. ADAMS ESQ charges a retainer of $1 to low-income clients. Our cases are accepted on contingency, and our fees are paid by school districts or other local agencies only if we are successful. Therefore, we must be constantly vigilant in order to ensure timely payments from these agencies.

Learn to use QuickBooks or some other bookkeeping software and become accustomed to working with numbers, no matter how distasteful. Pinpoint your target market so that you can efficiently market your services. You may be a fabulous legal advocate, but those skills *do not translate* into being a good businessperson. For example, spending hours or even days researching and perfecting your legal argument or real estate contract is expected of a sterling attorney of your caliber. However, in running your firm, you will need to make snap decisions and rough judgment calls regarding business projections, and you will need to fire people on the spot. Rumination is rarely an option. Solid business planning and enlisting early advice from skilled professionals in accounting, human resources, technology, and insurance will provide a good knowledge base to help in the decision-making process.

Create systems. As a public interest law firm, we had to learn how to operate "lean and mean" without compromising our commitment to excellence. One of the keys in achieving this balance was to create systems. Since our practice is cyclical (roughly tracking the school year) we devised and implemented systems that allow us to expand and contract our capacity as necessary. The best resource on the importance of creating systems that I have read is *The E-Myth Revisited*, by Michael Gerber.

Embrace technology. It's important to research and invest in a good case management and billing system that is fully integrated into your accounting software. That way, you can track your productivity and that of your attorneys and staff, accurately and effectively bill your clients, and pinpoint areas for improvement. There are a number of free and low-cost software and web-based programs. However, when choosing an application, make sure it is right for your business and meets your needs. "Free" is not necessarily cost-effective if it is not reliable or secure.

3. Dive In.
After you've dreamed and planned—now get started. Don't be paralyzed by the thought "what if I fail?" This was particularly daunting for me as I was transitioning from a high-profile position as an entertainment attorney to a field of law that I knew very little about. I was so concerned about doing a good job that I hesitated to start at all. When I finally did summon the courage to jump in, the water was just fine.

Surround yourself with cheerleaders. Many of my well-meaning colleagues tried to convince me to abandon the idea of opening my own practice—after all, I already had a dream job. They suggested that I was too old to start a new firm in a different area of law, that I would be overwhelmed with paperwork, that the school districts were too powerful, and that the hearing officers (now administrative law judges) were all on the side of the school districts so parents could never win. Thankfully, I had 100 percent support from my family, who never doubted that ADAMS ESQ would one day be a thriving practice.

You're never too old for a mentor. One of the things that I did after my practice hit a rough spot was to consult with an advisor from the SCORE program, which is part of the Small Business Administration. My SCORE mentor was a retired CFO of a large multi-national corporation. His advice was excellent and was critical to the success of our practice. I was also mentored by a retired founder of a technology company. His advice was to focus on solving one problem at a time and to then move to the next problem. Work constantly on refining your business processes and focus on one thing at a time until that one aspect is in good shape. Don't worry about perfecting it, as that will simply drive you nuts.

4. Enjoy the Journey.

Building and running ADAMS ESQ has been a roller-coaster ride with incredible highs and lows, successes and setbacks. Throughout this adventure, I've enjoyed what I do and the children that ADAMS ESQ represents. Our clients may not be able to pay large retainers, but they reward us with prayers, referrals, and—my favorite gift of all—a copy of their child's graduation announcement.

JEAN MURRELL ADAMS is the managing attorney of ADAMS ESQ, a special education law firm, with office locations throughout California and Nevada. She graduated from law school in 1986 and founded her firm in 2002. *www.adamsesq.com*

- JOANNE R. STERNLIEB -

"I love what I do....When I've been approached with partnership opportunities at large and small firms, I have turned them down."

On September 11, 2001, I looked out my office window approximately 40 blocks north of ground zero and saw the World Trade Center implode. I was nine months pregnant with my second daughter, and I decided then that I would finally follow my dream and start my own law firm. I always wanted to have my own firm—even before I was married and had children. However, 9/11 and wanting more of a work/life balance after having children gave me the courage to go out on my own. I had practiced trusts and estates law as an associate, and then counsel, at a large New York law firm for over 12 years. A year after my first daughter was born I left that firm for a part-time job as a senior estate planner at an asset management firm, where I worked for two and a half years. In June 2002 I left to start my firm.

The first thing I had to determine in deciding whether to start my own firm was whether there was a need for my services. Was there a niche that I could fill? When I was at my previous two employers, I was often asked by friends and colleagues for the names of trust and estate lawyers for themselves, their families, or their clients. They were looking for attorneys with good backgrounds and experience, who charged reasonable fees, and to whom they could feel confident referring clients. I knew I could fill that niche.

Once I made the decision to explore starting my own firm, I looked at a number of factors: (1) Who would be my referral sources? (2) Who were my prospective clients? (3) How would I market my services and network? (4) Would I limit my practice to estate planning? (5) What would my start-up costs and overhead be and would I be able to afford them? (6) Would I be able to replicate my income? If so, how long would it take? Would I have enough savings to tide me over while my practice was growing? And (7) how much would I charge for my services? Would I charge by the hour or would I charge a flat rate?

I attended a seminar on starting your own law firm at the New York City Bar Association. I then began speaking to solo practitioners. I also spoke to former colleagues and T&E lawyers at large firms to see if they would refer clients to me. They said "yes" and, true to their word, former colleagues, lawyers at large firms, and clients have become the largest sources of business for me.

I started my practice working at my dining room table, taking almost any client, charging low fees, and making accommodations for those who couldn't afford my rates. As my practice grew, I needed more help. The biggest challenge I have faced since starting my firm is how to expand my practice without overextending myself. For the first several years I worked night and day (taking time out to spend time with my girls)—defeating the purpose of starting my firm, which was to have more of a work/life balance. It was grueling. I hired a law student to work part time as a legal assistant. But that wasn't enough. I needed a lawyer. I was reluctant to hire a lawyer even on a part-time basis because I didn't know if I would consistently have enough work to keep her busy. My solution was to use lawyers who work for me as independent contractors on an "as needed basis"—from their homes, on their own schedules, and whenever they want. These lawyers have no set hours, no billable hour requirements, no guaranteed hours, and no guaranteed pay. Since I use, and pay, the independent contractors only when I have work for them, they are not a fixed cost.

Now, eight years later, I have six amazing women with stellar credentials working with me—a lawyer who works four days a week, a full-time paralegal, and four lawyers who work as independent contractors (three of whom have children and have chosen not to work at a traditional law firm so that they can spend more time with them).

In addition, I am counsel to a small, full-service corporate and litigation firm (with tax, labor, bankruptcy, broker-dealer, securities regulation, and intellectual property practices) where I handle their trust and estate work. This arrangement is beneficial to me since it enables me to help my clients with their other legal needs.

Once you decide who your prospective clients are, it is easier to target your marketing to them. Initially, my typical client was a young couple with a new baby who needed wills and didn't have extensive assets. I marketed then to new mothers groups. Although I still have a lot of young parents as clients, now most of my clients are investment bankers, hedge fund managers, and professionals with more significant wealth. Many of these clients also have young children and need wills, but they have greater wealth and need more sophisticated planning. My target audience has changed.

When I started out, several times a month I went to "marketing" or "networking" meetings (e.g., lunch at an accounting firm with other professionals that doubled as CLE credit). Now that my practice has grown, I don't do any marketing and I participate in fewer networking activities.

At first, the financial impact was much harder than I anticipated. I was used to getting a paycheck every two weeks. Not only was money not coming in, it was going out toward start-up costs. Clients don't always pay on time, and the income isn't steady. The first two years I relied on savings. I work out of my home so I have very low overhead. When I started out I met clients at their homes or in their offices or I rented office space on an hourly basis. Now, I usually meet clients at the office of the corporate/commercial law firm.

For standard estate planning services I usually charge a flat fee, and I tell clients what the fee will be up front. Now that my practice has expanded, I have raised my fees to be competitive. However, my rates are still significantly cheaper than other lawyers with my level of expertise at large firms.

My advice to anyone wanting to start her own firm would be to get experience first. Develop contacts and referral sources. Do a budget to determine how much money you need to live on. Try to project what your costs are going to be—startup and ongoing costs. Think about how you will feel in an office or working at home all day and not coming into professional contact with others. Decide if you are ready to take on nonlegal tasks, and if not, make sure you have the funds to hire someone to do them for you. You have to realize that you are no longer just practicing law—you are running a business, which takes a whole different set of skills than we were taught in law school.

Am I glad that I started my own law firm? Absolutely. I love what I do. I have more control over my life, more flexibility, and better work/life balance than I ever had before or that I could imagine having working for someone else. When I've been approached with partnership opportunities at large and small firms, I have turned them down. But there are downsides as well. If I don't bring in clients, I don't get a paycheck. I work incredibly hard. Sometimes I realize how much easier it would be to put on a suit, go to an office, and pick up a paycheck at the end of the week. I think it's a matter of choice. I have what is most important to me—work/life balance and a practice that I love.

JOANNE R. STERNLIEB is the founder of the Law Offices of Joanne R. Sternlieb in New York, New York, where she focuses on providing estate planning and trust and estates services to individuals, banks, and trust companies. She graduated from law school in 1987 and founded her firm in June 2002. *www.jsestateplanning.com*

- Deborah Hrbek -

"You need to learn to weather the inevitable cycles of good times and bad with dignity, to stay positive, to remain true to yourself, and never to compromise your integrity."

The best part of owning an independent law firm is the unconditional autonomy that such a practice provides. I am the master (or rather the mistress!) of my own universe. I can take on the kinds of clients and the types of cases that most appeal to me. I can decline work that I find tedious. What a rush I felt when my very first private client paid me for my work; someone was actually giving me money because I was able to perform a valuable service for them. I was not on a salary; it was completely different from just being paid to show up and do what I was told. What a thrill it was when I submitted my first application for an order to show cause that went out without being reviewed by a supervisor. I must have read it over 50 times. But once it was done, once it achieved the desired result, I felt an unparalleled sense of accomplishment.

Traditionally, when men go to law school or embark on any professional career path, they expect that one day they will be their own bosses inside or outside a major law firm environment. Women often have quite different expectations. Or society often has different expectations for us. Either way, when we own and operate a successful law practice, we prove to everyone, including ourselves, that we can do it.

There is a freedom that comes with self-employment. I can get a mani-pedi in the middle of a weekday afternoon. I can run errands or take a relative to the hospital, I can roll into the office at 11 a.m., and I can take personal days without asking anyone's permission. Except that I can't do any of these things, at least not as often as I'd like. To be successful in my own practice, I have to be extraordinarily self-disciplined, and the inherent contradictions abound. There may be no boss to scold me, or even to wonder where I am mid-afternoon when I should be at my desk. But if I am not accessible when potential clients are trying to reach me, they will go elsewhere. There may be no billable hour threshold required of me, yet if I don't meet a certain self-imposed minimum then I won't be able to pay my bills. There is no one else to blame, I am accountable to no one. Except that I am accountable to myself and, as is the case with many women, I am my own harshest critic.

Owning my own practice has been as exhilarating as it has been terrifying. The potential rewards are high. I get to keep 100 percent of the proceeds, and I control the overhead. Yet the concomitant risks are even higher. There is no safety net when cash flow is low. I have to take full responsibility for business development, getting the legal work done, being responsive to clients, and making sure that I actually get paid. In some sense, we solo practitioners are uniquely vulnerable. It is not just the fact that we have to get used to having no regular paycheck. When work is slow there may be no money to take home whatsoever. There is no partner with whom to spread the risk, whose business interests are aligned with our own, who can help carry the slack, who can provide us with spillover work when we need it most. There is no one to help make major business decisions, to provide reassurance that we are heading down the right path. Time and again we are reminded that the price of complete autonomy is complete responsibility and often a sense of isolation. We have the freedom to pave our own path to success and the opportunity to enjoy the supreme satisfaction that success brings. Yet at the same time we have the freedom to fail.

I started networking during a slow spell, to maximize the utility of my down time by using it to build new business relationships. And thankfully, I have found that networking really works. I have developed new referral sources for my practice that have helped increase my client base and improve my bottom line. As an added bonus, I have found there to be many non-monetary benefits of networking for a solo practitioner. I now have a community of peers with whom I can not only cross-market and cross-refer, but to whom I can address the stupidest of my questions. I have a broader network of colleagues with whom I can share business dilemmas and experiences and tips. We exchange information about how to get the best health insurance and malpractice insurance. We turn each other on to affordable bookkeepers, computer repairmen, remote receptionist services, and second-hand furniture stores. We help one another resolve difficult staffing issues. We provide one another with a truly empathetic shoulder to cry on when the phone stops ringing.

The potential for creativity in a solo practice has been among the greatest sources of satisfaction for me. As an independent businesswoman, I have had the opportunity to create a business that reflects my own vision, my own values, my imagination, my personality. There are the classically fun girlie aspects of the business, like decorating the waiting area, selecting the font and the color and the texture of the stationery, and planning the office parties. But I have found that even the most menial tasks have become outlets for creativity. My firm's image and reputation are invested in the manner in which the legal back is printed, the way the telephones are answered, and the tone of my retainer agreements. Never having been one for paper organization, I have found that I now truly care about the way my filing system is maintained. I enjoy the inventiveness of developing systems that need to be in place for the efficient management of my caseload. Unsurprisingly perhaps, administrative tasks such as billing (a tedious task when one has a salary that is not directly related to one's billable hours) have become an unprecedented source of interest. I am now quite fascinated by, and happy to engage in the investigation of, effective strategies for bill collection, contacts management, and time management systems.

During the recent economic downturn we have all suffered enormously. For small firms, there is less margin for error. The sudden impact on our cash flow is as threatening as it is for any small business. Yet the tiny size of our practices has enabled us to bob and weave and become more efficient almost overnight. Because we make our own decisions, we do not need to have big meetings and reach a consensus before we downsize our office, our staff, or our marketing expenses. Because we are our own bosses, we do not have to fear the fall of the axe when layoffs are announced. We are resilient because our survival depends on it. We may be uneasy, but we can cling to the illusion that we are in control of our own destiny, which, in and of itself, is empowering in times of economic stress. We get creative: we add new practice areas to our service offerings, we explore collaboration opportunities, we scheme, and we strategize. We are strong because we have been empowered by the very autonomy and responsibility and confidence that have kept us standing on our own two feet every single day of our self-employed careers.

For me at least, there is no question that the pros of an independent practice outweigh the cons. To succeed, you need to keep your overhead low, be a risk taker, stay open and flexible, and keep your eye on the prize. You need to learn to weather the inevitable cycles of good times and bad with dignity, to stay positive, to remain true to yourself, and never to compromise your integrity. By taking the helm of the flight path of your career through the operation of your own enterprise, you will attain all the professional satisfaction that you can possibly hope for.

DEBORAH HRBEK is the owner of Hrbek Law LLC in New York, New York, where she practices arts and entertainment law, matrimonial law, and mediation. She graduated from law school in 1989 and founded her firm in 2002. *www.hrbeklaw.com*

- EILENE BROWN -

"[Y]ou are not an island unto yourself. Your colleagues will prove to be some of the most beneficial resources that you can have as you face each day and each new case."

My journey to start my own practice was on a slightly winding road. All I knew was that I was burned out from big law practice litigation and I needed a long break. I thought, what would I do? Defense litigation was all I had known for the past six and a half years after graduating law school. Then, I also began to think, are you crazy? You are on the "partnership track." You are at a pretty well-known firm. You have a pretty decent salary, with perks. Are you crazy? What will people think? But the little angel on my shoulder kept saying go for it, this can work. You are single, young (at that time I was not quite 30), and have no children. Your only responsibility is you. When will you ever have an opportunity like this? "Take the money and run." The "money" being my hard-earned end-of-the-year bonus.

So, thus started the germination of my plan to not only leave the law firm at the end of the calendar year, but also to relocate to Maryland, where members of my family had recently moved and settled.

When I got to Maryland, I was happy at first, living on my bonus, taking a long vacation to clear my mind and dream of the future. Then, reality hit me. I have to eat and keep a roof over my head. At some point, I have to earn a living again. Then all of the visions of the law firm long hours, multiple litigant cases, and fighting for the sake of fighting popped back into my head. I got burned out just thinking about being burned out again. So, I thought to myself, what else? What can I do and still keep my sanity and make a living at the same time? For the first time ever, I began to get familiar with and cozy up to the phrase "quality of life." Yes, just possibly, I can still utilize my hard-earned degree and still have a quality of life.

So I began to think about how I could have a quality of life and use my skills and training as a lawyer. As I thought and meditated and journaled, I discovered that there were indeed some areas of the law that I enjoyed going back to my days as a law student at Brooklyn Law School *and* there were some skills that I had picked up along the way that were comfortable and familiar that suited me well. I began to recall the classes I enjoyed most, which were family law and probate, and then I began to think about the common thread that those particular areas of law afforded that most suited me—and I realized that my strengths and affinity lean toward the "counselor" part of being a lawyer. Connecting with and helping people sort through legal issues and procedures at some of the most difficult and challenging times of their lives. So, my current practice's areas of probate and family law began to germinate.

Eight years later I am still here, practicing and enjoying the path I am on. I have attained my goal to practice in areas that I enjoy and to have a quality of life. I enjoy the clients with whom I interact and have come to help over the course of my solo practice. I have even had an opportunity to do pro bono work in the areas of domestic violence, adoptions, and guardianships. All of these experiences have been truly rewarding and gratifying.

While there have been numerous joyous and satisfying moments throughout my practice, there have been some challenges. But thankfully, the rewards have outweighed the challenges. I won't bore you with the mundane details of day-to-day practice as a solo attorney. I will only say, by way of guidance and to give you some direction, that you should network, network, network. Although you may be practicing as a solo, you are not an island unto yourself. Your colleagues will prove to be some of the most beneficial resources that you can have as you face each day and each new case. After all, we are in the "practice" of law, which means that practice makes you better and better and better. That "practice" should include your learned colleagues. You can pull from their experiences and knowledge as you research and grow your own body of knowledge and experiences.

In closing, I must admit that the journey as a solo practitioner is not easy, and sometimes it gets lonely. But I hope that your journey is as rewarding as mine has been, and I encourage you to keep the course, stay true to your purpose and your calling, and it will all be well worth it.

Kind regards and kudos to you!

EILENE BROWN is a solo practitioner and owner of the law practice known as E. Brown Law, LLC in Bowie, Maryland, where she focuses on probate and family law. She graduated from law school in 1991 and founded her firm in 2002. *www.ebrownlaw.com*

- R. Denise Henning -

"I have learned to listen to that nagging voice . . . when I am about to make a decision that is not the right one. It takes time and experience to learn to trust and depend on your intuition."

The Henning Law Firm, P.C. was established in February 2002. We represent plaintiffs who have been victims of personal injury, wrongful death, or transportation-related injuries such as tractor-trailer accidents and highway defects. We have a proven record of prevailing in our cases, including an $8 million wrongful death verdict, a $6 million arbitration award, and numerous six, seven, and eight figure settlements for clients.

We believe in providing exceptional service and communication to our clients. We are zealous advocates for our clients because they are entitled to first-rate representation. We are persistent and stubborn while at the same time being professional and ethical. We work hard and smart. We don't fight about every little thing because we pick our battles wisely and fight those that bring the most reward to the client and their case.

Our clients are mostly people who have never hired a lawyer. Something tragic has happened and they have to figure out how to pay medical bills and provide for their family without the wage earner of the family or without the physical well-being to do the job they used to do. They could never afford to hire a lawyer on an hourly basis. I have had the honor of helping the most wonderful families and the great pleasure of developing relationships that survive past the end of the case with many of my clients.

When I founded The Henning Law Firm, I decided one of the most important tenets of the firm would be to always show employees respect and appreciation. I established a firm culture that is team-oriented, supportive, and flexible, in which each employee is treated fairly regardless of whether he or she is a legal or nonlegal staff member. I remain dedicated to providing my employees with more than fair compensation, health insurance, a retirement plan, and time off that affords everyone a high quality of life.

At The Henning Law Firm, we work on every case as a team. We hold regular case strategy meetings during which we brainstorm and strategize. Everyone contributes during these sessions. I believe my employees feel good about being included and about having their ideas valued. We also provide the best service for our clients when we work in this manner because more ideas and strategies are considered.

We have structured our firm procedures so that each client will always be informed about the progress of his or her case. Telephone calls are returned promptly. While we always strive for an early settlement in our cases so that clients can be immediately compensated, some cases may require two to three years to be resolved or go to trial. During that time, clients are sent a copy of every letter that we receive and a copy of every letter that we send out. If a pleading is filed in a client's case, he or she will get a copy of it. It is our client's case, not our case. Clients are entitled to know exactly what is going on in their case, and we are 100 percent committed to keeping them informed.

One of the difficulties of working solely on a contingent fee basis is financing cases while paying the firm's overhead during the lengthy time period that it takes to prepare a case for settlement or trial. In a semi-truck case or a wrongful death case, it is not unusual to spend $100,000 or more to get the case to the point where serious settlement negotiations take place or to get the case ready for trial, which can take one to three years. During that time, the firm carries the expenses of the case. We extensively investigate each potential case before we agree to take the case because if we lose the case or are unable to recover, the case expenses will not be reimbursed and we won't get paid for our work. We are very honest with our potential clients and tell them immediately if we don't think their potential case is one that can be won, saving both of us the time and expense of pursuing a case that can't be won. We have overcome the challenge of financing by building a strong relationship with our banker and being efficient when incurring case expenses.

In almost every case, the defendants are represented by large defense law firms that have many lawyers and staff members. Large firms have the ability to file numerous motions and briefs because they have abundant human resources to assign to the case. The Henning Law Firm has dealt with this by having on our staff a lawyer who devotes almost all of his time to research and writing so that we can file motions and brief issues and respond to the motions and briefs that are filed by the defense. This approach has made a huge difference in the success of our cases because we are able to put pressure on the defense by filing our own motions, and we are in a position to respond quickly to motions that are filed by the defense. This is unusual for a plaintiffs' firm because most plaintiffs' firms would not be willing to increase overhead in order to have an attorney who devotes his or her time solely to writing and research. This approach provides us a depth that other plaintiffs' firms do not have.

I am often asked for advice by young lawyers who are starting their own practices. The first thing I tell them is to trust their intuition. Learning to trust one's intuition can be very expensive, but it is an invaluable lesson. I have learned to listen to that nagging voice that raises the caution flag when I am about to make a decision that is not the right one. It takes time and experience to learn to trust and depend on your intuition. The most important aspect of trusting my intuition is when we are deciding whether we should agree to represent a potential client. I feel compassion and sympathy for almost every client, but I can't represent every potential client. If I meet with them in person, I want to help them, even if I shouldn't take the case. I now do a better job of screening the potential clients on the phone and referring them to other qualified lawyers so that I don't end up taking too many cases or cases that don't fit my area of expertise.

Building a law practice is a life-long endeavor. Hard work and long hours are essential to your success but most crucial is honesty, integrity, and your word. The greatest piece of advice I can give young lawyers is to work hardest at building and protecting your reputation.

R. DENISE HENNING is the founder of The Henning Law Firm, P.C. in Kansas City, Missouri, where she represents plaintiffs who have been victims of personal injury, wrongful death, and transportation-related injuries such as tractor-trailer accidents and highway defects. She graduated from law school in 1992 and founded her firm in 2002. *www.henninglawpc.com*

- CHERYL A. BUSH -

"[M]y experiences as a founding partner of a smaller boutique firm and equity partner at a big firm had taught me some important lessons on how to run a successful and competitive law firm."

Building your own law practice and starting your own firm are a little like making a really good batch of cookies (which I am known for among family, friends, and colleagues). It's all about the right mix of ingredients, proper tools, creativity, dedication, and knowing when to stop before getting burned. It is not some *Field of Dreams* experience, where if you build it they will come. Expect to work harder than you anticipated, and to start your own firm, you have to be a good lawyer—so be that first.

I began my career at a large, well-known firm in Detroit, which was a good learning experience for me personally and professionally. While at this firm, I chose to stay away from the elite, higher-profile cases because I knew that as a young lawyer, I was unlikely to get anywhere near a courtroom. Instead, I chose to dive into tort cases and did so with great enthusiasm. This decision helped me gain more trial experience than the lawyers I was competing with, the respect of my colleagues, and the knowledge it takes to be a bet-the-company trial lawyer. The majority of my tenure there was spent expanding my knowledge base and fine-tuning my advocacy skills, along with navigating my way through the big firm bureaucracy and layers of hierarchy (also known as red tape). As my practice developed and client list grew, I became an equity partner, but the more I worked with support staff and young lawyers, the more I realized the big firm environment did not fit my long-term goals. After 10 years, I left big firm practice for a partnership at a smaller boutique firm of trial lawyers.

Over the next eight years, I learned that even in a smaller firm, divergent viewpoints can form among lawyers in terms of how to run a law firm. Some were more comfortable with the big firm approach to law firm manage-ment, while two of my partners and I wanted to implement a different, more hands-on approach. So I opened my own firm with two trusted partners and colleagues, while the others returned to a local big firm. As the task of starting a completely new firm loomed large, I realized that my experiences as a founding partner of a smaller boutique firm and equity partner at a big firm had taught me some important lessons on how to run a successful and competitive law firm.

Starting my own firm was not a whole lot different than perfecting my chocolate chip pecan cookies: it's all about finding the right blend of ingredients and perseverance, trying new things until the proper mix is found. Like good cookies, where certain elements are critical for a successful batch, I believe there are critical ingredients needed when starting your own law firm. My recipe incorporates both management philosophies and practical considerations. Your firm will only be as good as the people who work for you, so it is critical you become a good boss—someone who promotes a team management style. Treating people fairly and with respect will go a long way toward making everyone feel they are a vital part of your team.

An important part of promoting a team environment is making sure your employees enjoy both working at your firm and the people they work with. I try to promote this in two ways: (1) by giving credit where credit is due and not hogging the spotlight, particularly in front of clients, and (2) laughter— we laugh a lot at our firm and often play practical jokes. But then again, we are largely a firm without hierarchies, which may or may not work for you. Reward employees based on merit, and avoid promotions based on a lock-step approach. Finally, I urge you to be a realistic employer—when you can. That is, make sure you understand how long it will take to complete an assignment before handing out a deadline.

So, how do you find this great team of employees that are going to make your firm an unparalleled success? Well, with respect to hiring staff—I only hire really smart people no matter what the job is. Remember, college degrees are not always necessary or an indicator of work ethic or intelligence. Some of my best paralegals began as administrative assistants, with no formal paralegal or college degrees (you should check your state law regarding paralegal requirements), who were promoted, based on merit, as our business grew.

To do your job really well and build your firm and client base, it is critical you hire an impeccably trustworthy, part-time person to handle your books week to week. A good referral source is the accounting firm you hire to take care of your tax returns. With respect to hiring attorneys, do your best to avoid using legal search firms—they are very expensive and the results are mixed. One way my firm has recruited excellent associates is through a $1,000 annual scholarship we offer to a local top law school for students interested in our practice—trial work. Another option is to pay attention when attending motion call or depositions and look for less experienced lawyers who do a really good job—you may want to hire them someday.

Now that you have the proper mix of ingredients in place, you can utilize your highly motivated team to help you grow a diverse client base and start marketing your new firm. After working through this most recent economic downturn in Michigan, I urge you to start, and never stop, marketing because it's no place to save a nickel. As part of your marketing and client development efforts, keep in mind the biggest complaints clients have about lawyers in big firms, and strive to keep yourself and your firm above the competition. For example, return calls promptly and be available.

There is no recipe book for opening your own law firm, but I do have some practical considerations for those of you just starting out. I am not a pessimist at heart, but things may go more smoothly if you assume everyone is trying to rip you off. You'll be pleasantly surprised when they don't! That said, here are some practical tips when starting out:

- Limit personal guarantees whenever possible (office lease, etc.).
- Avoid signing any long-term contracts for office equipment, software, leases, etc., and remember that timeframes are always negotiable.

One of the more frustrating surprises I encountered was learning that the cost of our initial software did not include the service of that software. So be aware that you may be able to buy the software, but if you don't purchase a service contract, there will be no one to answer your questions. Also, encourage your staff to learn how to handle the reset-the-server-type issues, so that support is always available.

- Don't sign up with a huge computer assistance company. Instead find a good, local computer person who moonlights in computer services. You will become their priority client, and they will work harder to impress you. Call other small firms in the area and ask who they use for computer assistance.

- Create business and marketing plans and stick to them.
- Build a website (domain name filing) that speaks to who you are and what your firm is capable of. This will act as one of your most important marketing tools.

I hope you find my recipe for success a useful one because truly, I love what I do, the people I work with, and the clients I serve. Plus, I get to make rules like no flip-flops in the office, then apply a double standard to myself. (I love wearing flip-flops!) I constantly strive to diversify our practice and grow my firm without ever sacrificing the personal relationships I have with my team. Because of this, six years later, in the midst of a significant economic downturn, we are still here.

Good luck!

CHERYL A. BUSH is the majority owner and managing partner at Bush Seyferth & Paige PLLC in Troy, Michigan, where she focuses on complex product liability and commercial litigation. She graduated from law school in 1984 and founded her firm in 2003. *www.bsplaw.com*

- POORVI CHOTHANI -

"I wanted to establish an Indian law firm with international capabilities and standards, so I took the New York bar exam. . . . There is no limit to what you can achieve with hard work once you have crossed the hurdle of self-doubt."

Early Years—Solid Foundation

My formative years played an extremely important role in building a strong character and eventually a strong career. I was the second born among three daughters at a time when a daughter was not as welcome as a son—especially not a second daughter! Despite this I thrived!

We were raised in a simple environment that imparted platinum values of discipline, honesty, strength, integrity, and character. My father, a strong supporter of education, at a time when families lived in the same home for centuries, moved so that we got a good education. Once again, when my father realized that the environment at the only college in town was not conducive to women's education, he worked hard to establish a new college—the Emerald Heights College for Women. This small college gave me myriad opportunities to participate in activities and enabled me to take up leadership positions.

Soon, unfortunately, my family ran into bad times and money was scarce. The enormity of the problems hit me when we did not have the equivalent of three dollars for a five-day college trip. This was the turning point when I realized the importance of money and education and resolved to pursue a professional degree.

On graduating from college I moved to Mumbai to join law school and lived with an aunt who provided some financial support. I trained as a secretary and eventually worked for $12 a month, which paid for some expenses.

The Influence of Previous Practice on Opening My Own Firm

On graduating I started out as a trainee with Rohit Kapadia, a leading lawyer, and continued working as a junior counsel for about $20 per month. In the meantime, I got married to Rohit, a progressive and supportive husband from an extremely conservative family. At this time several of my classmates were on their way to the United States to pursue an LL.M. at Harvard. I craved to go, but the cost of such an education and my personal circumstances made it impossible.

In those days, legal work was hard to come by, and women lawyers were not taken seriously. Striving for work/life balance became that much harder after my daughter and son were born. I was forced to take sabbaticals, during which I worked on gaining knowledge and contributed to society. But the idea of having a significant legal career always stayed with me.

Making the Decision to Start a Firm or Practice

My dream of pursuing higher education in the United States lay dormant until my daughter graduated from school. In 2002, at the age of 39, I joined the LL.M. program at the University of Pennsylvania Law School. Having been in solo practice, it was clear that growth is limited when you are on your own. Before leaving India, I carefully examined ways in which I could optimize my career after the LL.M. and resolved to start my own law firm if nothing better came up.

This resolve was reinforced on graduation while working with a U.S. law firm. I wanted to establish an Indian law firm with international capabilities and standards, so I took the New York bar exam and got admitted to the New York Bar. This was difficult but helped me practice New York and U.S. federal law in India in the name of LawQuest. LawQuest's clients were for U.S. immigration work in the beginning but steadily evolved, and within a short span of time we included practices in intellectual property, real estate, corporate and commercial law, transaction law, family law, global migration, and Indian employment law, to name a few. LawQuest plans on opening an office in New York City in 2012.

LawQuest today, with three partners, four associates, and several support staff, is a law firm that offers the flexibility that women need to maintain a work/life balance. This seems to attract women associates and employees, resulting in an all-women law firm!

Business Development by a Women-Owned Firm

Practice development and rainmaking cannot be very different for men and women, and I prepared for this in a focused manner. In the initial two years I focused on developing the U.S. immigration practice by meeting people, holding seminars, having round table discussions, and writing articles. Once this was buzzing along, I added different areas of practice. Broadly, I initiated or enhanced one rainmaking activity every week.

Cognizant of the importance of networking, I joined clubs and business associations that I had earlier shunned. This resulted in two immediate advantages—it raised my profile in business and social circles and resulted in direct or indirect work. Helping organize events and inviting good speakers further helped raise my profile and eventually led to leadership positions, again resulting in indirect referrals. All the while, I kept writing articles for various publications, including for *The Economic Times*, India's premier business daily.

LawQuest soon developed its own monthly newsletter and more recently launched a blog and Twitter post. Frequently answering questions on LinkedIn and www.allexperts.com helped raise our profile on the Internet, resulting in inquiries initially and work eventually.

Access to Resources and Building a Billing System
As my husband's business grew with some help from me, we incorporated companies that invested in real estate by buying offices at multiple locations. We generally leased these out for additional income. LawQuest initially used a part of one such office, and as the practice grew I took over one of our own offices for a moderate rent.

Striking a balance between the fees charged by independents and small firms in India and the rate of fees as a U.S. licensed lawyer was very difficult. I started out modestly and gradually increased the fees.

For the most part, clients can either choose hourly billing or flat fees. This works fine, though there are occasions when we work much more than expected and some where we finish before expected. Billing is still done manually; we are in the process of identifying an electronic billing system suitable to a small law firm.

Hindsight Is Always 20-20, Ongoing Challenges, and Introduction to Philosophy for Relative Peace
I wish I had started earlier! And, I wish India's economic boom had come earlier! It feels everything I have achieved could have been better and bigger if I had started my own firm earlier. There are a thousand things I still want

to do, and the opportunities available in India are quite mind-boggling. Other than that, I cannot be at a better juncture in both my personal and professional lives.

The challenges I face are keeping the team at LawQuest motivated, ensuring productivity because we usually do not track billable hours, and maintaining client relationships. Managing the firm's growth without losing out on quality and prompt services requires ongoing efforts. Also, as I go along I strive to gain peace and work with equanimity.

In this my pursuit of Vedanta, an ancient Indian philosophy, since 2003, under the tutelage of A. Parthasarthy, has been extremely important. Vedanta teaches the art of composed living through one's own thought process and broadens a person's intellect as it trains one to think things through. Further, led by the conviction that the body, mind, and soul need to be continuously nourished, I practice yoga and subject myself to a strict regimen of exercise. I read books on spirituality and self-improvement and periodically read light fiction and nonfiction too.

My message to the readers—there is no limit to what you can achieve with hard work once you have crossed the hurdle of self-doubt!

POORVI CHOTHANI is the founder and managing partner of LawQuest, a general business law firm in Mumbai, India, handling intellectual property, corporate, real estate, dispute resolution, commercial, and immigration matters. She graduated from law school in India in 1984, received her LL.M. in the United States in 2003, and founded her firm in Mumbai in 2003 to address U.S. and local business law matters. *www.lawquestinternational.com*

- Karen L. Giffen -
&
- Kerin Lyn Kaminski -

"Jumping off the cliff like Butch and Sundance was worth it. We hope that our legacy will be that we inspire people, and in particular women, . . . to define success on their own terms."

Do you remember the scene from the movie *Butch Cassidy and the Sundance Kid* when they were poised to take that dangerous leap off the edge of the canyon? They decided to jump together, and so did we. That jump is what starting our women-owned law firm felt like. When we started our business we did what Butch and Sundance did—we started running, did not look back, and went whooaaaaa as we launched. They landed safely, and so have we. Here is our story.

We spent over 15 years working with an established and well-regarded law firm in Cleveland, Ohio. The firm primarily represented closely held businesses throughout the state of Ohio. As members of the firm's management committee, we were in the process of analyzing how to bring in more business in the coming years. Frankly, we were not enthusiastic about how we would develop business. At about the same time, one of our Fortune 250 clients told us that some of our work was going to be given to a minority-owned firm. We were shocked. This was a great client. The matters were interesting, and we thought the client relationship was very solid.

The client contact explained that while she loved working with us, she had a diversity initiative to hire more women and minorities. The idea was to empower women- and minority-owned law firms in a very direct way. The client contact then candidly revealed that while she wanted to shift some work to women- or minority-owned firms, finding qualified firms to fit the bill was a challenge, and in Cleveland there were no women-owned firms who were doing the work we were doing.

After learning that, we began to ponder, if we were going to have to change the way we marketed ourselves anyway, why not do it as a women-owned law firm? While the answer might seem obvious, it was daunting. Could *we* actually do this? Between the two of us, we did not have a portable book of business that was sufficient to make a living. So we would need to not only learn how to run a business but also develop work very quickly.

We discovered that being a lawyer and running a business are two very distinct skills. We had a lot to learn about running and marketing a business. It takes something more than being a good lawyer. We have identified five main things we think helped us successfully launch our firm.

First, we did our homework. We found a market niche that needed to be filled. We investigated and learned that many Fortune 500 companies were beginning to require their outside counsel to institute diversity best practices and to document actual change in their diversity metrics. Many companies were deciding to hire women- and minority-owned firms rather than wait for the larger firms to diversify. We traveled to New York and met with another women-owned firm that had been successful. We also discovered that there were no women-owned law firms that did our type of commercial litigation in Northeast Ohio. So it seemed that the timing of our launch should be as soon as possible.

Second, we knew we had to immediately begin developing business. We knew we did not know how to develop business and were not skilled at marketing. So we hired a business consultant to teach us how to get our message to the right people. Together, we created a business and marketing plan. That plan was the roadmap that we followed. Central to the plan, we developed a set of agreed-upon business values. The plan had a mission and a vision by which we could judge decisions. We decided to limit our practice areas to what we did best: litigation. Even early on, we turned down work. That was not easy to do. Looking back, it was the right choice to stay on the path of only doing what we knew we could do well.

Third, consistent with our business plan and target audience, we concentrated on developing clients that were large companies with in-house counsel. We had learned that we enjoyed working with in-house counsel because they seemed, more than nonlawyers, to appreciate good outcomes and to recognize when we had saved money or solved a problem. Given that we wanted to create a firm that would give us the most possible job satisfaction, we decided to build our firm around the needs of in-house counsel.

Fourth, we built our own definition of what it means to be successful and included as a critical component that our firm be actively engaged in community services. We ask ourselves and all of our employees to be involved in the community. We model that for our employees and have committed time ourselves to community service. For example, Kerin Kaminski became the fourth woman president of the 180-year-old, 5,000-member Cleveland Bar Association, and Karen Giffen serves as treasurer for the National Association of Minority and Women Owned Law Firms. These organizations serve as a networking opportunity in Cleveland and throughout the United States and enrich the professional lives of the lawyers in our firm.

Fifth, and by no means last, we have had the fortune to find people who are not only great lawyers and employees, but also wonderful people who share our values. Often we are asked if we have any men. It always makes us chuckle because the question itself demonstrates how unique women-owned law firms still are. Yes, we do and always have had men working with us and as partners in the firm. Our goal is to be as diverse as possible in all respects. We have come to believe that the more diversity of thought, the better product we are able to deliver to our clients.

When you ask us what it all comes down to, we really believe that you must

- find a market you can serve;
- define your vision and mission;
- identify the characteristics of your ideal client;
- become immersed in your community; and
- recruit and retain great individuals.

As we look back to when we started the firm in 2003, we had two small offices and a secretary between the two of us. Today, we now have 22 employees occupying newly renovated class A office building space that overlooks the Rock and Roll Hall of Fame on the shores of Lake Erie. We are proud of our growth.

We remain a women-owned law firm committed to the vision and values we set as the core of our firm culture—championing excellence, teamwork, diversity, and professional growth. Vital to our success is a willingness to be loyal, responsive, and dependable. We continue to foster development of a relationship with our clients where we demonstrate that we have a vested interest in their success.

The future looks bright. Jumping off the cliff like Butch and Sundance was worth it. We hope that our legacy will be that we inspire people, and in particular women, to take a different path and to define success on their own terms.

KAREN L. GIFFEN and **KERIN LYN KAMINSKI** founded Giffen & Kaminski, LLC in Cleveland, Ohio in 2003. Ms. Giffen, a 1989 law graduate, focuses on employment, securities, and commercial litigation. Ms. Kaminski, a 1984 law school graduate, focuses on real estate, employment, and commercial litigation. *www.thinkgk.com*

- Antoinette M. Tease -

"Experience has taught me that competence, responsiveness, and drive are more determinative of success than gender."

I am a solo practitioner in Billings, Montana. I have one employee, a legal assistant, and I specialize in intellectual property law. I started my own firm in 2003 and since then have developed a worldwide practice in which revenue has grown each year. I practice in a rural state where you can count the number of patent attorneys on one hand. As far as I am aware, there are only two other female patent attorneys in the state. The fact that I am a woman has not hampered me professionally; the fact that I have a specialty in a state in which that specialty is scarce has been a key to my success.

There was no single factor that propelled me to start my own practice. It was a combination of things—boredom with my job as in-house counsel, the fact that clients from my former firm were still calling me, and the fact that my eldest son was about to start first grade. Regardless of what motivated me, I felt it was time to strike out on my own. I prepared a simplistic graph to show my husband what my financial picture would look like. If I could make enough money to cover my expenses, then the rest would be profit. The key would be keeping my expenses low. I convinced my husband that we should renovate a room in our house for use as my office, I launched my website, and I was off and running.

Working from home has had both economic and personal benefits. The economic benefit is that my overhead is approximately one-third that of my peers. The personal benefit is that I am home when my sons, ages 10 and 13, get home from school every day. I have allowed only a select few clients to visit my home office; the rest I meet with at the Petroleum Club, a downtown professional club I joined. This arrangement has worked very well for me and my clients.

When I first started my practice, my only asset was a desktop computer, and I had no outside help. I have found over the years that there are four areas in which it is absolutely crucial to have good help: computers, website, accounting, and administrative. I have listed these in the order in which I engaged these profes-sionals. I had been in-house counsel for a software development company, and the first contractors I hired were a couple of guys from that company to set up my computer network. Next, I hired a professional acquaintance to launch my website (my 13-year-old son now does my website work). I managed to generate my own invoices for a while, but that soon became overwhelming, and I asked the accounting firm that had been handling our personal tax returns to take over my billing.

For the first few years of my practice, I had an arrangement with the Montana Business Incubator (MBI) whereby they provided secretarial assistance for $50 a month. I am deeply grateful to MBI for the support it provided because it took awhile for me to feel stable enough financially to hire my first employee. My legal assistant is my only employee, and I do not anticipate hiring any other employees in the near future.

In terms of business development, I believe the single most important method of generating new business is to be responsive to your existing clients and to be good at what you do. Never learn the law on the client's dime. Know your stuff and be efficient with your time. Treat clients the way you would want to be treated, particularly in terms of billing. Because Montana is such a large state geographically, I do not bill clients for travel anywhere in Montana or Wyoming.

I also take every opportunity to make presentations to groups throughout Montana and Wyoming. For example, I have spoken at programs sponsored by the Montana Manufacturing Extension Center, the Montana Business Incubator, TechRanch, the Montana World Trade Center, various marketing and paralegal groups, and the Montana State Bar. There are similar organizations in every state, and they provide excellent opportunities for you to distinguish yourself as a specialist in an area of law. I never charge for my speaking engagements, but I also never pay for the opportunity to speak.

The American Bar Association Section of Intellectual Property Law (ABA-IPL) has been a phenomenal professional development outlet for me, not so much in terms of direct referrals, although there have been a few, but in terms of making me a better lawyer. Simply because I am a limited resource, I have been more selective about the speaking engagements I accept on a national level, but those that I have accepted have all been through the ABA-IPL Section. In addition, thanks to a referral from a woman who chaired the ABA-IPL Section a few years ago, I have now had the opportunity of acting as an expert witness in patent infringement litigation.

Another fruitful marketing tool for me has been my electronic newsletter, Intellections. I maintain my own database of contacts, which has now grown to over 1,000 people, consisting primarily of clients, referral sources, and foreign associates. I find that my newsletter not only serves to let potential clients know of my areas of expertise, but it also prompts existing clients to contact me about new matters.

No discussion of my business development practices would be complete without mentioning the relationships I have developed with the U.S. senators from Montana and Wyoming. Senator Max Baucus (D-MT) invited me in March of 2008 to testify before the U.S. Senate Finance Committee on the enforcement of intellectual property rights at our borders and beyond. That experience was meaningful not only in terms of the substantive testimony I provided, but also in terms of my credibility as an expert witness. Senator Mike Enzi (R-WY) sponsors an Inventors Conference each year in Wyoming, and I have had the privilege of speaking at that conference since its inception. Senator Enzi's conference attracts individual inventors from throughout the state of Wyoming, and his conference inevitably results in new clients.

Since I hung my shingle seven years ago, I have never felt that being a woman has been a detriment. To the contrary, I believe the fact that I am a woman is one of the reasons I was retained as a testifying expert. In any event, experience has taught me that competence, responsiveness, and drive are more determinative of success than gender. I meet with a lot of farmers, ranchers, hunters, fishermen, miners, construction workers, engineers, and software programmers, the vast majority of whom are men, and not one of them has declined to hire me because I am a woman. They recognize immediately that I have the intellectual capacity to understand their inventions, and that is the single most important factor in their decision to hire me.

ANTOINETTE M. TEASE is a solo practitioner and registered patent attorney in Billings, Montana, where she provides intellectual property legal services to clients throughout the United States and around the world. She graduated from law school in 1990 and founded her firm in 2003. *www.teaselaw.com*

- LISA A. DUNNER -

---

*"The old adage 'life is short' so aptly fits in one's professional life.
Do what you want to do. Don't be afraid. Take risks.
Being small means having a bigger life."*

"Operation Dunner Freedom." That was the title I placed on the notebook of information I kept as I prepared to embark on a life as a solo practitioner. This notebook was my lifeline to independence; my lifeline to freedom; my lifeline to my own choices; my lifeline to happiness.

Maybe I was naïve, or maybe I felt like this was the only path for me, but when people tell me that it "took a lot of guts" to go off on my own, I tell them that I had no fear. How could I fear a life free of firm politics; a life free of the competitiveness of origination credit; a life with no billable hours targets? Since July 2003, I have never been happier as a lawyer. My only regret is not doing this sooner.

I have had to learn some things along the way, but for the most part I have been very fortunate. I still work very hard, but I do more than just practice law—I run a business. It is my business though. Success or failure is up to me, and I can measure my success not solely by how many hours I bill and how much money I make, but also by the quality of life that I now have—and, it is a very good life.

Making the Decision
My decision to go solo came about over time. It was the result of a number of events and feelings that led me to believe that it was the best career path for me. I would not have decided to go in this direction had I not experienced working in a big firm. It was my big firm experience that, in part, gave me the confidence to do what I wanted to do. I learned how to practice law in my prior firms, but I learned how to run a business on my own. I also had made partner before going solo, so I had the credibility in my clients' eyes to handle the work on my own.

What ultimately led me down this path was my desire to have better control over my life—not only the kind of work I wanted to do, but also to have the freedom to decide my own schedule. While I am competitive, I did not like the underlying competitiveness created in big firms by "origination credit" schemes, large billable hours goals, and firm politics—all things that I do not miss.

Having worked at three firms prior to starting my own practice and having been very unhappy at my last firm, I concluded that the grass could not be greener at another firm. I explored working in-house, but after a number of conversations with colleagues who had started their own practices, I was convinced that I should hang out my own shingle.

Making the Move

Two months prior to leaving my last firm, I started my "Operation Dunner Freedom" notebook. I made a list of every supply and piece of equipment that I would need to practice law, from paper clips to a copy machine. I also created a budget and wrote down my current personal expenses, as well as a budget forecast of what my business expenses were likely to be on a monthly basis. I had been told that I would need six months to a year's worth of finances to support my firm in case clients did not follow me and work was hard to come by. So, knowing that I would not be able to get a loan without a job (within the first two years of starting a business, it is extremely difficult to borrow from a bank), I opened up an equity line of credit with my bank. I figured that I could use the equity line to remodel my house if I did not need to use it for my new firm. I remodeled my house.

Starting Out

I worked out of my house for the first six months, since I was concerned about spending money to pay rent, and I did not really know what type of office I wanted or where it should be. However, working from home can be challenging, since house chores and the refrigerator can be distracting. As a result, I ultimately rented an office in a cute little area in Georgetown, Washington, DC. This turned out to be a good move since there were a number of businesses nearby, many of which needed my intellectual property expertise. I invested in some nice furniture and décor since I believe that appearances are important in this profession. I have always been cognizant of maintaining my big firm expertise and standards while operating on a smaller scale. I believe that this enhances my credibility as a lawyer, especially for potential clients that have not yet seen our work.

Where I Am Now

Seven years after I got started, my firm has doubled in size (I now have one associate), and I am looking to add a paralegal sometime soon. I have moved my firm into a brownstone I purchased a year ago, and I look out onto a cobblestone street surrounded by antique stores in the heart of Georgetown. My clients love to visit me, because it is a treat for them to get out of the hustle and bustle of downtown.

When asked about the pros and cons of having my own practice, I have a hard time coming up with the cons. The pros seem so obvious to me—I have the freedom and flexibility to run the firm the way I want and to live the life that I want; and, as long as we continue to do high quality work, referrals and new matters should keep coming our way. I suppose that what might be a con to some is a pro to me—that I have to wear many hats since I maintain a business while practicing law—but I enjoy juggling multiple tasks, and I find that entrepreneurial life is much more exciting than focusing on just one thing.

One thing that has remained consistent from big firms to small is that integrity and high ethical standards are important regardless of where you are. The old adage "life is short" so aptly fits in one's professional life. Do what you want to do. Don't be afraid. Take risks. Being small means having a bigger life.

LISA A. DUNNER is the managing partner at Dunner Law PLLC in Washington, DC, where she focuses on trademark, copyright, e-commerce, and unfair competition law. She graduated from law school in 1995 and founded her firm in 2003. *www.dunnerlaw.com*

- VERONICA BRINSON -

"First, I was a single mother. Second, I was running my own show. Third, I felt like there was room enough for me and the good ole boys. Even though I often felt as if the good ole boys were trying to run me out of town."

My Experience as a Lady in Law in Middle Georgia

Opening the Law Offices of Veronica Brinson on June 1, 2003 was like birthing another child. Operating a law office requires much nurturing, time, and resources. At the age of 31 as a single mother of two young boys, I took on this additional responsibility in Macon, Middle Georgia. Macon was not ready for me. I became a "Lady in Law." I often described myself as a Lady in Law because I believe that as a female lawyer I could be assertive while maintaining the softer touch and acting like a lady. I also expected to be treated like a lady—that is, with respect.

The Law Offices of Veronica Brinson has been a bittersweet experience and a wonderful lesson in survival. Seven years passed by before I knew it. My young boys became young men, and I realized that the law office shared an enormous amount of time that I could have given to the boys. However, it also allowed me the opportunity to home school the boys for a brief period of time at my office, as well as the opportunity to provide these young men, as well as other members of my family, internships and jobs. Having my own business also allowed me to provide opportunities to others who may not have otherwise had access to the legal community.

My experience as a business owner operating a law office in Middle Georgia has been tough. However, even though practicing law and owning a law office is a tough job, it can be a very worthwhile and rewarding experience.

Family
Being a Lady in Law requires a deep and personal commitment. However, one must balance running a law office with the demands of running a fam-

ily. It can be very easy to have misplaced priorities. Family should always be first. I recommend making the family part of the business so that they can understand the demands and rigors of the job. My children have always been involved in my business. As they got older, I found them positions in my business. It made both of my sons better appreciate what I do for a living.

The Commitment

I have worked harder for myself than I have ever worked for anyone else. Owning one's own law practice requires much commitment and much dedication. It requires a whole lot of faith. The journey is not a straight road. It will have its twists and turns. Stay focused and committed to growing and nurturing your business. The business served as the engine in my family. It was our source of revenue. The office became the family meeting place.

Me Time

It is so easy to nurture family, clients, and the business. I often sacrificed much of my personal time for others, until God gave me a couple of wake-up calls. Then, I realized that in order to take care of my business and others, I had to take care of me. After working six years straight, I had failed to take a vacation. I started putting in mini-leaves of absence from my work to take time to care for myself. In the end, it was worth it because after a good vacation, I came back to work with more energy than ever.

Clients

Good clients are important to any business. We have utilized the telephone book and other forms of marketing to attract clients. However, I still prefer the good ole word of mouth. It is important to select your clients, just as it is important for them to select you. Each year, we would organize an annual client appreciation event to show our clients how much we appreciated them. Client screening is very important. A good client will put a big smile on your face. However, a client who is not properly screened may not be a good fit. It is okay to acknowledge that a particular client is not a good fit for the working relationship and to find a way to amicably end that relationship.

Practicing Law in Middle Georgia

Practicing law in Middle Georgia was a very challenging experience for a lady like me. First, I was a single mother. Second, I was running my own show. Third, I felt like there was room enough for me and the good ole boys. Even though I often felt as if the good ole boys were trying to run me out of town.

I did not realize that my assertiveness at times would be misunderstood. I was often told that I was "too young" to hold certain positions. For example, I became a judge at the age of 32. Second, I ran for mayor at the age of 35. I received many accolades. Each accolade brought many challenges. Practicing law in your own hometown can be tough too, especially when you were born on one side of the tracks and you are now operating on the other. I had to constantly remind myself that I had worked hard for my law degree just like everyone else, and with hard work and determination I would be entitled to a piece of the pie too. By a piece of the pie, I meant the opportunity to pursue my dream as a Lady in Law running her own business.

Running my own law office has been a great lesson in business management, marketing, survival, faith, the balance of work and family, managing conflict, and customer service. Don't expect it to be easy. However, you can really make lemons into lemonade in this business with some creativity. At the same time, you can be a blessing to many others.

VERONICA BRINSON is the owner of the Law Offices of Veronica Brinson, LLC, with offices in Atlanta and Macon, Georgia, focusing on criminal, personal injury, and domestic law matters. She graduated from law school in 1999 and founded her firm in 2003. *www.attorney-brinson.com*

- R. SHANTI BRIEN -

---

*"I found that women happily give their time to help . . .
strategize a case, practice an argument, edit a brief, or just
answer a simple question."*

I consider building my own practice to be one of the greatest accomplishments of my life. It has not been easy. In fact, when I make a mistake—file something wrong, leave an argument out of a brief, or stumble in an oral argument—sometimes I think it's too hard to be a solo practitioner. Several times I have cried in frustration and disappointment: it's just too hard with no one to blame but myself; too lonely, too stressful. But when I win in the face of a horrible standard of review, when the court publishes a decision in my favor, or even when I lose and my client writes to me and thanks me for my dedication and patience and persistence, I know that this is the right path for me.

During an internship in law school with a public defender's office here in the Bay Area, I discovered that criminal law fascinated me. The stories are so real; the problems, so urgent. The clients are at once the most hated and the most ignored people in our society. I felt compelled to help them.

But with two small children, I didn't have the energy, time, or stamina to become a trial attorney. I began to ask everyone I knew—internship supervisors, family friends, law school professors—for advice on family-friendly part-time jobs. One recommended applying to the courts for appellate appointments. Appeals would provide the flexibility that my family life demanded with the intellectual and professional challenges that my brain demanded. I soon discovered that this was not a part-time job; this was a practice. I set up my own firm, complete with liability insurance, letterhead, a website, and a load of office supplies. I worked from home, but I had hung out my virtual shingle.

I received appointments through the state courts, which provided a stable, albeit small, paycheck. I also worked on marketing my business through my website and through contacts with trial lawyers. Networking has never been my strong suit, but it is an essential skill for a solo practitioner. It continually challenges me. But even small amounts of effort into marketing—sending a letter to all of the trial attorneys telling them I am available to handle referrals, for instance—have developed into well-paying retained work.

Networking through the local bar association, professional seminars, and friends of friends not only provides a source for referrals, but also practical resources as well. I could not have made it without a few valuable mentors whom I have called upon again and again. I found that women happily give their time to help other women strategize a case, practice an argument, edit a brief, or just answer a simple question.

As my business grew, I knew I needed help. I started by hiring a couple of law students and recent graduates to do legal research projects for me. I gained valuable assistance at a great price and added other women to my expanding virtual firm. I now work with a smart, hardworking, stay-at-home mom. She quit her job at a big firm to have her children but wants to keep a foot in the legal profession. She works from home, too, and we do most of our business via e-mail. Another mom summarizes trial transcripts for me. Two other accomplished lawyers work on a project-by-project basis.

I think my career and my practice could be more successful and more lucrative. But I've chosen to make my family a priority. I have the freedom to drive for my kids' field trips and take them to the doctor without scrambling for child care or worrying about my billable hours. My kids also know that my career is important and that their mom works hard every day, helping people. Sometimes I'm stressed and tired, or even crying, but I have found a balance and built a business, and I consider those two incredible accomplishments.

R. SHANTI BRIEN is a solo practitioner in Oakland, California, focusing on criminal appeals and habeas proceedings in California and federal courts. She graduated from law school in 1999 and founded her practice in 2004. *www.shantibrien.com*

- MELANIE DAMIAN -

"It's rare that a woman is entrusted with bet-the-company litigation. . . . [T]hat will change. My advice to women thinking about it is to, as Nike says, 'just do it.' It is totally doable and completely worth it."

After eight years and more than 18,000 hours of working in a mid-size law firm, I realized that the business model would never allow me the freedom to grow into the professional I wanted to become in either my work life or my personal life. The business model of that firm essentially involved the very senior partners bringing in business and everyone else working on it. At some point around year five it became clear, at least to me, that those senior partners were the only employees of the firm that could control the direction of the firm and, relatively speaking, their personal lives. I decided that was who I wanted to be and that I couldn't become the senior partner with my own business from where I was sitting (in my office doing everyone else's work).

I began to look at how the "rainmakers" did it. What things did they do that the other lawyers didn't. Then I looked at other firms and their leaders and how they succeeded. I am a believer in looking to role models, and if you can get them to tell you how they succeeded, even better. There were very few women to look at as role models in business litigation in Miami, so I looked at the male rainmakers. There were and are discernible patterns to their success. One element is certainly being a good and ethical lawyer. However, to have your own business, you need to let people know you are good and ethical by getting out of the office and in front of potential clients and referral sources. When I looked at the "rainmaker" résumés, I noticed bar activity was always prominent in their backgrounds. While most of my role models were no longer active, they all were bar leaders at some level—either the local, state, or national level, if not all three—over sustained periods of time at some point in their career. Each also became an expert in at least one area of the law, speaking, writing, and debating with other lawyers throughout the country.

This expertise gave the rainmaker exposure within the profession and often outside the profession through media outlets.

One such "rainmaker" advised me to join the ABA. I responded that I had been a member for years. He asked, "Have you ever been to a meeting?" I didn't even know what he was talking about. "What meetings?" He explained generally that there would be a big annual meeting in San Francisco, and I should check it out. So I did. I practice business and employment litigations. I looked at the Litigation, Business Law, and Labor and Employment Law Sections and was impressed with the quality of the programming and opportunities for participation in each section. Ultimately, I found a home in the Business Law Section and recommend it to anyone who asks. I am also involved in the Law Practice Management (LPM) Section's Women Rainmakers. In addition to Women Rainmakers, which is a great group, LPM has a lot of resources for starting and managing a law firm. In addition, the Florida Bar (and I am sure other state bars as well) has a lot of resources for starting a law practice.

In July 2004, after studying rainmakers and beginning to be involved in the bar, we (a male partner and I) took the risk and started the firm. At first we did not have enough work to keep ourselves busy. We took small cases and gave away a lot of time. But slowly, through constant effort and by providing good service to our clients and demonstrating our abilities, we developed loyalty among our clients and referral sources and slowly started to accumulate a good practice. Today, six years later, we have a very busy 10-lawyer litigation firm.

Because my partner is a man, I have never marketed the firm as "woman-owned." In general, being the senior partner and a woman has advantages and disadvantages. On the advantage side, at least from a marketing perspective, I am often remembered in the big crowd of male lawyers. And that can help, but only after you have credibility as a competent attorney, which requires more effort from a female than from a male attorney. Although strides have certainly been made, it's rare that a woman is entrusted with bet-the-company litigation. As more women start their own firms or otherwise build the business necessary to compete with their senior male rainmaking counterparts, that will change. My advice to women thinking about it is to, as Nike says, "just do it." It is totally doable and completely worth it.

My top 10 tips:

1. Hire a good legal secretary. Your time is better spent doing the legal work or going out looking for work than addressing envelopes. I know it's scary to take on the overhead, but you just have to trust me on this one. It's worth it even if you have to borrow the money to do it. This is the best advice I can give (and I didn't follow it myself right away).

2. Make a plan every year for your business (what kind of work you want to do) and marketing (how you will get it). The plan should be specific, including month-by-month descriptions, and you should check it regularly to make sure you are meeting your goals.

3. Think and act long term. It's a marathon, not a sprint. By way of example, don't charge clients for the initial meeting or regular status calls. The clients appreciate the investment in them and will be loyal clients and great referral sources.

4. Attend at least two marketing activities per week.

5. More than quantity (see #4 above), make the marketing events something you like doing. If you don't like it, you won't do it, and you won't be consistent. Consistency is what really matters.

6. Your marketing activities can be whatever you want. You don't have to play golf at the country club to bring in clients. Go to wine events, school socials, book clubs. It really doesn't matter as long as you are not alone in your office or at home on the couch.

7. Work with people you like. Personally, I think having a partner is better than solo practice because you have someone with whom to discuss theories and legal argument and who will keep you in check when your argument might be overly myopic. Also, it's just more fun—provided you pick the right people.

8. Do the work you like. You will be better at it, and everything else will follow.

9. Ask for work. This is very hard for women. We are terrible advocates for ourselves. Watch how men do this. "Hi, how are you?" "Fine. How are you?" "I am good. Also, I am a really good lawyer and you should hire me. Here is my card." I am not even exaggerating. You can be more subtle, but you need to ask. Try: "I think I can help you. Give me a call to discuss."

10. Put yourself in front. Volunteer for leadership in cases and in community activity. Then, most important, when something goes well, take credit. Women have trouble with this too. We are all about sharing and noting others' contributions. Whatever...if you don't take credit, someone else will, and they will get the clients. Work on this. It matters.

MELANIE DAMIAN is a co-founder and partner at Damian & Valori LLP in Miami, Florida, where she focuses on business litigation, including matters involving officer and director liability, corporate governance, securities, real estate, professional negligence, and employment law. She graduated from law school in 1996 and founded her firm in 2004. *www.dvllp.com*

CHAPTER 6

2005–2008

Accelerating into the Recession

"After the story about the 'all-women' firm ran, we received a flurry of e-mails, phone calls, and letters. We didn't appreciate until then . . . how many people—men and women alike—would be inspired by a group of women who chose freedom over stability."

—Partners Jane Taber, Dawn Estes, Jessica Thorne, Lori Carr, and Melanie Okon

---

The letters from 2005 through 2008 show an explosion of break-outs by women founders. Among the 21 writers in this four-year period, five had more than 25 years in practice, six had from 15 to 24 years, three had 10 to 14 years, four had five to nine years, and three had fewer than five years of practice experience. For the first time, senior women broadly moved to start their own firms, and the distribution across ages evened out.

The writers in this chapter generally do not refer to the economic downturn as a motivating factor in their decision, and indeed it may not have been directly. But the economy is mentioned by some writers in the context of their success, noting that "recent layoffs and closures" show that "the corporate model can leave the individual lawyer vulnerable" and witnessing their own achievement "despite a down economy."

The writers in this period voice increasing impatience with traditional compensation systems and constraints in the practice they might pursue. In answer to that concern, one writer and her three partners started a new business model, articulating the mission of "killing the billable hour." They created a firm based on the pure principle of value.

Several came into their own firms from strong backgrounds in specialized practices, including the Department of Justice, the INS, and

---

commercial litigation. The more junior writers share the interest in specialized practices, including workers' compensation and family law. One of these, dismayed at the collateral harm to children of families in divorce, founded her firm with the motto: "*divorce done differently.*"

Many of these writers address the importance of changing their practice environment to one where, as one writer puts it, "both the substance of my daily work and culture of the workplace reflected more of me—my vision, my values, my style." It is during this period that a writer first gives voice to a theme that is quietly discussed in this decade: that making the decision to start her own firm "is probably the best opportunity [the woman] will have to further [her] legal career."

In proof that the marketplace had quickly matured for women in charge of law firms, there came a moment in 2005 when the partners of a male-founded firm realized that the firm had morphed into a majority woman-owned firm the year before. The partners discuss what they believe went right in their firm to permit this to have happened naturally.

Far from a story of sad recession decisions, the explosion of voices in this four-year period offers strong encouragement. "The opportunities are there."

- BETH L. KAUFMAN -

---

*"The firm that I walked into on April 3, 1978 . . . was comprised
of five male partners. . . . I was the first woman associate. . . .
Today, the firm . . . is a certified women-owned law firm of
11 partners, 10 counsel, and seven associates."*

Becoming a Women-Owned Law Firm

The firm that I walked into on April 3, 1978, my first day at my first job as a
soon-to-be-admitted lawyer, looked very different than it does today. Then,
it was comprised of five male partners, most emanating from large New York
law firms, in office space in one of New York's original skyscrapers. I was
the first woman associate, fresh out of law school. In the early summer of
2005, when the firm's financial statements for 2004 arrived, we learned that
women owned more than 50 percent of the firm's equity, which qualified the
firm for women-ownership status. Today, the firm still is in the same building, has opened an office in Chicago, and is a certified women-owned law firm
of 11 partners, 10 counsel, and seven associates.

A firm that allows women to develop professionally, while shouldering other
responsibilities—to children, spouses, and parents, for example—that
inevitably fall on their shoulders is one that has the potential to become a
women-owned law firm. In the early years of my career, I had three children
in pretty rapid succession and worked in ways and at times that did not fit
the traditional model—late into the night, from home; on weekends with
my children at the office with me. Throughout those years, our firm did more
than just tolerate those habits. Once I proved that I was a good lawyer who
wanted to take on responsibility and could produce a first-class work product,
the firm *encouraged* me to meet my family responsibilities as well, provided
the resources I needed in the evening and on weekends to get my work done,
and often rescheduled meetings so that I could attend. Work assignments
were made with regard to merit—expertise and experience, prior dealings
with a particular client—and not gender. The clients with whom I worked and

with whom I maintain friendships to this day all knew about my children's exploits, and they delighted in the stories; the firm never hid any of that from these clients (as some firms seemed to do), deciding, quite correctly, that it all was a part of who I was and would be a part of the relationships I was building with clients.

For me and others at our firm, professional development meant involvement in national, state, and local bar associations; for me and other women, the national bar association involvement often meant travel—with families—to meetings. My own career thrived at our firm; the nature of the work was so stimulating and challenging and our clients involved in such interesting businesses, and so helpful and supportive, that I wanted to do a first-rate job and pushed myself to be my own harshest critic and taskmaster. The result? Great results for very pleased clients and great experience and exposure for an increasingly experienced lawyer.

Having achieved this level of success as a lawyer and within my firm, after eight years of hard work and three pregnancies and childbirths, I became an equity partner. Still relatively young (not quite 32 at the time) and unsophisticated, I did not understand that my partnership status was economically feasible only because of the loyalty of clients who were important to the firm and the generous spirit of existing partners, who made sure those clients thought of me as their primary lawyer at the firm.

It took me many years to realize the responsibility that being a partner carries with it, particularly at a small firm. Again, this is true for both men and women, but I believe its ramifications may be somewhat harder to grasp for women. Certainly in the late 1980s and early 1990s, there were few women partners among law firm partner ranks, no matter what size the firm.[1] And there were even fewer women who were equity partners, and fewer still who held leadership roles within their firms.

I set out to assume the responsibilities that came with partnership in the same way that women usually take on new responsibilities—whether at

---

1 Nor are the statistics much better today. According to the October 2010 *Report of the Fifth Annual National Survey on Retention and Promotion of Women in Law Firms*, issued by the National Association of Women Lawyers and the NAWL Foundation, women lawyers in the nation's 200 largest law firms make up approximately 15 percent of the equity partner ranks, 80 percent of the largest law firms report that they have *at most* only two women on the firms' highest governing committees, and women equity partners earned only 85 percent of what their male counterparts earned.

work, in the home, or in community organizations: I painstakingly learned all aspects of the business, the economics, the business development dynamics, the human resources concerns and demands, and the competitive environment in which our small business operated. I worked to maintain good relationships with our excellent staff—indeed, to a large extent, I had matured as a lawyer with their support, and many had watched as I raised my children. One even remembers pulling out my first gray hair! But I had to figure out and navigate the new relationship of employer-employee with each of them, without losing the personal connections.

I quickly learned that excellent legal work for existing clients, for which I may receive some management, but not origination, credit under our firm's compensation formula, was not, by itself, going to lead to the success I wanted to achieve—for myself and, more importantly than I then knew, for the firm. I knew that I had to develop business in different areas from existing clients, so that I could share in the origination credit, or I had to develop new clients for the firm, for which I would receive full origination credit.

Although I usually was not aware of it, I was being mentored as a business developer during my associate years and my years as a young partner. Doing excellent legal work, networking to establish relationships within existing corporate clients and with potential new corporate clients as in-house lawyers left to go to other companies, networking with other lawyers in professional organizations—all keys to successful business development—were all supported and encouraged by our firm. But I had to learn something that does not come intuitively to women: I had to learn how to ask for work from those clients. Whether it was fear of rejection, or a sense that if I was a good lawyer, the work should just come to me (as opposed to any other excellent lawyer—and there are many of them), or an inherent shyness, I am not sure, but no matter how many times I heard from consultants at programs and on panels that women just have to ask for work, I could not bring myself to do so directly. This was the case even though I thought I had mastered the economics of how we did business, and I knew and understood completely how important new business and new sources of business were to a law firm. I plugged away, indirectly soliciting new business from existing and new clients, in my own (discreet) way. Slowly but surely, I am learning to be more direct. I also am learning that a few gray hairs and ascension to a leadership role within a law firm facilitate being able to do this successfully.

One of the most delightful by-products of our new ownership status was the wonderful messages of support and encouragement we received from colleagues, judges, and clients. One in particular led to another significant development for our firm, our expansion to Chicago.

We often are asked the question why our ownership status matters. On the most fundamental level, it does not—our lawyering skills, good judgment, and successes are what matter. But we like to believe that most lawyers have good skills and good judgment and are successful in their areas of practice. Our women-ownership status distinguishes us because it reflects a culture that is the polar opposite of that of the large law firms surveyed in the NAWL survey—a culture instilled in our firm by some enlightened male lawyers, that goes back to the late 1970s, that rewards and encourages excellence in a gender-neutral way, that promotes and encourages the advancement of women lawyers, and that lets them ascend to be leaders of their firm and the profession.

BETH L. KAUFMAN is a senior partner at Schoeman, Updike & Kaufman, LLP in New York, New York, where she focuses on complex commercial litigation, employment matters, and product liability defense. She graduated from law school in 1978. Starting as an associate at the firm, she advanced to senior partner, and on the eve of 2005, she and her partners realized they had become a majority women-owned law firm. *www.schoeman.com*

- ALEXANDRA DARRABY -

---

*"Those who categorize such endeavors as passions,
it seems to me, miss the point. Austerity enables efficient
management of resources to maximize effect."*

The Muse of the Art Law Firm

The Muse

It was J. M. W. Turner's iridescent glorious light that lit the journey to the Art Law Firm. Turner's phosphorescent paintings, glowing in the gray of a London day, emblazoned the then-unknown career path that lay ahead. There are certain magic moments in life when the psychic and the visceral merge, and this aesthetic mind meld occurred in a tired and worn museum gallery, largely empty, aglow with Turner's dazzle. That magic moment of meeting the muse occurred years before law school and graduate school and a decade or so before a field recognized as art law existed. I did not yet know where art would take me or how it would get me there. But like Saul's conversion to Paul on the road to Damascus, the transcendent and mesmerizing moment amidst the Turners committed me to choose a certain kind of life over a certain type of career. And that life was to be lived looking at art, thinking about art, and dialoguing on art. Art is the universal media of revelation, and that is the intrinsic power of art, from the Paleolithic to present day.

Traditional Law Practice: Recommended

The rest of the story, at least the law part, is more banal. I maxed out as many art credits as permitted during law school and went to work in a law firm, where associates were rotated through departments. Unaware of just how well this training would serve later on, there was an opportunity to problem-solve in different areas of the firm's practice fields—corporate and nonprofit law, tax, litigation, administration, and arbitration. For those who aspire to open a law firm, there is no better exposure to best practices, a diverse workforce, and variegated legal specialties than a big firm, or at least a firm sufficiently organized to offer that experience. The law even today is still a practice of apprenticeship.

The Gallery: The Road Chosen and Risk-Taking

Everything you do at every given time comes together at life's various crossroads. The key is to recognize the signposts and choose the right path. Life's directions are not charted by GPS. Two roads beckoned, one straight and wide, of billable hours and big bucks, and the other curved and windy, with no particular road map and no certain end. My choice was clear. I left the day-to-day practice of law and followed the muse (from which the word "museum" derives). I chose an entrepreneurial path that would place me in a community of people who, like me, lived their lives immersed in art. I became an art dealer and gallery owner.

Entrepreneurs open law firms, and entrepreneurs take risks. In homage to Robert Frost, and to those considering founding a law firm, there is a lot to be said for the path not traveled, but it is definitely riskier—and at times lonelier—than the route well-trod. To open a private practice, like any entrepreneurial venture, you must believe in yourself and the persons with whom you partner, and you must intuitively understand how to do the right thing. What I learned in the gallery and as a junior lawyer formed the basis of the art law practice. Foremost, the client is always right. In art and entertainment practices, the principals are in business with their clients. Understanding art and the art business is understanding the clients' interests and business. Achieving successful results for the clients is success for the firm.

IRS and the Birth of Art Law

During the years I was learning the art business—and gaining new respect for the meaning of that business school term, "on the job training"—certain people were taking tax deductions for donations of artworks to institutions. Ordinarily, this would not be noteworthy. Deductions for charitable contributions on federal income tax returns are provided under the Internal Revenue Code. But the deductions for those artworks, according to the IRS, were too substantial and based upon inflated art values, inflated in some instances to the point of tax fraud.

From the prosaic ledger sheets of books and accounts (for this occurred before computerized recordkeeping and QuickBooks), art law was born. The vocabulary of art law began in the tax lexicon of scary words like deficiencies, overvaluation, interest, and penalties. It is ironic that an image-based field was launched from numbers, columns of figures, and balance sheets. Or perhaps not. Coincidentally, as in *art imitates life*, Turner dwelled on financials and was derided for his belief in art as business.

Academia and the Art Law Treatise

When I was invited to apply for an art law position at a law school, I'd never heard of the field. It sounded like a lark. But as it turned out, the day-to-day business of the gallery—the deals, artists, clients, copyrights, museums, collaborations, projects, collections acquisitions, auctions, sales, import-export, customs and permits, international trades—is the very essence of art law. In organizing to teach, it became clear that there was not a source book for the myriad of interdisciplinary threads that comprised my art business experience and that they could be woven together into a field, like entertainment law. Selecting materials, I proposed a book and was offered a contract for a treatise. The practical and the juridical of art and law became forever bound. Requests to consult and testify followed. The life-choice sojourn in the arts had incidentally created an area of expertise.

Founding the Art Law Firm

As the art market soared, art law became a beacon. By the twenty-first century, art law was a page one business story, not just culture. Art law was everywhere, and so it seemed timely to transition the consulting practice into a law firm. My business was already established in a building redesigned by Frank Gehry, a space imbued with great karma. I did not advertise. I never had a website designed until last year. Open the practice, and the clients shall come.

Firm Realities

Maintaining a firm practice, like operating a gallery, analyzing a case, or evaluating art, is an austere undertaking that requires an open mind and prescient vision. Those who categorize such endeavors as passions, it seems to me, miss the point. Austerity enables efficient management of resources to maximize effect. The business model I use gives my clients access to the top lawyers from firms of all sizes and specialties, across this country and in many countries of the world. As I learned from a corporate executive who could and did hire whomever she wanted, choose people you like. The boutique practice of art law, as I structured my practice, enables firm clients to have a full range of legal services from hand-picked teams. I retain not only gifted colleagues who are the most appropriate on any given matter, but they are people the clients and I enjoy collaborating with on our team.

Further Musings

Life offers choices, and opening a law firm maximizes choices. Founding a firm gives women choices that working at a firm, or for a company, does not. Women who wish to control their destiny are women who understand that destiny can be crafted and a calling, and each of us measures achievement by different markers. The Art Law Firm is something that was both a life's work and a momentary decision. It is a chance to give back to the Muse.

ALEXANDRA DARRABY is a principal in the Art Law Firm in Los Angeles, California, and founder and president of Creative Vision Strategies, LLC in New York, New York, a strategic planning company, founded respectively in 2005 and 2010, both entities dedicated to representation of international clients in the arts, architecture, new media, and urban redevelopment. She graduated from law school in 1979. *www.artlawfirm.com; www.creativevisionstrategies.com*

- BARBARA A. BURR -

"Each decision triggered a fear about the budget. I drafted two budgets. . . . At some point, although I don't remember when, I stopped sketching my business plan on every available napkin."

On February 1, 2005, I opened the Burr Law Firm, a very small law firm (it started as just me and my laptop) specializing in family matters. While I knew from the start that starting my own firm would be both frightening (mostly on the financial front) and exciting (mostly on the professional front), I did not imagine just how fulfilling it would be personally.

My History

In the fall of 2001, after 11 pretty wonderful years as a civil rights lawyer, I started my career in family law. As a civil rights lawyer, I had the great fortune of working in the Civil Rights Division at the U.S. Department of Justice. At Justice, I loved wearing the "white hat," fighting for fundamental rights of fairness and justice, and I was thrilled by the incredible authority I was given from the first day. After Justice, I moved to the National Women's Law Center, where I focused on the important work of expanding possibilities for women in groundbreaking matters. Again, I was thrilled by the amazing opportunities, such as drafting an amicus curiae brief for the U.S. Supreme Court. Notwithstanding the profound professional satisfaction of these two terrific legal jobs, I found myself longing to represent real people in more everyday matters, where I could make a tangible difference in real lives. I envisioned working in a very small firm, where both the substance of my daily work and culture of the workplace reflected more of me—my vision, my values, my style.

After a lot of soul searching, I decided to move into family law. I joined a small family law boutique. After three years, I found that I loved family law, that I loved helping real people who were going through a bad patch, that I loved the combination of old-fashioned legal counseling and financial expertise that family law required.

At the same time that I loved family law, I found that I was not happy. When I moved into family law, my son was one year old. As I developed my family law practice, my son graduated from toddlerhood. While working at the firm, I often felt conflicted. When I was at work, I longed to be closer to my kid, volunteering at the school or picking him up early on Friday afternoon. But when I joined my kid's class for a field trip, I remained in fear of the voice mail message from my boss asking me where I was, telling me (and I quote), "I need you here all day, every day." If I had been in court or at a settlement conference, I wouldn't have been at my desk all day. So why was it unthinkable that I could be both a successful family law lawyer and an involved mom?

The Decision

I knew there was a better way. I knew that if left to my own devices, and my own priorities when it came to my schedule, that I could do both.

Scared is an understatement for how I felt about the idea of starting my own practice. I am fortunate, though, in that I am married to an incredible man who truly believed in me—in my right to a workplace that made me happy and in my ability to pull this off. So, in the coming days, as my mind wandered to "What if I fail?" I very deliberately replaced my self-doubt with my husband's complete faith and forged ahead.

After the Decision

Having made the decision, I started researching *how* to open a firm by talking to a few good people who had started their own firms and who generously shared their experiences. At the time, the DC Bar employed a very helpful attorney-advisor, Reid Trautz, who spent hours talking with me about the nuts and bolts of opening a solo practice. Also, a very complete "how-to" on opening a law practice is Jay Foonberg's *How to Start and Build a Law Practice*.

Opening up a firm entails a number of decisions. Some exciting: Home office or sublet? Stick with PC or switch to Mac? Splurge on a Herman Miller desk chair or not? Some more mundane: Operate as a PLLC or Sub-S? Which carrier for liability insurance has the best rates?

As fun and exciting as some of these decisions were, each decision triggered a fear about the budget. I drafted two budgets: Start-up costs (those one-time costs that won't repeat—the security deposit on the office sublet, the new furniture, the new computer, the new software, treatises to fill my bookshelf, the costs of registering the business entity) and the monthly expenses (rent, phone, utilities, Westlaw or Lexis, office supplies, etc.). I then tacked onto my monthly budget what I needed to take home.

If I Build It, Will They Come?

Having figured out how much I needed in monthly revenues, I then calculated—and recalculated, again and again—how long I could operate and cover my monthly budget before I *needed* a new client. I must have sketched out on a zillion napkins each active matter that I expected to follow me to my new firm and the number of hours of work needed to complete each matter. I then divided my estimated gross revenues by my monthly budget and determined the number of months I could expect to last. Fortunately, surprisingly, new clients actually appeared at the door. At some point, although I don't remember when, I stopped sketching my business plan on every available napkin.

The Hustle

The worry about how to get new work is unavoidable. One of my most joyful surprises, however, is that successful marketing does *not* involve having to "sell" myself to all of my friends, family, and colleagues. What I found was that I just needed to do good work wherever I was and let people see that I was a competent, reliable, and likeable member of whatever group or community I belonged to. And people seemed to assume that I would bring similar skills and qualities to my legal work. So I began "the hustle": serving on volunteer committees at my kid's school, serving on the board of the Women's Bar Association and other professional associations. Trust me, I call this "the hustle" for good reason—it is time consuming and, given that you must do quality and substantive work (not just show up for meetings), it is demanding. But it is also rewarding, fun (you spend time where you want to be and with people you like), and you happen to be creating referral sources wherever you go.

Managing the Growth

Having successfully run my own law firm for five years, I still struggle with the fact that time is precious, and I still juggle being a fullish-time lawyer with being a fullish-time mom. I now have three full-time employees—one attorney and two paralegals. As it turns out, managing a staff also requires time, which of course is what I have precious little of. But I adore my current staff (and I learned the hard way how difficult it is to find and keep employees you adore), and while it turns out that managing staff is not my favorite task, I also learned that I must invest time in managing in order to reap the rewards of a great staff.

In the end, it is all about the balance—balancing time for doing my legal work, time for managing the staff, and time for my family. The urge to grow bigger is tempting, but growing means tipping the balance such that more time must be devoted to managing my staff. Accordingly, I'm holding tight for now.

Enjoying the Vision

As I already said, time is still precious. And there are more days than I like to admit where I am returning e-mails at 4 a.m. But I have a nine-year-old who is a joy. And I am thrilled that I have yet to miss a game or a performance. By starting my own firm, by taking complete control over my calendar, now, wherever I am, at a conference room table or in the bleachers, I am always right where I am supposed to be.

BARBARA A. BURR is the founding principal of the Burr Law Firm in Washington, DC, where she focuses on family matters and collaborative divorce. She graduated from law school in 1989 and founded her firm in 2005. *www.burrlawfirm.com*

- MARY L. SMITH -

"When I became a partner at a women-owned firm, my partners and I tried to adopt a more collegial approach to billing credit."

Starting your own firm is a scary proposition. However, as I often remind myself, if you aren't a little nervous, then you aren't challenging yourself. While starting your own firm is intimidating, it need not be debilitating.

The best advice I can give to women seeking to start a solo practice or to establish a women-owned firm is to network, to plan, and to have patience.

I have worked in many areas in my legal career, ranging from the White House; the U.S. Department of Justice; national political campaigns; two large law firms; a Fortune 500 company; a nonprofit; and a small, women-owned firm. Each of them helped me in my practice at the women-owned firm in the areas of business development and networking.

When I was a senior associate at one of the largest law firms in the country, I hired a consultant on my own dime to help me with business development. My firm, at the time, did not provide any business development assistance to associates or, for that matter, to partners. The consultant with whom I worked advised me to develop a plan and to devote a set amount of time to business development each week, even if I had time only to send one or two e-mails a week. I can certainly relate to young lawyers who say that they don't have time for business development given the grind of billing hours. At that time, I was billing over 2,100 hours per year, but I told myself that I needed to make time for business development. And, this advice is even more apt if you are starting your own practice or joining a women-owned firm.

Whenever someone tells me that they don't have time for something, I arrive at the same conclusion: that project or activity is simply not a priority for that person. One of the adages by which I live my life is this: People make time for things that they deem important.

Another piece of advice the consultant gave me was to become involved in bar activities. At the time, I had not really thought of that on my own. Nonetheless, I did take her advice, and I have to say that that piece of advice has transformed my life.

Through my bar activities and attendance at bar programs, I have expanded my network tremendously. I now have a national network of lawyers that I would not have otherwise met. I have met some truly impressive persons, including legal icons, through my bar activities. This network helps with business development through referral of cases and persons who can serve as references for my work. In fact, I met the women with whom I worked at the women-owned firm through my bar activities. My speaking opportunities have also expanded greatly through my bar work. By attending panel discussions, I met many in-house counsels, including general counsels of some large, multinational companies.

By the time I became a partner in a women-owned firm, I had a large network from all the bar positions that I had held and from my bar activities. And, I continually work to nurture my network. I try to stay in touch with people on a regular basis and not only when I need something from them. So nurture and do not neglect your network.

One of the lessons I learned from the big firm where I worked was that there were disincentives for younger lawyers to be able to develop business. Once a company had been a client of the firm, even if it had been several years ago and even if there had been no active work for several years, the original attorney who brought the client to the firm in the past would receive the credit for a new matter originated by a younger attorney, even though the original lawyer played no part in bringing the new matter to the firm.

As there are only so many companies, and my previous firm was one of the largest in the country, as you can imagine, most of the companies I was approaching for business were already past clients of the firm, and I would receive no credit for bringing the client to the firm. Nonetheless, I persisted, and I was able to bring a few matters to the firm, including representing several members of Congress before the U.S. Supreme Court in the University of Michigan affirmative action case, which my firm heavily marketed as a coup for the firm.

When I became a partner at a women-owned firm, my partners and I tried to adopt a more collegial approach to billing credit. With one of my partners, we agreed to split any billing credit for matters that we both worked to obtain. I would really encourage you to make some kind of arrangement at the outset with your fellow partners at a women-owned firm. It will help to guide the business development of the firm as a whole and will work to minimize resentments. Even though the women-owned firm where I worked was very small, it still often happened that my partners and I were approaching the same business contacts for work, as we had similar networks. After the fact, we would often find out that we were approaching the same people. So, to have an agreement in advance regarding billing credit is not only advisable but is also smart business. I think it provides the right incentives to try to obtain business rather than to prevent someone else from obtaining it.

Business development takes patience and luck. You need to stay on your contacts' radar screens. So continue to reach out to your contacts. Learn the businesses of potential clients, and then convey to them how your skills and experiences will help their businesses.

From being an in-house counsel, I have an inside perspective on the concerns of clients, ranging from legal needs to issues of billing. If you have started a solo practice or are a partner in a women-owned firm, you will not be able to bill at the rates that the large law firms bill. It is beneficial to try to provide value to your clients in economical ways. Lower billing rates will serve as an incentive for potential clients to hire you or your firm. Also, be amenable to alternative fee arrangements such as flat fees and bonus payments.

It does not happen overnight. For one potential client of mine, I had been trying to obtain work from her company for two years before she invited me to submit a request for proposal for legal services. Be patient and keep at it.

Have faith in yourself, and you will succeed with patience, determination, fortitude, and good humor.

Warm regards.

MARY L. SMITH is currently Counselor at the U.S. Department of Justice, and her past experience includes stints at the White House, as in-house counsel at a Fortune 500 company, and at both a large, international law firm and a women-owned firm. She is an enrolled member of the Cherokee Nation and graduated law school in 1991.

- ROSANNA BERARDI -

"For all the time and energy we spend planning and thinking through our options, it's often those spur-of-the-moment decisions that end up putting us on the road to our best future."

Eyes Wide Open: Finding Your Passion on the Road Less Traveled

Life is funny. For all the time and energy we spend planning and thinking through our options, it's often those spur-of-the-moment decisions that end up putting us on the road to our best future. I've learned that on the road to independence, it's important to keep your eyes open for the paths less traveled and watch for opportunities that can lead you to your passion.

Find the Right Path, or Create Your Own

In 1992, I was a junior at Canisius College, a small Jesuit college in Buffalo, New York. I was an English major because I was bad in math and science. I was walking down the hall by the career services office and noticed a posting from the Immigration & Naturalization Service (INS). They were looking for summer co-op students to work at the local international border crossings. The pay was $10 per hour, which was great in the early '90s. It sounded interesting and paid well. I applied, was hired for the summer of 1993, and 17 years later am the managing partner of my own immigration law firm in Buffalo.

My experience with the INS began in 1993 as a co-op student. It was my job to assist the immigration inspectors with the inspection process. I had no idea what I was in for. I will never forget as I watched an immigration inspector deny a Canadian nurse admission to the United States. It sounds harmless enough, but the nurse had sold her house and all of her personal effects in Canada to take a U.S. job offer. She had nothing left in Canada and was hysterical. The inspector would not let up. He was mean and bordered on bullying. I felt so bad for her. I can still recall her expression after all of these years.

As the summer progressed, I watched the inspectors question people, review documents, and make determinations about applicants' admissibility to the United States. I was exposed to foreign nationals from around the world. It was also my job to write up I-94 cards, which are the entry documents that visitors receive upon entry to the United States. I had to write them by hand, which seems like no big deal, but on a Saturday in the summer, I would write hundreds of them for Asian and European tourists. This was a pivotal learning experience, as it was my first time witnessing passports and visas and, more importantly, dealing with the international community. I also witnessed peoples' dreams in action. They would show up at the border to apply for admission to the United States to work, visit family, or tour the country. The immigration inspectors, with their enormous discretion and authority, could quickly grant that dream or extinguish it.

As I continued to explore my post-graduate options and my career with the INS moved forward, it became clear that teaching was not for me and that a law degree seemed more suitable. I also realized what an amazing job I had landed. I worked for the INS, one of the premier government agencies under the Department of Justice. I recognized that, while I didn't necessarily want to be a lawyer, I did want to obtain a degree that would allow me great flexibility in my career, hence the early attraction to teaching. I entered law school in 1997 and was transferred to the INS Litigation Office, where I assisted INS attorneys with the prosecution of their cases. It was a great experience. I learned rudimentary office skills—how to change the toner in a printer, how to load paper in the copier, how to write good file notes—all things that are important to good office management. I also witnessed immigration trials in which I learned the decorum of the court and appropriate interactions with the immigration judge.

In 1997, I graduated from law school, and my first legal job was as an assistant district counsel for the INS in New York City. Each day, I was responsible for prosecuting illegal aliens before 32 different immigration judges. It was a fast-paced learning environment, and my caseload was 70 files per day.

My government experience established a strong foundation for my immigration law career. I left the INS in 1998 and headed back to Buffalo, where I became the immigration attorney for SUNY Buffalo and then a senior associate at a large multinational law firm. I was selected for both jobs due to my government experience and my understanding of the system, its players, and overall processes.

Today, I am the managing partner of a full-service immigration firm in Buffalo, and still find that my clients select me, in part, due to my government experience. Because of my background, I have an intimate understanding of the government processes and mindset. I have a firm grasp on the documentation related to each case, due to my experience when I was the person writing the I-94 cards and examining passports.

Observe Along the Way

If you are unsure of your career path, the best advice I can give you is carefully examine your current work environment. Everything in life happens for a reason, so if you're not at the perfect job today, look around and see what you can learn from it. How does the copy machine work? How is work assigned and delegated? How does your office currently bill their clients? Look and learn. You will be surprised how much of this information will act as the foundation of your own business someday. After all, Julius Caesar said, "Experience is the teacher of all things." Also, pay attention to management styles. Use every experience as a learning opportunity. If you are unhappy about your boss's current management style, think of what you would do in a similar situation. Someday you will be the boss and will need to develop your own style and rapport with your employees.

Build Your Business Around Your Passion

I remember my parents always saying "do what you love." I never fully appreciated this statement until I launched my own law firm in 2005. I began Berardi Immigration Law out of my two-bedroom apartment, with a computer and some basic office supplies. I started to live my passion on a 24/7 basis. For many years of my career, particularly at a large law firm, I was unsure as to whether I really wanted to be a lawyer. I had even applied to graduate school to obtain my teaching certificate, after all. However, when I started my own practice, my passion became very apparent. I truly loved being an immigration lawyer—it was the setting of the job that had left me uncertain. My own practice provided me with the perfect opportunity to help foreign nationals realize their U.S. immigration dreams. I was able to work with them on a personal level and focus on their cases, not billable hours.

Five years later, I am one happy immigration lawyer. I work hard, but on most days it does not feel like work. Rather, it feels like breathing, a natural act that my body and brain are programmed to do. I am living my passion and would continue to be an immigration lawyer even if I won the lottery. My work is my passion and thankfully so because I couldn't imagine spending this much time doing something I hated.

The road to owning a law firm is a challenging one. It requires long hours, experience, and education. But by keeping your eyes wide open, taking in the scenery, and following the little traveled, but oddly attractive, side paths, you *will* find your passion and shape your business along the way.

ROSANNA BERARDI is the managing partner of Berardi Immigration Law in Buffalo, New York, where she focuses on U.S. immigration law. She graduated from law school in 1997 and founded her firm in 2005. *www.berardiimmigrationlaw.com*

- AMANDA GREEN ALEXANDER -

"A federal court judge. . . .said, 'find a "go-to person" who is available on a moment's notice to assist without asking a million questions about your reasons.'"

Just Plain Good Advice

I began my law firm nearly five years ago. I was doing family law cases while employed full time. Eventually, I decided to venture into practice full time. I located the perfect office space, signed my lease, and began selecting furniture. One day, while finalizing my lamp selections, my doctor called to advise me that we were expecting a little one; funny thing about God—when you ask for blessings He has a way of bringing them down all at once. So after consulting with my then-silent law partner we decided that there was no turning back, and the firm would have to be successful because each of us had at least one mouth to feed. I operated the firm for nearly two years before the formation of Alexander & Watson, a small defense firm that handles primarily workers' compensation and employment matters in the state of Mississippi. We still remain committed to our family law clients and strive daily to fulfill our firm's motto, "to do justly, love mercy, and walk humbly."

Oddly enough, we were not as afraid as we thought we would be, or at least neither one of us would let the other know. Planning and seeking good advice were essential in beginning the firm. We soon learned that when entering a courtroom, boardroom, or docket room, we should instantly make friends with the people in the room. We would often explain to them, we are still trying to figure this out—*please help!* And that request would seldom go unanswered. If you are reading this book you are also trying to figure things out, and I hope this advice will be helpful to you along the way.

Seeking Advice

Before finalizing my decision to venture into private practice, I sought advice from a friend who was in private practice. His advice was invaluable and very practical:

1. Selecting your partner(s): If you decide to have a partner, make sure you all can talk about everything—your finances, family life, major decisions etc. This person must be someone that you can trust with all of this information and who complements your strengths and weaknesses. But most importantly, ensure that your partner's personal partner is on board. After all, you are about to seriously dip into their discretionary time, income, and sense of stability, so his or her partner at home must be *all in* as well. You must have this clearly defined from the beginning, so you do not encounter problems in the future.

2. POWER 3: Select only three individuals to share your ideas, concerns, and fears about starting your business. Each partner selects one, and then both partners decide on one person together. I would recommend a more seasoned attorney and/or businessperson. Only these three individuals will know your plans of getting started, your timeline, and the possibility of your leaving your current office/law firm—because you do not want to leave your office before you are ready.

3. Your POWER 3 will provide insight on establishing your office, including names or suggestions for billing/computer software, accountants, malpractice carriers, selecting staff, balancing work and life, pitfalls, possible start-up capital, small business friendly bankers, vendors for letterhead, website designers, technology support staff, and the like.

Administration of a Law Office
Remember, you will spend most evenings/nights in the early years working on good systems and less time practicing law, so you will need help. Later in my career, I began developing my own ideas about things to consider. Though this list is long, it is not exhaustive, and it is certainly a work in progress.

1. Business formation. Whether LLC, PA, PLLC: consult a CPA or tax attorney to determine the tax benefit.

2. Obtain malpractice coverage. Some companies offer many payment options including monthly, quarterly, and annually.

3. Select a good accountant/bookkeeper. Early in the practice, it is extremely important that you manage and sign all checks and monetary matters. Both you and your partner should have an internal checks and balances system to ensure proper auditing.

4. To help limit your expenses and maximize your income:

    a. Law office space: Ensure the space is within your budget and manageable. Obtain insurance on such space.

    b. Legal research software: Contact your local bar association to determine discounts on law search engines.

    c. Professional resources: Register with your bar association resource listservs.

    d. Phone systems/wireless/Internet/DSL: Explore all options. Based upon your income and needs, you can always upgrade, but it may be more difficult to downgrade. Most services require a contractual agreement for services for a period of time. Ask about promotions.

    e. Furniture: Explore used furniture options, such as retiring attorneys and/or office moving sales. Most of this furniture is solid wood and is offered at a great bargain.

    f. Computer systems: Consult your information technology person to determine best options for computer systems, networking capabilities, software options, fax/copier machines, etc.

5. Determine an amount that each partner will bring to the firm, whether in kind contributions, furniture, monetary, etc.

6. Determine the distribution of commission and salaries. A good example—after all expenses are paid, including salaries, the remaining funds are split three ways, one share going to each partner and one to the firm.

7. Determine the amount of money for emergency funds. It's a good idea to project three to six months of expenses to ensure the firm continues even if you have a bad month or two.

8. Determine your hours of operation, each staff person's responsibilities, etc.

9. Establish a key person insurance policy. The policy is owned by the firm and ensures that the firm continues in the event of the death of a key person.

10. Establish a solid partnership agreement that specifically outlines the distribution of stock, dissolution of partnership, disbursements to surviving partner's family, etc.

11. Establish firm goals and business development strategies. Periodically check in with your partner and staff to ensure the firm is managing well.

12. Establish weekly staff meetings to check in with staff on effective and ineffective systems.

13. Establish a database for forms, procedures, and checklists because much of your efforts as an owner/partner will involve development of systems to ensure the work is being done while you are away from the office.

14. Establish a telephone intake procedure. Track calls; it eliminates price shoppers and repeat calls and assists with your market strategy.

15. Decide your areas of practice. There are some cases you will know little about but can very easily figure out, and then there are others that you know in your gut you should *never* take.

16. Determine your ideal/typical clients. Are you appealing to consumers or businesses? Make sure your image is aligned with expectations. Never be afraid to decline representation; remember to trust your instincts.

17. Decide your market strategy. Call up friends for referrals to let people know your areas. A good brochure is helpful to have at your friend's desk for quick reference. Make your best advertisement efforts (and consult the Rules of Professional Conduct).

18. Stay connected with other lawyers, especially women lawyers. They will provide good advice on strategies, typical fees for services, and most importantly how to do it well.

19. Ensure your partner's ethical tolerance is compatible with yours. Select a keeper of the rules to answer those difficult ethical questions. After all, your law office is not much of an office without a license to practice.

20. Ask for help. As a mother of a very young daughter, I received wonderful advice from a federal court judge. She said, "find a 'go-to person' who is available on a moment's notice to assist without asking a million questions about your reasons."

Success is when planning meets opportunity. May your opportunity arrive in perfect and divine timing.

Best to you and your endeavors.

AMANDA GREEN ALEXANDER is a partner at Alexander & Watson, P.A. in Jackson, Mississippi, where she represents both self-insured employers and insurance companies in workers' compensation and employment matters. She graduated from law school in 2004 and founded the firm in 2005. *www.alexanderandwatson.com*

- DEMETRIA L. GRAVES -

*"As entrepreneurs we can sometimes be 'control freaks,'
which will only hurt us in the end! Trust me as I say . . .
delegate, delegate, delegate."*

How long have you been doing what you do and how did you get to be a family law attorney?

When I passed the bar I was naturally eager to begin my career. After considering many firms I selected a position in a small family law firm not far from my home. Like most first year associates at small firms, I was "thrown in the water" and had to quickly figure out how to navigate the family law waters and find the best strategies to effectively assist my clients. I soon realized that this was the hardest time of life that each client would face (next to a death in the family) and that it was just as important to tread carefully and be sensitive to their needs as it was to deliver good legal service.

Although sensitivity and honesty are extremely important, I felt strongly pressured to close more clients by making false promises and billing more hours while spending less time with each person than I felt was truly necessary. It seemed that I would need either to find a new firm where I would be allowed to practice my own style of family law or to open my own office.

While contemplating this decision, I was very fortunate to meet an attorney who felt the same way and who had just opened her own law practice. After I explained my situation, she was convinced that I should start a practice of my own. At that very moment, I decided that I would make the commitment not only to myself, but also to my potential clients to practice family law according to my personal standards. I would provide total attention to my clients' needs, deliver well-devised case plans based on such needs, and provide a thorough explanation of the process in clear, laymen's terms.

So it happened! On July 5, 2005, I opened my doors as a family law attorney in the San Gabriel Valley and have been going strong since that time.

If you had it to do all over again, what would you do different?
At the time I opened my doors, I did not have a clue about running a business. (And please understand you are running a business in addition to your law practice!) Honestly, I barely knew how to practice law! Because I did not know how to run a business, I did not understand the importance of marketing, budgeting/managing finances, business structure, support systems, and something that has become very important to me: *balance*! Listed below are tips I learned in my practice that I wish someone told me before I opened my doors!

1. Marketing: If you don't remember anything else written here, please always remember: "Marketing *is* your business!" And in all honesty, this is very true! If potential clients don't know who you are, what you offer, or how to find you, you will not have any business. In the beginning, I guess I was very naïve to believe that clients would just knock down my door once I hung my "shingle" and placed my name in the phone book. Boy, was I wrong! When you have made the decision to open your own practice, it is crucial to make marketing a very big priority and part of your daily routine. Even before you open your doors, start thinking about the "ideal client" whom you want to serve; begin to think about what benefit you offer to clients, why they should hire you and not someone else. Also consider the ways in which you will get the word out about you, such as a website, e-zines, social media, etc. This may sound extreme, but in my opinion you should spend between 15 and 20 hours a week on marketing. A great resource that I use is Client Attraction by Fabienne Fredrickson. I cannot promise that she will solve all of your marketing woes, but she certainly got me started on the right track! I wish I would have spent significantly more time on my marketing in the beginning! I'm now in year five, and I'm just now really getting accustomed to the marketing ideal. It makes a huge impact on the success of your business!

2. Business Structure: Business structure is also important for your protection. It is probably worth it to pay a CPA whom you trust to discuss how you should incorporate for your full protection and to decide which approach works for you and your present/future assets. If you meet with a CPA or decide to do it yourself, the following are very important questions: (a) Do I want to have a partnership with another attorney? What are the pros/cons of a partnership? (b) Do I want to be solo? (c) Do I want

to have an LLC or an S corporation? (d) How much legal malpractice insurance do I need? (e) Which structure best fits my needs? We never plan to face legal obstacles, but always be protected just in case! I did incorporate in the beginning, but I really did not put much thought into this and instead just let people "tell" me what I should do. I strongly encourage you to get all the facts and then decide what works best for you!

3. Organizing Your Finances: When you begin your practice, the three most important accounts to have, in my opinion, are the following: your trust account, your business account (eventually you may have more than one), and the most important—your business savings account. Your trust account will of course be used for retainers, settlement payments, etc. You *will not* commingle with your business account, nor will you "borrow from" your trust account. Be *very strict* with your trust account, and be sure to keep impeccable records. Your business account is for your business operating costs. Throughout your business, be sure to create a budget and really strive to keep your expenses low! Again, in my opinion, contacting a bookkeeper and/or a CPA when you begin to make money will keep you in line with your budget and help to make sure you are not overspending. Lastly, your business savings is extremely important for rainy days. It's okay...we all have them! But save up for those times. It doesn't have to be anything outrageous, and you can start with any amount that is comfortable for you and your checkbook, but give yourself a little cushion just in case! Because as business owners we will have our good and bad days, you may need to get a credit card in addition to your business savings account, but again, be very clear on what you need your credit card for, and do your best to pay off the balance as soon as you can.

4. Support System: It is very fun to have your own practice, but it is important to have other experienced attorneys whom you can call when you have questions and lean on when you have "trials" and "tribulations"! Also, as you grow and the cost fits in your budget, seek out competent support staff who can assist you with the daily operations of your business. As you grow you will see that you cannot do everything yourself, and you will need support.

5. Balance: I saved this one for last, but this is extremely important. When you open your doors you will feel the urge to work...work...work.... Which is okay, but you do not want to burn out before you really begin. One of

the biggest tools that I use is planning my day the night before. This way I am able to hit the ground running without being drawn in different directions. Will you have days that need special attention? Yes, but on a general basis that's the strategy that I use! The time not allocated for work should be designated for fun, family, friends, vacations, etc. You will see that you need your breaks so you don't burn out! As we discussed above, as you grow your practice, learn to delegate the tasks that do not relate to your lawyer genius (e.g., writing letters, billing, marketing, etc.). This will allow you to work on what you are paid to do, take some breaks, and still get done what you feel needs to get done. As entrepreneurs we can sometimes be "control freaks," which will only hurt us in the end! Trust me as I say...delegate, delegate, delegate, and most importantly, rest, rest, rest. And above all, don't forget to enjoy the ride!

I hope this helps! And please feel free to contact me with any questions!

DEMETRIA L. GRAVES is the managing partner at The Law Offices of Demetria L. Graves in Glendale, California, where she focuses on celebrity family law cases and bankruptcy litigation. She graduated from law school in 2004 and founded her firm in 2005. *www.attorneygraves.com*

- JOANNE W. YOUNG -

"'Big in law firms is not necessarily better."

Entrepreneurship in the Legal Profession

Whether the decision to establish one's own law firm comes from the need for independence and flexibility, client conflicts, or disillusionment with large law firms run like corporations—or all three as was my experience—the benefits are tremendous. An entrepreneur at heart, having focused on growth areas and actively sought out business since four years out of law school, I realized that the same entrepreneurial spirit, coupled with my expertise in an industry area and the people skills I cultivated in other practice settings, qualified me to open my own firm.

Three and a half years ago, my practice colleague and friend of over 15 years, David Kirstein, and I set up Kirstein & Young, PLLC in Washington, DC. Now, at age 60, I wish I had done it 20 years earlier! It's a challenge I highly recommend, and it is a privilege to share below the benefit of our experience. Specifically, I will touch on the rewards from being a legal entrepreneur, some prerequisites to establishing one's own firm, including client relationships and business development, and administrative requirements, followed by some observations. I conclude with some predictions for the future of entrepreneurship in the legal profession.

Rewards
The greatest reward for establishing one's own firm is the flexibility it gives you to practice virtually anywhere, at any time, and under the standards you set. With today's technology one can stay in touch with clients and colleagues no matter where you are—no small thing for those who look to balance work, family, and personal goals. Billing rates can be controlled and alternative billing arrangements pursued. You set your own standards for excellence in practice, for fairness with employees, and for uncompromised high ethical standards.

Prerequisites

I believe it is essential to develop expertise through practice experience as well as a positive reputation in a legal or industry specialty before opening a firm. Clients require specific expertise so "on the job training" is to be avoided. Find out what your passion is and pursue it *before* you hold yourself out in it.

My own path involved a judicial clerkship and trial work for the federal government, followed by an associate position in a law firm. Having seen the potential in airline deregulation in the late '70s, I sought out opportunities for Washington lawyers. I conceived, researched, and wrote articles geared toward those who would need my services. The Civil Aeronautics Board was doing a "road show" around the country, introducing communities to the deregulation scheme, and I was invited to come along to introduce private sector opportunities.

I went to the places clients would be and asked the questions everybody wanted answered, which invariably broke the ice. With business in hand, a large Wall Street firm approached me to help open and build their Washington office. Later I transitioned to two other firms, the last an international firm with 1,700 lawyers. However, conflicts made it difficult to bring in new business, which largely triggered the decision to establish K&Y. We left with the support of that international firm, being careful to observe its requirements and those of the bar for transitioning clients.

Another prerequisite is the ability to generate business. Every firm needs an entrepreneur/rainmaker. Clients and their matters come and go; running a business requires a continuous stream of work and billings. If you are not comfortable generating new business and clients, partner with someone who can generate work. I do believe women have an edge in legal practice. They can have a natural ability to inspire confidence and trust—essential ingredients for rendering professional services. They are less threatening compared to many men who can be intimidating to clients in trouble.

One of the strengths of gaining specialized experience before launching one's own firm is developing a client base that is loyal and willing to transfer with you. Clients do not want legal services interrupted and will naturally want to stay with a lawyer they know and trust. It is not necessary to steal clients from a firm from which you depart. Take only what is yours, and be careful not to burn bridges. Indeed, former partners can be an excellent source for referrals.

Taking time out to engage is important, not only in pro bono efforts to gain experience, but also to establish yourself as an elected leader. Given my focus on aviation and shipping, I became involved in and was fortunate to be elected to lead several organizations, including in my area—the Washington Foreign Law Society, the International Aviation Club, the International Aviation Women's Association, and the Women's Bar Association. The latter gave me the opportunity not only to network with other successful professionals, but also to promote their development and success including on an international basis. I highly recommend establishing informal networks with women in your area of interest.

Organizational Structure
Getting organized should not be viewed as a barrier to starting a small practice. There are helpful books and bar association support, as well as accountants and IT vendors who specialize in supporting small law firms. We chose to put a limited amount of capital up and do not use a line of credit to fund the business.

Critical to success at the outset and on an ongoing basis is timely billing and follow-up on collections. Clients understand your need to collect the money you earned and to which you are entitled.

Miscellaneous Observations
- Ask for help, especially on administrative matters, to keep one's time billable as much as possible.
- Don't be afraid to ask for business. Tell potential clients you want to show them how good you are. Ask satisfied clients to refer others to you and to make introductions.
- When client demand is more than your business can handle, seek out other lawyers on a contract basis. There are many terrific women lawyers taking time out for child or elder care, as well as older lawyers who want to stay involved.
- Unlike a large firm, you will not have other lawyers down the hall to help on matters beyond your expertise. This is an opportunity to refer this work to other lawyers, who in turn will refer you work. Referrals can be

your greatest source of new business and give you the opportunity to network with other lawyers in a new and promising way.

- Remember, you are not a threat to other lawyers. In your boutique practice, you do what you do well and stand ready to collaborate with other lawyers who do not have your expertise.

- It is important to draw lines and protect your personal "off duty" time. Finding ways to take "time outs" will be essential for your relationship with family and friends and your ultimate success.

Predictions

Based on the changes I have witnessed in the legal profession, I believe increasingly women (and men) will turn to small and medium-sized law firms for practice fulfillment. The younger generation of lawyers especially values balance in their lives and will not be willing to put in slave billable hours. "Big" in law firms is not necessarily better, and as we have seen from recent layoffs and closures, the corporate model for professional services can leave the individual lawyer vulnerable.

At age 60, I have found the right model for law practice at this stage of my career. Through participation on nonprofit boards, I am able to give back to the community both in the legal profession and generally to the disadvantaged. Setting my own standards for excellence and rigorous ethics in legal work, while treating employees fairly as team players, would be hard to give up, just as would be retreating from the independence and flexibility that come from being a business owner. At the right time in one's legal career, it is a choice I highly recommend.

JOANNE W. YOUNG is the managing partner of Kirstein & Young, PLLC in Washington, DC, where she focuses on regulatory and commercial law with a particular emphasis on aviation, shipping, antitrust, and international privacy law. She graduated from law school in 1974 and co-founded her firm in 2006. *www.yklaw.com*

- ALICE M. ANDERSON -

---

*"I've been solo for some four years now and have practiced for 18
years overall. . . . Client development was the primary focus of my
first year, and I keep thinking that next year it will be again."*

I've been a solo for some four years now and have practiced for 18 overall. Before that I worked for three different firms, one large and two small.
From a solo perspective, here are a few thoughts on the question, should I
open my own practice?

The first question I think is, are you a litigator? That may be a more involved
start-up, with different time, support, and financial demands than most
transactional and corporate counsel work. In my experience, a nonlitigator
can get up and running fairly readily.

Second, you have to prioritize your needs for this stage of your life: income,
schedule flexibility, the type of practice you want to have, independence, security, etc. Working for yourself may not offer what you need at first (income
in particular), so it's crucial to be clear on this. But if what you really need is
flexibility, or more time somehow so you can have a more gratifying life, it
can be a beautiful thing.

Third is whether you'll have clients from the outset. If this is uncertain, managing income expectations is important. You may exceed your prior income,
or you may not get back to that level for some time. You may not break even
the first year. Having a personal partner who's supportive and really understands the situation is a great asset. Client development was the primary
focus of my first year, and I keep thinking that next year it will be again.

Managing overhead is probably equally important. My expenses are low, and
I plan to keep them that way. A key question in this area is whether you'll
have employees; I think it's too often just assumed that you will, and the
liability, hassle, and management factors and other options aren't reviewed
closely enough. Technology and the availability of contractors have com-

pletely changed what's possible, over the last 10 years or so. Remember your confidentiality clauses, though, and vet your contractors.

You'll still need colleague input, especially if you're a solo. I consider myself incredibly lucky because I'm in a niche practice (tax-exempt organizations law) and have a small circle of great colleagues locally. I'm also on the listserv for the relevant ABA tax section committee. These two are my go-to sources when I really need that word from the wise.

You'll also need good computer support. Your systems will have problems, and you'll want to establish in advance a relationship with a good provider that you can later run to in emergencies. Finally, regarding staying atop everything: early this year I was concerned about the volume of projects and events on my calendar, so I posted a contract position on guru.com for a "progress report manager," and it's worked out well. She gets my weekly and daily task lists and status updates and keeps me pretty well on track. I find that just the act of reporting in daily to somebody else really clarifies what needs to be done and when.

I hope these thoughts are useful to you. Good luck, and fair winds.

ALICE M. ANDERSON is the principal of Anderson Nonprofit Strategies in San Francisco, California, where she focuses on the law of tax-exempt organizations. She graduated from law school in 1991 and founded her firm in 2006. *www.anpslaw.com*

- Cindy D. Salvo -

"The opportunity to do my own marketing was one of the reasons I started my own practice! I had run my own business before . . . and I truly missed the fun and strategizing in creating a successful advertising campaign."

Congratulations on making the decision to start your own law firm! It is probably the best opportunity you will have to further your legal career. Because, like it or not, law is still a male-dominated world. The odds of your making partner at other law firms have not improved much over the years, even though more than half of all law students today are female. Just visit some Big Law websites and calculate the male-to-female ratio of partners. The results are frighteningly uniform: in firm after firm after firm, only about 15 percent of the firm's partners are women. And that's a statistic that is not likely to change anytime soon. So, bravo on making what I think will be the right move to further your legal career.

The first thing you need to decide (besides choosing a name!) is what area(s) of practice you want to pursue. That was an easy decision for me—during my years working for large firms in New York and New Jersey, my practice area was always commercial litigation, and that is what I wanted to continue doing once I opened my own firm. But, for you, the decision might not be as easy or clear-cut. You may not want to continue doing what you have been doing but instead may want to reinvent yourself as a different kind of practitioner. Is there an area of the law that particularly interests you? Maybe now is the time to turn your practice in that direction. Of course, you will need a mentor or two in that practice area to turn to for guidance as you learn the ropes. I have always found lawyers to be exceedingly generous with their time when asked to mentor other lawyers. It is, thus, a very good idea for you to join one or more of the attorney e-mail lists out there. The ABA has a particularly good one, Solosez, meant for attorneys who are solos or who practice in small law firms. Solosezzers are always willing to lend a helping hand to one another.

Another thing to keep in mind when making the decision as to the practice area(s) you wish to pursue is whether you have any good referral sources to send you business in that practice area. If you don't, you may also need to pursue a practice area where you can advertise for potential clients if necessary. That way, if you find new business is not being referred your way in your favored specialty, you can reach out and find clients by yourself in other areas. Good advertisable areas of practice include divorce/family law or bankruptcy, as many people look for divorce or bankruptcy attorneys on the Internet or in the Yellow Pages.

The next thing you need to think about is where you want to set up your practice. It is very important to keep overhead low when you first open your law firm. This is crucial because, unless you are taking a lot of clients with you from the firm where you worked previously, the money is going to just trickle in for a while, and probably not in very large amounts. You may want to think about opening your first office in your home and renting virtual space in an executive suite so you have a professional address, receptionist, and conference rooms where you can meet with clients. (Note: Be sure your state's bar does not have a problem with this setup. New Jersey has said such an arrangement violates its bona fide office rule). While some solos I have spoken to have said they meet with clients at coffee shops or the library, I strongly advise against this. I believe you could lose a lot of potential clients that way. Think about it—would you have confidence in a professional you met with in a coffee shop? I wouldn't. So my advice is, spring for the executive suite conference room instead!

If you keep overhead low, your firm can be profitable from its very first day! Mine was, and soon I was able to move into my very own office space!

Another important thing to remember when starting your own law firm is that, once you do, you will no longer be able to be just a lawyer. You will need to become an entrepreneur as well. Because whether you are selling legal services or widgets, you still need to learn how to attract clients for what you are selling. And you need to learn how to spend your money effectively on marketing and advertising—no matter what your budget.

It is crucial to your law firm's success to put together a marketing/advertising plan because, unless you do so, no one is going to know you are out there. The opportunity to do my own marketing was one of the reasons I started my own practice! I had run my own business before becoming a lawyer, and I truly missed the fun and strategizing involved in creating a successful advertising campaign. But always be prepared to change your strategy if it is not working for you. When I started out, I thought I would market my law firm to other women-owned businesses. I felt confident that businesswomen would want to work with other businesswomen. Unfortunately, it didn't work out that way. Although I sent a mailing to a number of women-owned businesses in my area, to my surprise, I did not receive even one telephone call. But perhaps my approach was wrong. Perhaps the mailing wasn't worded correctly or didn't reach the right kinds of businesses. Marketing/advertising always needs to be tweaked until it is working effectively, and if it can't be made to work, it is time to move on to another strategy.

One of the simplest marketing strategies is creating a professional-looking website. Nowadays, a law firm loses credibility if it can't be found on the Internet. But be careful whom you get to design your website. I did a lot of research on website companies before choosing one that was able to put a site together relatively inexpensively. There are so many website companies out there, and the prices range from a few hundred dollars to $15,000 or more. And the $15,000 websites are not necessarily more effective in attracting clients than the ones created from a template for a few hundred dollars. In order to keep your start-up costs low, you should choose a company that can create something professional-looking for you, at a good price. Ultimately, you may want to jazz up your website—adding video, a blog, etc.—but, for now, you just need an attractive and informative website that educates the public in your practice areas. Remember too, a website should be helpful to potential clients by providing them with information they are looking for. It should not be a site that simply tells people how wonderful your law firm is.

Finally, be aware of the fact that there are opportunities available to you specifically because you are a woman-owned business. Just surf the Internet for information on women-owned businesses, and you will find a wealth of resources. There are companies that will loan you money at a better rate simply because you are woman-owned and companies that will want to do business with you to improve their vendor diversity. The first step is to get certified as a woman-owned business. There are several organizations that do this, and you should reach out to one of them as soon as you are up and running. I neglected to do this and have only recently applied for certification. Don't make the same mistake I did. Get certified right away!

In short, I wish you the best of luck in your new enterprise. I have never regretted my decision to start my own law firm—it's a source of joy to me every day!

CINDY D. SALVO is the founding partner of The Salvo Law Firm, P.C. in Fairfield, New Jersey, and Tarrytown, New York, where she focuses on commercial litigation, employment litigation, and trademark infringement litigation. She graduated from law school in 1997 and founded her firm in 2006. *www.salvolawfirm.com*

- PAMELA J.P. DONISON -

"It was a risky move in a litigious community where the family bar is known for its lack of camaraderie."

In 2005, I was a divorce litigator and associate at a small family law firm. I had been practicing for just six years (three in civil litigation, three in family law) and was already in the burn-out zone. My weight was up, morale down, and my stress levels were at an all-time high. It was not unusual for me to have multiple high-conflict trials each month, and my work hours were routinely over 70 per week. It seemed like I was sick a lot, and I was generally miserable. Then two things happened.

"Aha" Moment One

In March, 2005, I got a call from Dr. Jane (not her real name), pediatrician to the children of John, one of my high-conflict divorce clients, asking for a meeting. John and his wife had three young boys, ages 4 years, 3 years, and 18 months. The youngest, Jack, had been hospitalized several times between Christmas and March for asthma attacks. When we all met at Dr. Jane's clinic, she looked at each of us in turn and then said, "Jack has been very sick for the past three months, and his condition is not getting any better. The reason is that Jack is the youngest, weakest member of the family, and all of the stress of this divorce is making him sick. Every time you file a motion or have an argument, it affects Jack. I've brought you here today to let you know that if you continue in this way, I will not treat Jack or your other children because I will not be a party to the abuse that is happening between you."

At that, the wife became furious and said, "You see what I've been putting up with?" She points at John. "This is all your fault!" To which the diminutive Dr. Jane responded by rising to her feet and slamming both fists on her desk.

"Stop it right now." Pointing at each of us, she shouted, "You, you, you and you are all at fault. I am leaving the room and will give you five minutes to grow up and come to your senses. When I return, I expect you to have Jack's best interests in mind and not your own. And that goes for the lawyers, too."

I felt as if I had been slapped. I was as guilty as if I had cut off young Jack's airways myself, and that just wasn't acceptable. I was almost always successful in court and was in demand for these types of high-conflict custody battles, which meant that whenever I "won," some kid was "losing." I knew in that instant that I had to figure out another way to make a living because I couldn't live with the consequences of my actions. But now what?

"Aha" Moment Two

My brother-in-law, Gary, is a bona fide genius, inventor, and entrepreneur and is as blunt and to-the-point as anyone I've ever known. During one of our family vacations to Mexico, over sunset margaritas on the beach, my Blackberry was buzzing constantly. I was bitching about how unhappy I was with nonstop litigation, high-conflict families who were literally sucking the life out of me, working for a firm where most of my billable hour was going to fund someone else's retirement, and generally having no control over my time or my life. He cocked his head with a quizzical look and said, "So why don't you just leave and start your own practice? If all these other people do it, how hard can it be?"

So, Dr. Jane and Gary, I thank you both for giving me the whack upside the head I needed to see the light that was shining onto my own path. In July 2005, I began wrapping up my caseload and working on the start-up of my firm.

On January 1, 2006, I opened the doors to my practice with the motto *divorce done differently*. I decided that I would not litigate any more high-conflict cases and, instead, would devote my practice to mediation, collaborative law, arbitration, and negotiated settlements. It was a risky move in a litigious community where the family bar is known for its lack of camaraderie. A handful of my fellow family law attorneys were supportive, but most saw me as foolish (at best) and a detriment to their litigation livelihood (at worst). Some were downright mean-spirited and declared (behind my back) that I was an idiot who didn't know what I was getting into. Four and a half years later I am happy to report that things are going very well, despite my lack of experience, a downward spiraling economy, and the gloomy forecasts of those colleagues.

Over the past five years, I have coached about 10 other women attorneys on starting their own practices, and here's some of the advice I gave them about getting started.

1. Get a notebook and start writing. It doesn't have to be anything fancy, but a three-tab notebook is helpful.

   a. *Logistics:* These are all the things that need to be accomplished in order to go out on your own, like office space, phones, website, business cards, etc.

   b. *Forms:* You will need a draft of everything from fee agreements to cover letters to marketing materials. Having a bank of forms ready to go will keep you from scrambling at the last minute and making costly mistakes.

   c. *Vision:* This is *your dream.* What do you want your typical day to look like? If you could create the perfect assistant, partner, client, or case, what would the characteristics of each be? How do you want your practice to be perceived? Be *bold* and, above all, *be yourself.*

2. Take at least five superheroes to lunch. Choose people in your community who have created the type of practice or business model you admire, and pick their brains over lunch. Be up front about your purpose, and make sure they understand that you are looking for guidance about what doesn't work as much as what does. Both are important to your success!

3. Make friends with your banker. If you have never met your branch manager, now is the time. It is likely that you will need some financial assistance at some point in your business life, and the branch manager is the person who will go to bat for you when times are tough (like now).

4. Have a family meeting. You will probably work harder for less money in the first year of your practice than you ever imagined, so it's important that your family and friends are on board to help as needed. My husband (a nonlawyer) was incredibly helpful in everything from choosing office space to buying computers, particularly in the first year, and I would have been lost without his assistance.

5. Write a business plan. It may sound silly, but drafting a pro forma profit and loss, balance sheet, and budget will help you see the real dollars that are needed in order for you to be profitable. Don't forget, you're in this to make money! Also, it comes in handy to have this information if your

banker wants to see how you're going to use the line of credit you've applied for!

6. Plan vacations. Time away from the office is essential to your health, happiness, and the wellness of your practice. Don't skip the vacation just because you're in your first start-up year, but make sure you take your notebook!

7. Have fun. Life is too short to be unhappy, so enjoy yourself along the way.

PAMELA J.P. DONISON is the owner of Donison Law Firm, PLLC in Phoenix, Arizona, a boutique family law practice focused on out-of-court solutions. Pamela graduated from law school in 1999 and opened her firm in 2006. *www.donisonlaw.com*

- ANGELA BARKER -

"Be committed to continuous learning."

There are 10 essential elements to weathering tough times as a solo/small firm attorney:

1. Understand why you chose to become a solo/small firm attorney, and be fully committed to building your practice.
It is essential that you understand why you have chosen to become a solo attorney. You will not do well as a solo/small firm attorney if you believe it to be a fallback position or if you are only hanging out your shingle until the next opportunity comes along. The life of a solo practitioner is simply too hard and the risks are too great for you to not give it the full attention it deserves.

2. Understand that there is no real division between work and personal life. All is the same for a solo/small firm attorney. You are the face of your business, and you are constantly marketing that business.
You must market your business at every opportunity. You do not market in an aggressive or in-your-face way. Rather, let people know that you are an attorney and the type of law that you practice. For example, when going to a social function and a topic of interest comes up, make a comment in line with your business. For me, as a divorce, trust and estate, and real estate lawyer, almost any current event can be used for me to market my business.

3. Cut costs wherever possible.
Consider virtual offices or office shares instead of shouldering the overhead of a traditional office.

Consider part-time employees or, even better, contract employees, or outsource the work; I contract out most of my secretarial, accounting, website maintenance, technology repair, and marketing work.

4. Invest smartly and wisely in as much technology as you can afford.
Research before you invest in hardware and software. The right hardware and software can help you cut your overhead cost because you'll need fewer

employees, and it can automate routine practices and procedures, so you will spend fewer hours recreating standard forms.

5. Work six days per week, take the seventh day to spend with family, friends, or your favorite hobbies. Take vacations.
Lawyers are often hard-driving and intense. Attorney burnout leads to substance abuse. You must take a step back from your practice at least one day a week.

6. Charge what you believe your services are worth, and get a good proportion of the money up front.
You must charge what you believe your services are worth. If you do not price effectively you will resent doing the work for your client.

7. Be committed to continuous learning. You must take continuing legal education courses in your practice area, ethics, civil or criminal procedure if you are a trial lawyer, and law firm management.
You must constantly hone your craft. You must attend CLEs that are in your area of practice.

8. Be willing to take calculated risks.
Consider expanding outside of your practice area if your practice area is slow. However, always pair up with an experienced attorney in that area.

9. Create practices and procedures that will allow you to save time and to consistently create an excellent product.
- Streamline procedures.
- Have intake forms.
- Have checklists for your particular area of practice.
- Have a telephone script.
- Have a procedure for opening and closing files.
- Have a checkout procedure for the use of files by staff.

10. Carefully choose your clients, and do not take on a representation if instinctively you believe that you will have problems with the client's expectations or problems getting paid.
The initial client interview is key. A bad client will cost you untold hours of headache. Beware of the following traits:

- the client has unrealistic expectations about the merits of his case even after he has heard your advice during the initial interview
- the client lies or requests you do something unethical
- you are the second or third lawyer hired
- the client needs a lot of handholding or makes unreasonable demands on your time
- the client that for whatever reason you just don't like
- the client who does not want to give you his contact information
- the control freak—that is, a client that second guesses your every move

---

ANGELA BARKER is the founder of Angela Barker and Associates, LLC in New York, New York, and Rutherford, New Jersey, where she focuses on matrimonial law, trusts and estates, and real estate. She graduated from law school in 2000 and founded her firm in 2006. *www.angelabarkerlaw.com*

- KIM M. KEENAN -

"We often ignore the inner voice telling us that we were meant to be somewhere else. This is not an indictment of others who choose the obvious path but an affirmation of our individuality and the voyage that is sometimes our destiny alone."

For me, the road to a solo practice began with two female solo practitioners I met while still in law school. To this day, I remember the response one of them gave me when I asked her about her practice. It really was the typical question, and I fully expected the sort of cookie cutter answer you hear every day. Her response, "I only do what I want to do," has haunted me my whole career. The more senior my career, the more haunted I was by the notion that every day I could choose my assignments and select projects that excited me.

These two women, Mabel Haden, a co-founder and president of the National Association of Black Women Attorneys, and Suzanne Richards, the first female president of the Bar Association of the District of Columbia, were living proof that you could sustain and thrive in your own law practice despite the general notion that this was difficult to accomplish and rarely done by women. From my observation, they both determined what they did best, and they drew clients by providing the best service possible. Of course, the fact that these women carefully selected their client matters significantly improved their results.

After almost 20 years of practice, I needed a new challenge. I needed to know that I could create the brand and deliver the product. From the beginning, I had worked for brilliant lawyers, mostly men, who defined their respective areas of practice. So whether it was a federal judicial clerkship, the largest private law firm in the nation, or a nationally recognized boutique firm, I was trained by the best. Still, I was left with the nagging feeling that I did not want my career defined by an infrastructure created by someone else. The urge to do it my way and make my own choice was always there, and it refused to simply go away.

Starting my own firm was like jumping into the ocean. Initially, there is so much trepidation—okay, fear—when you realize that everything begins and ends with you. It is much easier to micro-manage how someone else runs their practice than it is to take the chance that you might do it better or at the very least develop an understanding of the requirements of a successful practice. This was my chance to create the big picture rather than managing the details.

As I look back on this experience, three questions are at the heart of every discussion I have had regarding starting my own practice. First, "where will you get clients?" Legal education is just beginning to understand that lawyers "sell" a service. So unless you have the good fortune to work with lawyers who understand that ultimately you must be able to attract business, you will have to teach yourself. Luckily for me, although few lawyers formally mentor on this issue, I had the opportunity to observe the best. In sum, you have to learn to inject yourself into the community in such a way that people understand what services you can provide and believe that you can provide that service in a manner that is excellent. If you are in a room more than an hour and you cannot subtly interject the nature of your practice into the conversation, regardless of your employment, then attracting business will be that much harder. I like to say, "when I leave a room people know what I do, and they have confidence in my ability to get the task done."

Second, "how will I manage a practice alone?" Before I made the decision to start my own practice, I had a network of other small and solo practitioners. A number of these lawyers coached me through the best and the worst of times. One in particular coached me through the process and offered support for my solo journey. This continues to be such a valuable resource that it is difficult to put into words. What a difference it makes to have someone demystify the process. Instead of sweating the small stuff, I could focus on the really big problems! So while working on litigation was still the same, I now had the responsibility for every aspect of the practice. Having a cheerful guide to take me through the process has been the difference between sanity and insanity.

Third, "how will I manage unpredictable cash flow?" The phrases "feast or famine" and "you eat what you kill" quickly move from cliché to mantra. I evaluate every conversation with a potential client in terms of cost-benefit analysis. Is this a matter that best uses my talent and resources, or would the client be better served by someone or something else? The answer to this question is often the difference between effective use of time and ineffective use of time.

Ultimately, reaching my goal of maximizing my career satisfaction requires that I continuously evaluate new opportunities and project how they will fit into my time. As a result, I have diversified my professional activities to include mediation, teaching, consulting, and writing to balance both my interests and my bank account. With each additional nuance, more and more my schedule is beginning to look like my goal of self-determination.

In some ways, starting your own practice is one of the ultimate acts of faith in you. When you are not sure whether your plunge in the ocean will eventually lead to dry land, working anywhere can start to look like a fantasy island! Panic does occur from time to time. The good news is that this is actually very normal. Even better, once you take a few deep breaths, you realize that you were always in the ocean, only now the oars are yours. You discover exhilaration upon creating your own professional limited liability corporation or choosing the health care plan that meets your needs. You bask in the freedom of truly charting your own course. At the end of the day, I am a more confident lawyer because I trust my judgment and I have really put it to the test.

As I look back over the last three years as a solo practitioner, my favorite accomplishment is the notion that I created my own brand. Every aspect of what I do and how I do it is stamped indelibly with my style. I truly believe that each time I do something new I revel in the fact that this is my choice and that the distance I can expand my horizons is limited only by my imagination. The practice of law is now the adventure of my choice and not the whim or choice of someone who cannot possibly understand that I cannot do everything the same way everyone else does it. It has taught me to respect the choices of other lawyers and how they set up and manage their own practices, and ultimately that respect is what makes this experience such a triumph.

One final thought: we often ignore the inner voice telling us that we were meant to be somewhere else. This is not an indictment of others who choose the obvious path but an affirmation of our individuality and the voyage that is sometimes our destiny alone. Bon voyage.

KIM M. KEENAN closed her firm, The Keenan Firm, in 2010 to serve as general counsel of the NAACP, the nation's oldest and largest civil rights organization, in Baltimore, Maryland. She graduated from law school in 1987 and founded her firm in 2007. *www.naacp.org*

- RENÉE A. RUBINO -

"If you remember nothing else from this letter, remember this:
ask a lot of questions."

Starting a new business can be very rewarding and at times very overwhelming. I started my law firm in June of 2007, entering the exciting world of independence. Whether you are thinking about starting your own firm, or have already taken that first step, congratulations—both are courageous moves toward an exciting future. Here's my insight into forming your own firm.

Do the Right Thing, and the Money Will Follow

Early in my career, I had the privilege of working for a prestigious New Jersey law firm. The managing partner said the following, which truly resonated and stayed with me: "Do the right thing, and the money will follow." It's only natural for new business owners to worry about getting the bills and employees paid every month. But I'm willing to bet that money wasn't your sole reason for starting your own firm (maybe not even the top one). It probably had more to do with independence, flexibility, a more balanced life, and working more closely with clients, as it did for me. Whatever has inspired you to take this step, stay true to those values. Remind yourself of them every day. Be fair to clients and employees, and give back to your community as much as you can. No matter what decision you are facing, "Do the right thing, and the money will follow."

Develop a Business Plan

I know you are tired of hearing that, but this is where a lot of entrepreneurs go wrong. They make the mistake of thinking that everything will "just work out." It's important for you to have an ultimate goal and a clear, realistic path on how to get there. I don't mean just thinking things over in your head. I mean taking the time to prepare a real business plan. If you cannot afford a professional to assist you with your business plan, you can use one of the many reputable software programs on the market. Some states, such as New Jersey, offer free planning advice and assistance to new business owners (e.g., the New Jersey Small Business Development Centers). Without a business plan you have no direction.

Even with a business plan, though, don't be surprised (or disappointed) if you need to change direction along the way, maybe even take a few sharp turns! Not every idea is going to work as anticipated. When that happens, take a step back, assess the situation, and see if you need to tweak your game plan. Maybe you need a new game plan! That's okay, too.

As an example, when I started my firm in June of 2007, I expected to develop the majority of my business in real estate transactions. If you take a moment to recall the turn of events in real estate and the economy in 2008, you've probably guessed that I had to revise my business plan and change direction. Conversely, the practice area to which I had allocated the smallest percentage of cases, divorce law, is now the firm's largest practice area. As that practice area grew, my administrative and staffing needs changed as well.

You have to be flexible and willing to see what works and what doesn't. It's a good idea to pull out your business plan every couple of months and ask yourself, "where have I been, where am I now, where do I want to be (this year, next year, in five years), and what steps do I need to take to get there?"

Be Willing to Take Chances, Fail, and Learn

When I was 25 years old, I was waiting on tables without a penny to my name. I knew I wanted to be a lawyer. I knew that meant college, law school, and student loans the size of a mortgage. But if I had had any idea as to how many roadblocks, challenges, and setbacks I would face, I may not have taken that first step. I realize now, 20 years later, that every setback was an opportunity, even if I didn't realize it then.

The same has been true for my business. I am sure that my business is successful in part because I have been able to learn and recalibrate after failed experiments. Don't be afraid to make mistakes, because you *will* make mistakes. As for some of my own, I cringe when I think about the thousands of dollars I threw away on what seemed like good "marketing" ideas at the time: magazine advertisements with no real target audience and fancy pens with the firm name on it, as if someone would see a pen and say, "yes, I'm going to hire this firm because I like the pen!" Here's what I learned. I'm a lawyer—not a marketing professional. If you cannot afford a marketing professional, as I could not at first, find colleagues to ask for advice. If you remember nothing else from this letter, remember this: *ask a lot of questions.*

Ask a Lot of Questions

Questions are key. You may not realize it, but we are all surrounded by intelligent, competent, generous individuals, who know many of the answers to our questions. I believe that most people have good hearts and want to help. I also believe that very successful people understand that the more we help each other, the better we all do. Don't be afraid to pick up the phone, call a colleague or acquaintance, and say, "if you have time for lunch, I'd love to ask how you developed such a successful business." Or, "I'd love to ask a few questions about staffing, administration, marketing, supervising employees, etc." Ask questions based upon what that person has accomplished and what you would like to learn. I have done it often, and I have never received a negative response. Whether I am asking questions, or being asked questions, those are the times I learn the most and feel most grateful for.

Network, Network, Network

I don't mean networking as in, "Hi, this is what I do. Here's my card." That's not networking, and I'd suggest you do not waste your time at those events (of which there are many). Real networking is getting to know someone, building a rapport and trust.

Real networking can be difficult at first. It's not something that comes naturally to most of us. But it's so important if you want to have a successful business. You have to let people know what you do and, more importantly, find out what they need. Let them see how you may be able to help them or someone they know. Our profession is ultra-competitive. You need to differentiate yourself. What makes you different? And don't say the service you offer—everyone says that.

For me, for example, it's that my clients really matter to me. Whether an individual or company, I want my clients to do well and succeed. I want us to work together. What happens in their lives matters to me. As you know, people come to us with their most pressing, and sometimes personal, problems. It's a privilege to be trusted with that. It's a privilege to do what we do for a living.

I would encourage you to build a network list in Microsoft Outlook or some other contact management system, such as Constant Contact. Then start communicating with your network consistently. Whether it's face-to-face, an e-newsletter, regular newsletter, or online forum, let them know you're here to stay.

In Sum

I encourage you to use your own values as the foundation of your business. Try to understand yourself in a way you never have before. What are your strengths and weaknesses? For me, I knew I was an excellent attorney. I did not know I had so much to learn when it came to starting and running a business. Having spent the first decade of my career in large law firms, I, quite frankly, never gave much thought to bookkeeping, marketing, office supplies, mail meters, or staffing. Suddenly, it was up to me to develop systems for everything in the firm and oversee them all. As a primer, there is one book that I highly recommend, *Attorney and Law Firm Guide to the Business of Law: Planning and Operating for Survival and Growth*, Second Edition, by Edward Poll (an American Bar Association publication).

Above all, trust yourself, have fun, and be grateful for this amazing opportunity. I know you will find the abundance you are looking for in all levels of your life. And remember...if you have any questions, feel free to call me.

With warmest regards.

RENÉE A. RUBINO is the founding member of the Rubino Law Group, LLC in Hackensack, New Jersey, where she focuses on family law and collaborative divorce. She graduated from law school in 1994 and founded her firm in 2007. *www.rubinoesq.com*

- GRETCHEN LE VAN MANDEKOR -

*"The opportunities are there for us if
we have the courage to take them."*

If I had to name just one trait, one quality of character above all others that I would encourage you to develop within yourself as you contemplate the possibility of pursuing a career in law not as someone else's employee but as the leader of your own firm, it would be this: fearlessness.

But let me be clear about what I mean by that. I am not suggesting that you seek never to be afraid. First of all, that isn't possible, at least not in a life with meaning, a life of growth and accomplishment. We can avoid fear only by avoiding any and all possibility of failure—and we can avoid that only by foregoing every challenge and opportunity that life offers us, the very things that make life worth living in the first place, on both the professional and personal levels. Risk is an inescapable part of any fully lived life, and fear is a rational and ultimately unavoidable response to risk.

So rather than hope for a life free of all doubt and worry, I urge you instead to embrace Arianna Huffington's definition of fearlessness as "not the absence of fear, but rather the mastery of fear. It's about getting up one more time than we fall down."

If my story can offer you anything to emulate, it is not that of a person who has never been afraid but of one who refused to let fear be the deciding factor in her most important decisions.

After my first year of law school at the University of Oregon, I was offered a stipend through the Global Graduates Program to spend a summer in Dakar, the capital of Senegal, assisting with an agricultural research project sponsored by the United States Agency for International Development and doing independent research on the evolving laws relating to polygamy in Africa. Yes, it was an exciting opportunity, but I won't expect you to believe that it wasn't also intimidating for someone just a couple of years out of college to travel alone thousands of miles from every place and person I had ever known and to submerge myself into a culture that was light years removed from that of Oregon, as well as those of Vancouver, British Columbia, and Montreal, Quebec, where I had grown up and gone to college, respectively. My ability to speak French fluently made assimilation into Senegal somewhat easier, but still I was at first painfully aware of being an outsider.

Ultimately, however, it was that very sense of "otherness" in the beginning that made the experience finally so joyous for me. I returned from Africa with a renewed belief in myself and in what I was capable of. I strongly agree with the renowned trial lawyer Gerry Spence when he says, "Every triumph is preceded by fear. Fear always initiates the act of breaking free."

When I graduated from law school in 1999, I took a job with a small litigation firm in southern Oregon near the California state line. We have all known new associates in similar situations—some of us have probably been such types ourselves—who have contented themselves with menial tasks in their first jobs, doing tedious legal research under fluorescent lighting, hoping and waiting for a lucky day when their supervisors will decide to give them a chance to do real legal work in court for an actual client.

For better or worse, however, I have never been the type to sit quietly in the background and wait passively for fortune to smile upon me. Rather than live Thoreau's life of quiet desperation while wishing for better things, I got in my supervisors' faces and demanded real responsibility from the beginning. I'm not naïve—I knew that such an approach could put me on the fast track to the unemployment office if my supervisors proved to be chauvinists or men intimidated by female strength. But I was lucky—my mentors respected and rewarded my assertiveness, and in a relatively short time I had acquired both a level of trial experience and a book of business well beyond those of many of my contemporaries.

Although I was happy at my first firm, growing up in Vancouver meant that I had city life in my blood, and eventually the siren song of Portland's noise and crowds became too enticing to resist. I went on to work for two of the most respected defense firms in Oregon's largest city before finally deciding three years ago that the time had come to set off on my own.

Again, I had no illusions of guaranteed success—as I stepped through the aircraft door, leaving behind the security of a steady paycheck, I was well aware that my chute might not open. The "jump" was especially frightening to me personally because I was taking it as a single parent of two small children, my daughters Minga and Bibi, now six and three, respectively. But the possibility and the hope of three things steeled my resolve to take that step: greater autonomy, a potentially larger income, and an escape from office politics. Three years later, I am able to tell you with gratitude, relief, and pride that I have achieved all three. My practice is thriving and my firm is growing. When one of Portland's most respected senior defense attorneys recently passed away, 65 of his cases were directed to my firm for further handling.

Can I promise you that you will enjoy similar success if you take the step that I did? Of course not. I took a risk, and if you follow a similar path, so will you. For some that gamble will pay off, while for others it may not. As the novelist Walker Percy has observed, "Where there is chance of gain, there is also chance of loss. Whenever one courts great happiness, one also risks malaise."

Nor will I tell you that running an office, even a successful one, is always easy or always fun. I have come to the conclusion that there are certain inescapable headaches inherent in having to supervise others. As much as one would like to dream of having a support staff that one could simply set loose and leave to their own devices, there will never be perfect employees for the same reason that we as lawyers seem never to be able to find perfect clients: because there are no perfect human beings. I have resigned myself to the fact that, between being a mother and being a boss, I am fated always to be in "parent" mode in one capacity or another.

One genuine note of encouragement I can offer you, however, is that I have not found my corporate clients to be less willing to entrust their cases to me because of my gender. In fact, I have found the opposite to be true: Many of them, in the interest of promoting diversity, actively seek out representation by firms run by women. Many of us are familiar with the story of Sandra Day O'Connor, the first female justice on the U.S. Supreme Court, who graduated third in a class of 102 at Stanford Law School after two years rather than the usual three, only to find that the only private firm in the state of California willing to give her employment of any kind would offer her a position only as a legal secretary. Justice O'Connor is still alive, but already her story feels like ancient history. There are still bumps in the road ahead toward total equality, to be sure, but O'Connor and other women of her generation have made the path smoother for those of us following them. The opportunities are there for us if we have the courage to take them.

If you feel within yourself the same fire and drive that I did to become the captain of your own ship and chart your own course, I can only urge you to go for it and never allow fear to hold you back.

GRETCHEN LE VAN MANDEKOR is a partner at Mandekor Lewis LLC in Portland, Oregon, where she focuses on personal injury and employment litigation. She graduated from law school in 1999 and founded her firm in 2007.

- JANE TABER, DAWN ESTES, -
- JESSICA THORNE, LORI CARR, -
&
- MELANIE OKON -

"Opening your own firm is one leap of faith, and, once you're open, you will keep making them. In fact, your risk-taking muscles will get a workout like you never imagined. Some leaps will pay off."

What were we thinking? We were partners at a large Dallas law firm, with a stable salary and hundreds of support staff. What would make us potentially sign away our retirement and open our own firm?

We simply wanted to have something to call our own, but little did we know when we hung our shingle in February of 2008 that our little firm would be an inspiration to the businesswomen in our city. The hours have been long and the challenges many, but if we had known then what we know now, we would have done this years ago.

Like most new ventures, though, it didn't start out booming. It started in a box-filled office, on a Friday night, with a bottle of Dom Pérignon. As we were sprawled on the floor, sipping our champagne, our new neighbor (a late night DJ on a classic rock radio station) popped his head in to welcome us. We must have made an impression on him because he informed his radio audience that his new neighbors were a bunch of female attorneys who sit on the floor drinking wine.

It wasn't necessarily the image we were trying to convey, but we took the mention as a public relations coup and, hopefully, the start of some good free publicity.

We thought we would spend the first days at our new firm getting settled in and spending only part of the day practicing law. Our plan was to forego paychecks (for the partners) for the first six months and keep our admin staff to one for the foreseeable future. Little did we know that our clients would gladly come with us to the new firm and that referrals (mostly from our former partners) would begin almost as soon as the doors opened.

Our marketing plan was simple: we're smart, competent lawyers able to give our clients the same level of work they could get at a big firm. Our being women never entered into our "brand." But the universe had different plans.

Within six weeks of opening, we got a call late one afternoon from the local NBC affiliate asking if we would be the subject of a news story that evening. We did our best to be nonchalant, but as soon as we hung up the phone, we raced around the office, putting away boxes, making the lobby presentable, and pooling our cosmetics bags for a quick touch-up.

After the story about the "all-women law firm" ran, we received a flurry of e-mails, phone calls, and letters. We didn't appreciate until then how many people contemplate doing just what we did and how many people—men and women alike—would be inspired by a group of women who chose freedom over stability.

And then a second call came, this time from a local magazine editor. Would our firm be interested in being the subject of the feature story in the next month's edition focusing on the best lawyers in Dallas? We jumped at the chance and, again, were stunned and moved by the feedback. Somehow, we had become minor celebrities in the Dallas legal community, and for several months afterward, we were consistently introduced as "the all-women law firm featured in *D Magazine*."

The positive publicity was nice and helped give us a jump start, but the real work was still ahead. Looking back, there were a half-dozen tactics that—in retrospect—proved to be the difference between success and failure. If you're contemplating such a move, these are our recommendations:

1. *Surround yourself with competent administrative assistance* so you can serve your clients at the level you expect and they deserve. Do your homework, check references, and don't assume a productive individual in a large firm translates to competency in a smaller firm (where job descriptions can be much broader). Provide benefits to your employees so you can hire the most competent talent on the market.

2. *Get out in the community,* and announce your firm's existence, expertise, flexible rates, and anything else of importance and different from your prior firm. Don't assume someone isn't a referral source; people who would never refer to you when you were in a large firm will suddenly consider sending you work once you're in a different environment.

3. *If you don't have financial expertise to handle the firm's finances, get it.* A law firm is a business, and it needs to be run like one.

4. *Get a professional and user-friendly website.*

5. *Get women-owned certified,* and join groups that will help you use that as a marketing tool.

6. *Correct hiring mistakes sooner rather than later.* You can't hide bad employees in a small firm, so their potential negative effect is enormous.

Now, these are all very concrete suggestions, but as anybody will tell you, most of life's successes are more visceral than tangible. So here are our more philosophical offerings:

Don't be afraid to follow your instincts. Staying in that financially secure, but unhappy, position generally isn't better than taking the leap of faith to do something you're passionate about. Money usually follows passion, although it may take a couple of years (or more) to fully realize the financial gain. Staying in a job for fear of loss of income only leads to a stressful day-to-day existence and an unfulfilling job. And in today's economy, that "secure" job may not even have that going for it.

If you contemplate opening a firm with others, *make sure you have a track record of working with them so you know you have the same aspirations and philosophy for the firm.* If everyone is working toward the same goal, your likelihood of success is much greater. The last thing you want is a business divorce.

Opening your own firm is a leap of faith, and, once you're open, you will keep making them. In fact, your risk-taking muscles will get a workout like you never imagined. Some leaps will pay off, others won't. Let us share with you an example of one that paid off in spades:

Shortly after we opened, we were asked to sponsor an event honoring the 25 most influential women and the 25 largest women-owned businesses in the

Dallas/Fort Worth area. We didn't have the money, frankly, but we figured that by the time the bill came due, we would. So we signed on the dotted line and crossed our fingers.

At the event, when it was our turn (as one of the three sponsors) to hand out the awards, we gave a *Reader's Digest* version of our "creation story," and 1,000 pairs of hands began to clap. And they kept clapping. Slowly, the audience rose from their seats and gave us a standing ovation. As we gazed across the thundering sea of applause filling the room, we were finally as proud of ourselves as our supporters were.

It's been two years now, and the glow of our grand beginnings has been replaced by the reality of practicing law. But that's a good thing. As it turns out, we didn't have to wait six months for our first paycheck; it arrived after four months. We're now up to a dozen lawyers, our website is up, and there are no more packing boxes in the lobby.

But, amid the daily grind, we know we're more than just a law firm. Taber Estes Thorne & Carr is *our* law firm. And that's a distinction that will never be lost on us.

JANE TABER (J.D. 1982), **DAWN ESTES** (J.D. 1989), **JESSICA THORNE** (J.D. 1995), and **LORI CARR** (J.D. 1988) are founders and partners and **MELANIE OKON** (J.D. 1999) is a partner of Taber Estes Thorne & Carr in Dallas, Texas, founded in 2008. The firm focuses on representing businesses in litigation, business disputes, agreements, transactions, and employment matters. *www.taberestes.com*

- Kathleen Balthrop Havener -

"We not only can but we must *take charge of our careers and mold them into careers we are proud to pursue. . . . We* can *make our firms very pleasant places to work."*

I have bad news and good news. The bad news is that, having spent almost 100 percent of my extra-curricular time since I became a lawyer promoting diversity in the profession, I have concluded that—while women lawyers (and racially and ethnically diverse lawyers and openly gay and lesbian lawyers and lawyers with disabilities) are at least as good and often better than our male (and white straight able-bodied) colleagues—true diversity in the profession-at-large will not be achieved in our—or even perhaps in our daughters'—lifetimes. The large firms, the corporate law departments, even the mid-size regional firms that are the big fish in their own somewhat smaller ponds simply aren't moving quickly enough. The barriers are too deeply imbedded in the legal culture, and in the whole of American culture, for things to change on the timetable we might desire.

The good news, though, is very good. We not only can but we *must* take charge of our own careers and mold them into careers we are proud to pursue. We *must* take charge of our own lives and make them into lives we want to live. And there is even more good news. We *can* make our firms very pleasant places to work. We can represent the clients we choose (presuming they choose us). We can work among colleagues with whom we are comfortable and who will do anything and everything they can to ensure that we succeed. (Madeleine Albright said, "There is a special place in hell for women who don't help other women," and Gail Evans wrote *She Wins, You Win: The Most Important Rule Every Businesswoman Should Know*; both teach us that helping other women is to help ourselves.)

We can work near our children's schools and day care centers. We can exercise at times we choose and with nary a questioning look or a frown of disapproval. We can do our grocery shopping at respectable hours—and without racing around the store—and spend our weekends doing things that renew and restore us. We can start cooking again for our families and start eating things that are good and nutritious and hot that don't come out of boxes with fortune cookies or on plastic trays. We can take on the pro bono work we want to do without filling out forms and obtaining the approval of a committee. We can follow our own performance and control—to some extent—what we earn.

In response to your headshaking and disbelief, I quote a notable personage with whom we all are familiar: "Yes we can!" I know it. I'm doing it. In March 2008, with one client and one large complicated case, I started my own firm with my former firm's blessing, and I did it within four days. All my other clients followed me as soon as the announcement was made. Almost exactly six months later, my husband—a lawyer who is mobility-impaired—joined me as my law partner.

Because we can, we practice from our home and have thus reduced our carbon footprint dramatically. We do our own administrative tasks, but we don't pass on those costs to our clients. In fact, we don't charge for any "soft" costs—long-distance telephone calls, faxes, legal research—because those are built into our rates. To our relief, we don't need to record those costs in a manner that ties them to specific matters. We *have* hourly rates (because some clients still want them), but we prefer to work on a flat fee or retainer arrangement since—in theory at least—it provides a steadier income. Since our first two years coincided with the worst financial crisis in recent memory, we haven't yet begun to make the money we did while employed at big law firms, but we will, and the time isn't too far away. So long as our ship comes in and our accounts receivable are caught up *before* we have to stare down the wolf at our door, these two years of hardship have been worth the joy of being in charge of when and how I accomplish my work and how I live my everyday life.

The rewards of independence are immeasurable. Never do I wait to start a project until the deadline is so tight it squeaks. My ability to remain involved in the ABA and our state and local bar associations is limited only by whether or not the funds are available for me to participate. In fact, I manage my own schedule entirely—limited only by the courts. If you've never worked for yourself, it's impossible to imagine the freedom.

Of course, there is also fear. The pressures to keep the work pipeline full and the receivables actually *received* are sometimes a bit unmanageable. But there are things you can do to relieve the pressure once you have a few prosperous months under your belt. One is to open a second business account that I refer to as "the summer fund." We all know that—in the summer—legal work can slow down. Judges go on vacation, as do their law clerks. It's harder to schedule depositions because people's summer schedules so often conflict. If receivables tend to run dry at a particular time of year, keep three months of your payroll (or what you want to collect in a month) in the summer fund. When you deplete it, replenish it as soon as you can. It's akin to saving for your quarterly estimated tax payments—those dates come and the money needs to be there. Several personal injury lawyers I know put the summer fund aside when a contingency case is decided in their favor and they collect a sizeable fee. But knowing that the business has a cushion can truly ease your anxiety about an emergency computer crisis or suddenly learning that your malpractice premium is due in full when you thought you could pay by the quarter.

Another way to relieve your anxiety is to *network*! Not only does having a cup of coffee or lunch or attending a bar meeting or a community social event keep your name in the forefront of the minds of those with whom you interact there, it's also fun and even reassuring. You don't need your big firm's name behind you. Your own name and attitude inspire the confidence of those who will refer business to you. They trust you, not the name of your firm. They know their clients will be carefully handled because they know that you are a person they can trust.

I have nothing against big firms. They don't run their businesses or deal with employees the way I choose to (or the way I would if I ran one of them), but they're obviously filled with great lawyers and great people who have steady and reliable incomes and safe and secure lives. But they are certainly not the road to independence. They certainly don't "care" about you and what's happening in your day-to-day life. They shouldn't. It isn't their job.

A former colleague once said to me—with great sympathy—when I had to make a difficult choice between my home life and my work, "Everyone has a 'backstory,' and none of us knows the details of the next person's difficulties." But I do know my own backstory. I know what's going on in my life, when a nephew is getting married, or when a daughter is having a baby, even at least an inkling or a warning of when someone's health may need my attention.

Since I went out on my own, those details of my life that didn't matter to my employer before are now part of the calculus of every decision I make. My life—not just my career—is in my hands now. And the handling of my life is gentler now. I am more serene. I haven't cried in two and a half years about work, and I don't expect to anytime soon. One of my grown-up daughters calls it "Mom's 'No More Tears' Career." Enough said.

Best wishes.

KATHLEEN BALTHROP HAVENER is a member of The Havener Law Firm LLC in Cleveland, Ohio, where she practices complex commercial litigation, and her partner and husband focuses on business strategy, taxation, and transactional matters. She graduated from law school in 1991 and founded her firm in 2008. *www.havenerlaw.com*

- AMY B. BELLER -

"Sometimes we are stressed, to be sure, but . . . at least we are working for ourselves, building a practice and running it the way that we want, with the freedom to make our own decisions."

It is my honor and privilege to share with you my insights (for what they are worth) on forming my own law firm.

I am a 1992 graduate of Hofstra Law School and spent the first 12 years of practice at large firms in Manhattan before relocating to Florida. Despite doing "all the right things," that is, writing and speaking for the bar, networking, working hard, and taking on increasing responsibilities, equity partnership eluded me. After stints at two Florida firms, I found myself at a crossroads: take another non-equity position at yet another firm where, again, I would be working in a male-dominated bureaucracy where I might or might not be appreciated, or do something else. For years I had dreamed aloud with friends and some colleagues how great it would be to strike out on my own. But, being the major breadwinner in my family of three, with a mortgage and all of the expenses attendant to a comfortable life, I was petrified. I was generating some business of my own, but at that point it wasn't enough to be self-sustaining. How would I pay my bills? What would happen if I couldn't make it? Was I setting out on a course of financial ruin, not just for me but for my family?

I struggled with these concerns for weeks. It was one of the hardest times in my life. I vacillated on a daily, sometimes hourly, basis between taking one of several job offers or actually hanging a shingle. I would look at office space in the morning and interview at a firm in the afternoon. It was a difficult, schizophrenic time, and I knew that it was fear holding me back from making the decision I wanted to make. Although I had a lot of family support, I discounted the confidence my family expressed in my ability to develop a successful solo practice as either their not understanding the law firm business or their being unrealistic about my potential.

The turning point for me was a weekend away with women
friends knew about my struggle, and because many of them are in
field, I was willing to hear what they thought. To a (wo)man, each of my
friends urged me to take the risk of starting my own practice. They reasoned
that, if it didn't work out, my skills, background, and experience would be
intact, and I would be just as able to land a job in six months or a year if I had
to. They argued that I had laid all of the groundwork for a successful law practice and that if I didn't give it a shot at age 43 (with one or two large clients
that I knew would follow me), I never would. I credit my friends for giving me
the courage to do what I knew in my heart I should do.

Once the decision was made, I felt like a huge weight had been lifted, and I
knew pretty clearly what had to be done. First, I contacted some colleagues who
had solo or small firms and asked for advice on everything from stationery to
computers to professional liability insurance. I found a reasonably-priced office
sublet in a suite with a small firm, also owned by women who seemed to share
my basic values and professed a willingness to give me guidance as needed.
Wanting to keep overhead low, I made arrangements with my new suitemates
to use their phone system, their copy machine, and their office furniture, and I
decided I would handle all of the administrative work myself until I had some
money coming in. I opted to purchase a billing program (TABS) that I already
knew so that I would have one less thing to learn, and I got from a client the
name of a bookkeeper who set me up on QuickBooks. I opted to splurge on
beautiful, engraved stationery and business cards, so that people would not
think I was practicing law out of my kitchen. I also decided to list my new firm
with Martindale-Hubbell online, which is expensive but, in my view, necessary
if you want to establish a higher-end practice. I sent out announcements to
everyone on my contact list and then some. I used GoDaddy to create my own
(albeit simple) website.

To my great surprise, once news of my new venture spread, I started getting
work in from a variety of sources—former colleagues in New York, larger
firms in the area (referring smaller cases or cases on which they had conflicts), even friends and family. I was astounded at and moved by the number
of people who seemed to want to help me get on my feet. I also learned that
there apparently had been a lot of work over the years that had not been
steered my way simply because the referral source had some issue or other
with the firm employing me at that time. Before I knew it, I was in need of

an assistant, and I hired a recent college graduate who would be headed to law school as a summer clerk at a very reasonable rate. This gave me some time to find the right paralegal/assistant, and I ended up hiring someone I had worked with before at a prior firm. Pretty soon, I was using the services of a contract attorney to assist me and had more work than I ever thought I would in the first year of business.

Two years later, my firm has grown to two partners (a close friend whose practice was a perfect fit with mine joined me several months ago), two full-time paralegals, one contract paralegal, and plans to hire an associate attorney. My partner and I generally work 12-hour days and frequently work on the weekend just to keep up with our caseload. We have become more strategic in our marketing efforts (i.e., which bar functions, social events, and networking lunches we attend), and we share the administrative work between us. Sometimes we are stressed, to be sure, but at those times we try to remind ourselves and each other that at least we are working for ourselves, building a practice and running it the way that we want, with the freedom to make our own decisions. Although we have been approached by firms inter-ested in having us join them, we wouldn't consider giving up what we have even for the attractive conveniences and comforts of a big firm.

So, having gone through all this, the best advice I can really offer is this: don't let fear stop you. If you have paid your dues by establishing yourself as a qualified and experienced lawyer, and you have been good to clients and friends throughout your career, the probability is that you will be successful in your own practice. Of course, it's wise to have a backup plan and to be con-servative and deliberate in your initial expenditures. Solicit help and advice from others—you will be surprised at how happy people are to help you. Be flexible in the cases you take early on while building your practice, but don't be afraid to decline a matter that you are not comfortable with. Read books on starting your own law practice, taking the suggestions you find sound and rejecting the others (not all plans fit all practices). Don't be shy about telling people you meet in your "regular" life that you are a lawyer with your own firm and what kind of work you do. Make sure you acknowledge referrals appropriately, and keep the referral source apprised of your success on the matter. Don't be reluctant to admit when you need help, and know where to find it. Keep everything in perspective—even if your law firm venture doesn't work, it isn't the end of the world. And, finally, although it isn't always easy, try to keep your sense of humor—it's gotten me through a lot of very trying times.

Best wishes for your success.

AMY B. BELLER is a partner of Beller Smith, P.L. in Boca Raton, Florida, where she focuses her practice in the area of trust, estate, and guardianship litigation. She graduated from law school in 1992, founded her solo firm in 2008, and co-founded Beller Smith in 2010. *www.bellersmith.com*

- NICOLE NEHAMA AUERBACH -

"When three other like-minded large firm lawyers started talking about a new firm to offer alternative billing arrangements and provide value to clients facing complex litigation, I knew that it was a once-in-a-lifetime opportunity."

If you are reading this letter, it means that somewhere deep in your soul you crave change and adventure, and for that I applaud you. But let me get one thing out on the table from the beginning: starting a law practice is not for the faint-hearted. It is a remarkably amazing experience, but stress-free it is not. If you choose to read on, terrific. If not, I completely understand. There's something comforting about a 2,000+ hours/year billable requirement.

After 15 years of practicing law at a large law firm in Chicago, I decided to leave my cushy partner office and put it all on the line for something I could call "my own." The truth is, I had become disenchanted with the model that had sustained large firms for years. I could not understand why clients would blindly accept annual increases in lawyers' rates, with no commensurate benefit for the added cost. I strongly believed (and still do) that the billable hour model creates an inherent conflict between lawyer and client, as it is in the client's best interest to work efficiently and resolve litigation quickly, while the opposite is true for the lawyer. And so, when three other like-minded large firm lawyers started talking about starting a new firm to offer alternative billing arrangements and provide value to clients facing complex litigation, I knew that it was a once-in-a-lifetime opportunity.

Now, about two and a half years into "the plunge," I can assure you that it was well worth it. Despite having had 15 wonderful years at my prior firm, I can honestly say that I have never looked back. There were, however, some things that I wish I had known when we started this endeavor, a bunch of things we did right, and some not so well. Keep in mind that this is based on my experience only—so take it with a healthy-sized grain of salt.

A Little Background
When the four of us started Valorem (it means "value" in Latin) in January 2008, people thought we were crazy. When I mentioned that it was our mission to "kill the billable hour," there were several people who thought we were flat out mad. Two years and several hundred front page mainstream press articles later, I can only surmise that we were simply ahead of our time. I'm not sure if I mentioned that my other three partners were men, all 10 years older than me. Luckily, despite knowing only one of them well, we all get along splendidly. So that's the first lesson:

1. Make sure that you not only like your partners but that you like them enough to see them day in, day out, good mood or bad. A good test is this: if you were stuck in an airport with your partners because some volcano in Iceland spewed ash that delayed your flight for, um, about 16 more hours, would you be able to resist wringing their collective necks?

Space
Because our practice highlights collaboration at every level, we chose to build out two floors in a tower of an old Chicago building. The lesson there:

2. Estimate that it will cost at least two to three times more than you were told or anticipated. Also, think about how you want your firm to be in several years, not just right then. Luckily we planned to plan to grow, and now, with nine attorneys, paralegals, and staff, we are thankful we got the extra space. Still bummed we cut the shower though. Oh, and don't let the guys pick the paint color or the furniture. Plumbing and piping, by all means, but anything aesthetic, nope.

Expenses
3. Whatever business plan you first drew up, slash in half your expected revenue and double your expenses. Then, and only then, might you be in the ballpark of how things will likely go at the start. Also, even if there are only a few of you, have at least one person in charge of approving expenditures over a certain dollar amount. Otherwise, all of the partners will decide on their own that they need another white board, and before you know it, you've spent $50,000 on stuff you probably didn't need right then. And don't let the guys make the ultimate decision on technology—we have more flat screen TVs than a Best Buy showroom. Remember, you are no longer living with a large firm budget. If you do well, all that stuff can come in due time.

Getting Paid

4. Probably the biggest shock to overcome was the decrease in income in the beginning of the endeavor. Realistically, I would say that you will need at least two years to really see the revenue side of things. As I told my friends, I own a lot of nice orange chairs. Hopefully my kids will enjoy sitting on them instead of going to college. The bottom line is that as the owner, you get paid last. There were months when we didn't get a distribution, and those were very tough months. (See #1 above again).

Have Fun

5. Yes, owning your own firm is a serious prospect, but why bother if you can't have a little fun? For us, it was important to have a very non–law firm website. We also created programs like "Lunch with a Cool Person," where once a month we invite a cool person to come to speak with the whole firm over lunch. We also have weekly "collabostorms" on Fridays over lunch where we discuss an issue relating to a case or the firm or use it as a training opportunity for our younger lawyers. We also entered the *ABA Journal's* "Peeps in Law Part Deux" contest, where we had to create a diorama with a legal theme, made out of Peeps, those marshmallow sugar concoctions you see around Easter. Our "Trial of Former Illinois Governor Rod Peepovich" not only made the top five, but won first prize after national voting!

Communication Is Key

6. I have always believed that there are few problems that can't be solved with adequate communication. That is true tenfold in a new firm. Do not assume that everyone is on the same page, and do not assume that everyone understands the mission, the passion, and the goals. Especially as you grow—we doubled in less than two years—make sure that you keep people informed about the mission, the expectations, and what is needed to make the business a success.

It's Well Worth It

Despite the hard work, the responsibility, and the moments of stress, it has been extremely rewarding, and I am so proud I did it. My parting words: (a) don't sweat the small stuff; (b) vow to compromise; (c) laugh, play music, have fun; (d) make client service your priority, and you will do just fine; (e) it's a work in progress—if you have to tweak something, tweak; and finally, (f) build in some "me" time—your health and well-being are critical to the success of the firm.

Best of luck!

NICOLE NEHAMA AUERBACH is a founding member of Valorem Law Group in Chicago, Illinois, where she handles litigation in federal and state courts and in arbitrations across the country. She graduated from law school in 1993 and founded her firm in 2008. *www.valoremlaw.com*

- APRIL L. HOLLINGSWORTH -

"I am still exploring this world I've created for myself, enjoying taking on Goliaths, and getting better and better at what I do."

Everyone has their own reasons for considering starting their own firm, and it is, indeed, a very personal decision. One should thoroughly weigh the pros and cons from an individual perspective before taking the step. I can tell you that it was the best decision I have ever made.

I started my solo practice a year and a half ago. I had been working for a small firm for six years and had become a partner (one of four, with two associates). We practiced plaintiffs' employment law, and for six years, I loved it. But no matter what I did, I never quite got the feeling that my partners and I were on the same page with regard to what we were trying to accomplish and how we were going to go about it. In retrospect, I believe our priorities were just different, and the other partners and I just did not understand where each other was coming from.

Eventually, things came to a head when the other three partners asked me to withdraw from representing a client that I had represented for four years. As with most of my clients, I was emotionally invested in that particular client's case. We had won an ERISA case on his behalf in federal court and were pursuing different claims based upon a unique theory in state court. We had always known the state law case was a bit of a long shot, but if we won, we would make good law. Pursuing it was never a financial calculation for me, but for my partners, who were not working on the case with me, it was. For reasons that were never clear to me (we took many other long shots), my partners decided they were done with the case.

The problem was, the case was before the Tenth Circuit Court of Appeals at that time, and our opening brief was due in a matter of days when the other partners asked me to withdraw. I knew that to do so would have left my client in a very bad position, and I simply could not bring myself to do it. Instead, I recruited an empathetic friend to co-counsel with me on the case to placate my partners, and I spent the next two weekends drafting the brief, as it was not possible for my friend to get up to speed on the case in the short amount of time we had to file it. Meanwhile, it was suddenly crystal clear to me that I had to leave the firm and go out on my own. I never wanted to be put in that situation again, where I felt I had to sneak around to do what my heart and my head told me was the right thing. By the time the reply brief was due on the appeal, I was on my own.

I had never argued a case before the court of appeals, and in that particular appeal, I had not asked for oral argument, mostly because of my client's limited funds. Much to my surprise and delight, the court asked for oral argument on its own volition. The friend who joined me in the case and I went to Denver for the argument, together with our husbands, on our own dime. While I was waiting to give the argument, I looked around and realized that although there were several other women who sat at counsel table during oral argument on other cases, I was the only woman to present the argument during my session. I also realized that had I remained at my old firm, I likely would have also sat at counsel table, too, while the (male) senior partner at the firm presented the argument. I have never been so proud of my decision to go out on my own as I was at that moment.

There have been many other surprising benefits of going solo. I did not expect, for instance, that I would appreciate so much the ability to work when my brain is on, which is generally much later in the day than for most people. I generally spend my mornings working out or running errands. I also did not anticipate the difference being solo would make in the relationships I have with my clients. Because I now choose which cases I take, I feel like all of my clients are my partners and my friends. I do not work for anyone just for the money. The relationships that I have with my clients have made me a better lawyer because I want to try that much harder for them. In turn, my opposing counsel often recognizes my passion for what I do, and they have become my biggest referral source. But the most significant benefit to me of being my own boss is actually the one I was going for: having the freedom to tilt at windmills to my heart's content. It feels so good to be able to take a case because it's important, because I believe in my client, and because we should win, even if objectively, the odds are against us. As one might expect given this philosophy, I have had heartbreaking losses in addition to exhilarating wins (and settlements) but best of all, no regrets.

From all of this, you might correctly conclude that I am not a particularly business-minded person, and I acknowledge that the extent to which I detest the administrative requirements of running a business came as something of a surprise to me. I found myself, for instance, drafting a summary judgment motion as a way of procrastinating billing clients. The best advice I could give someone who identifies with my motivation for starting her own practice is to plan for this likely contingency in advance. Get a billing program in place, and get someone other than yourself to handle your billing (and other accounting) before you open your doors because in my experience, as soon as the doors are open, there are plenty of motions to be drafted or letters to be written or other ways to avoid doing that which you hate. And realize that you may never get rich practicing law to fulfill your heart but that the rewards are much more than financial.

I cannot say whether I see myself doing this forever. I can imagine a day when the adversarial nature of the business or the heartbreaks will become tiresome, and I'll think of some less stressful way to make a living. I have also considered that perhaps being a judge would be a better way to make the world a fairer place. But for now, I am still exploring this world I've created for myself, enjoying taking on Goliaths, and getting better and better at what I do. I've got a ways to go to become the best I can be, but that's my goal, and if I ever get there, maybe I'll look for something else to do. Meanwhile, I'm still waiting on that decision from the Tenth Circuit, but no matter the outcome, it was all worth the ride.

Good luck to you on your voyage.

APRIL L. HOLLINGSWORTH is the owner of Hollingsworth Law Office, LLC in Salt Lake City, Utah, where she focuses on plaintiffs' employment law. She graduated from law school in 1996 and founded her firm in 2008. *www.aprilhollingsworthlaw.com*

- KATHERINE E. FONG -

"I am just about to the point of needing to take on a part-time paralegal, so I am going to look into that shortly."

I am no stranger to hard work. Ever since I was 16, I have had a job, often two, and for a few crazy periods, even three. It became apparent just how hard I have worked when filling out my bar exam application—I had to attach three extra appendices just to list my past jobs in the last 10 years. Two of the three years of law school I worked full time and went to class at night. All of this work experience played a large role in my decision to open my own practice. I had really had my share of answering to others, and I longed to be my own boss!

Prior to law school I worked for a year at a prominent personal injury law firm in Manhattan, and I found I really enjoyed that type of law. Since the majority of my part-time jobs over the years were as a restaurant waitress, I developed a real knack for working with the public, and I enjoy helping people. During and after law school I worked in bankruptcy law and construction law, but I knew plaintiff personal injury was what I liked most. My husband, whom I met in law school, is also a personal injury attorney at a large firm in Hartford, Connecticut, so with his backing I decided in the spring of 2008 to open my own personal injury practice. Fong and Associates, LLC opened in 2008 out of my house, as I wanted to try to keep overhead costs low. I had simultaneously placed an ad on Craigslist looking for a conference room I could rent out on an as-needed basis, and a Hartford area bail bondsman responded and offered his conference room. I have yet to utilize that conference room, as all of my clients have preferred that I come to them and either meet at their house or a nearby coffeehouse, but it is good to know I have that room if and when I need it.

In the beginnin,g business was slow. In Connecticut, where I practice, there is no "no-fault" threshold, which means anyone can bring a personal injury claim resulting from a car accident no matter how big or small the damage/injuries.

As you can imagine then, the personal injury practice area is saturated with attorneys. As stated earlier, my husband works at one of the largest, most well-known personal injury firms, and you can turn on the television and see one of their ads any hour of the day. I had to brainstorm on how I could compete with these big firms and bring in business. At first I tried both local newspapers and larger regional ones, but these became costly without a lot of results. So after a time I canceled them, and my first few clients came from acquaintances.

My big break came when a former co-worker of mine needed some legal advice regarding his son. I helped him at no cost, and since he had recently joined an insurance brokerage firm, as a thank you he began to recommend me to clients of his who would call to report getting into a car accident. If they were not at fault, injured, and thinking that they may be looking to hire an attorney, he referred them to me. Then business really started to come through the door!

Since then I have had to hustle. I was and still am the attorney, paralegal, case manager, and secretary of Fong and Associates, LLC, but I can't emphasize enough how great it feels to work hard and then to have the satisfaction both personally and financially of seeing the fruits of your labor. I can tell you that as a solo practitioner, you have to be willing to go above and beyond. For instance, my cell phone is both my business and personal phone, which can be both a blessing and a curse: a blessing in that I can get calls and messages directly and don't have to wait to get back to the office to receive my messages; a curse at times when clients take getting a hold of you so easily for granted and call or text you during the early morning hours or late at night.

Regardless of how it impacts my personal life, I try to encourage the feeling in my clients that their case is my only case, so that I exceed their expectations and inspire them after their case is finished to rave to their friends about how much of a "hands on" attorney I was. Some of my clients have remarked how they have often felt lost in the shuffle of the bigger firms in prior dealings with attorneys, and they liked how I got right back to them whenever they had a question. I have some tough, frustrating days, though, when I am negotiating two or three cases and a client is calling me constantly to see if an offer has come in on his case. On those days I long for the buffer of a secretary to field that call, but again, it comes with the territory of being a solo practitioner.

I cannot speak to other practice areas or locations, but my two best sources of business, aside from word of mouth recommendations from past clients, have come from joining a variety of networking groups and developing relationships with auto insurance agents. It is imperative as a solo practitioner, especially a woman in what is a male-dominated practice area, to get your name out there. Every chance you get you should utilize networking happy hours, referral groups, chambers of commerce, etc.

Another tip I can give from my own experience is to be sure to have a strong firm website. If someone recommends you to someone else, and your name is not familiar, then the person seeking representation is most likely going to look you up on the web to see what experience you have and your practice areas. That may give them the first impression of your ability before they even contact you. Also, when one of your cases wraps up and your client is happy, ask them to write a short testimonial. In this day and age, you can find a review of pretty much any kind of business online, and having testimonials on your website shows not only you are a successful attorney, but also that you have experience and other people have taken a chance on you! I have seen some of my fellow solos' websites, and I have cringed over misspellings and poor grammar. Be sure to include relevant key words so that when searches are done regarding your practice area, your website will pop up.

Looking back, I am pretty happy with the choices I have made and the progress Fong and Associates has made in the two years it has been open. My business plan for the future is to continue trying my hardest to get my name out there any way I can and to give each of my clients the type of attention that makes them feel like their case is my only case. I am just about to the point of needing to take on a part-time paralegal, so I am going to look into that shortly. I am excited and looking forward to Fong and Associates, LLC continuing to grow and expand for many years to come. If you are thinking of opening your own practice, be prepared for a lot of hard work and to have to rub elbows with a lot of people to get your name and your firm's name out there. I can tell you it pays off and is *so* worth the effort!

KATHERINE E. FONG is the owner and founder of Fong and Associates, LLC in Windsor Locks, Connecticut, where she focuses on personal injury law. She graduated from law school in 2004 and opened her firm in 2008. *www.fonglawct.com*

CHAPTER 7

2009–2010 PLUS ONE

Diversifying the Practice Areas, Broadening the Seniority of Founders

---

"In 1929, Virginia Woolf published her famous essay 'A Room of One's Own,' urging that a woman needed money and a place to truly call her own—financial and personal independence if you will— to develop intellectually and flourish as a writer. My response to the financial crisis some 80 years later was to start 'a firm of my own.'"

—Christine C. Franklin

The broad distribution of writers among all age groups continues in this last group of 17 writers. In this group, seven writers had 20 or more years in law before they started their own practices. A number are younger; seven writers founded firms with less than 10 years' experience.

The recession appears in several of these letters as motivators. Yet these writers are buoyed by their enthusiasm for their new ventures. Some describe changes in the profession as motivators to leave traditional firms. In the words of one writer, "the legal services climate is changing, and a smaller firm allows us to provide the same . . . client service with greater flexibility." Another explained, "we are not distracted by the competition to log in more billable hours or generate more business than our colleagues."

This group of letters includes some from women who left in-house positions. One salutes her champion, also a former corporate attorney, who is turning the firm over to her as he retires. And during these two difficult years, just as in good times, women altered their practices in order to meet the needs of family members who need them.

Practical details are spelled out with care in several letters. One of these points out, "[W]hatever the reason, there is ultimately only one way (not 50) to leave your firm: well prepared." Details of financial challenges in meeting firm expenses are frequently addressed in this set of letters.

Regardless of the form of practice, or the time in a woman's career when she may break out of traditional practice, these letter writers both live and teach the fundamental point about the independence of women in private practice. "Expecting others to take care of your career, promote you, or make your professional dreams come true is only a crutch. You need to be able to stand alone."

As if to set the stage for the decade just begun, the final letter announces, with a click of ruby slippers, the exhilaration of realizing the power of self-determination and the freedom of starting a new firm based on years of relentless dedication to achieving success in a traditional firm. The writer founded her firm on 1/1/11.

- MARIAN COVER DOCKERY -

"Because I am a senior lawyer . . . I have built an incredible network . . . that has proven to be an invaluable base of referrals. Starting my own firm was the logical next step...in this bad economy."

Let there be no doubt that starting my own firm has been for me a wonderful journey, replete with more rewards than I could ever have imagined. Because I am a senior lawyer (over 50) and started my own firm just about one year ago, my decision was an easy one. First, I am an empty nester, as my daughter has completed college and her master's degree and my son just completed college. This makes starting a law practice much easier than it would have been if I had done so 10 years ago. Second, I have worked in the corporate arena, government law offices, and corporate management, which gave me advantages in starting my own firm. I have built an incredible network of lawyers, in-house and in law firms, that has proven to be an invaluable base of referrals. Starting my own firm was the logical next step and in this bad economy, I believe it was the right decision.

I started my firm as a solo in July of 2009. My partner joined me in January of 2010. When I started my firm, I thought that securing clients would be the biggest challenge. Instead, that has been the least of my worries so far. The biggest challenge is juggling handling the business side of the practice and practicing law. Unlike a firm, you do not have the support staff, the mailroom, and the on-site computer support to rely on when your computer blows up, nor do you have the secretary who is always available right next door to assist you with copying, scanning, and faxing. Although my firm has a paralegal and legal secretary, my partner and I have a virtual law office, and everyone is off site. Before you hang up your own shingle, understand that you must learn to effectively delegate and identify the experts to assume responsibility for those tasks that you are not capable of performing. Identifying those key persons who will be a permanent part of your law firm business, including the accountant, the tax attorney, the webmaster, and the paralegals, is a much more difficult task than you may think. If you are solo, and many attorneys do choose this path, I say to you good luck. It is not a bad choice, but I discovered that for me having a partner has more positives than negatives. You have a sounding board, more expertise, more capital, more ideas, and another source of referrals, not to mention more moral support. Also, practicing became more fun. At the end of the day, it is so important to have someone you can call and discuss some of the crazy events of the day.

Our firm eliminated the biggest challenge for most law firms—overhead! We reduced it substantially by forming a virtual firm. We pay for conference space and a receptionist service and work from our home offices. This is not always the most ideal situation, but at least we are able to pay our bills. The downside of the virtual office is it sometimes means doing virtually everything yourself. You have to replenish your own supplies, mail the brief at the all-night post office, and do your own typing and labeling of exhibits if you are working past midnight.

When you start your own firm, your income will not be as much as your income with a larger firm, unless you get incredibly lucky and land that *big* case right away. Another challenge is that you must research insurance and disability, as well as other benefits, software, and equipment for your office (computers, scanners, faxes, and copying machines), but this is what it takes to run a business. Some expenses may disappear because you cannot afford them, such as CLE conferences to exotic places, but other expenses will not disappear, such as your bar dues, which you must pay for out of your own pocket if your firm has not generated enough capital to cover these costs. Firm retreats to glorious cities are also a thing of the past.

But the upside is that at the end of the day, the practice is yours; you make the decisions, and you don't have to tolerate a lot of personalities that leave much to be desired. You are in charge, and if you are willing to put in the hours and work like a Trojan, I think you will find that the positives far out-weigh the negatives when you start your own law firm.

Best wishes and good luck!

MARIAN COVER DOCKERY is managing member of Marian Dockery & Associates LLC in Atlanta, Georgia, where she focuses on labor and employment law and diversity training. She graduated from law school in 1977 and founded her firm in 2009. *www.mdockerylaw.com*

- Eileen E. Buholtz -

*"Managing your law practice is your best
tool to make you a great lawyer."*

You Are in Charge

Managing your law practice is your best tool to make you a great lawyer. You should not advise your business clients until you have managed your own business.

Your Law Practice as a Business:

1. Follow the law on everything.

    a. File your business and personal tax returns, and pay your taxes.

    b. Comply with all copyright laws, and pay for all software subscriptions and licenses.

    c. Comply with all laws including income tax, withholding, employment, employee benefits, workers' compensation, and wage-and-hour.

    d. Pay your employees on the books as employees, make all appropriate withholdings, and file all appropriate reports.

    e. Require all hourly employees to turn in weekly time sheets (no pro forma sheets), and document that they take all mandated breaks.

    f. Insist that all documents be properly signed, notarized, and/or witnessed.

2. Set goals for everything, and measure your progress. Establish an annual budget, and compare income and outflow against it monthly. Monitor the amount and type of legal matters that come in. Track your marketing efforts with objective results.

3. Develop antennae for mistakes, shortcuts, and failing health or mental acuity in your office. Document your concerns, make decisions, and take action.

4. Choose a business entity that insulates your practice from your personal assets, and maintain sufficient malpractice insurance.

5. Market yourself, and read everything by Seth Godin on that topic.

6. Have a succession plan. If you are a solo practitioner, properly authorize back-up counsel, and nominate an appropriate executor in your will with authority to wind up your practice.

7. Establish an operating account into which you deposit all of your business income and out of which you pay only your business expenses.

8. Open a line of credit to cover operating-account cash shortfalls, and protect against overdrafts.

9. Retain a CPA to do your income taxes and a qualified bookkeeper to do the data entry; monitor the work of both.

10. Maintain a schedule of deadlines for tax and related filings and due dates for bills.

11. Maintain written bookkeeping procedures that include pertinent names, mailing addresses, account numbers, contacts, URLs, user names, passwords for each vendor and authority, and descriptions of how all important bookkeeping activities are done.

12. Personally know where things are filed in the bookkeeper's office.

13. Open all bank statements and invoices, and review all transactions. Between statements, go online to spot-check account activities. Inspect the images of canceled checks and the endorsements on the back.

14. Use computerized practice management and time-and-billing systems. Know personally how to use them.

15. Regularly monitor everyone's use of time. Require that all timekeepers contemporaneously record their time and that they personally input their own time into the system.

16. Maintain a database for conflicts checks with all names associated with all files, and require all staff and colleagues to keep it up to date.

17. Run a conflicts check before accepting any new matter, and document that the search was done.

18. Regularly review all work delegated to other attorneys and staff. Delegating relieves you of only 50 percent of the work and none of the responsibility for it.

19. Look at every vendor and contract to see if you can get it for less or do without. Review all contracts whether new, renewal, or replacement for "gotchas" and "oh by the ways." Usually your current system or subscriptions can already do what is being offered.

20. Retain a software consultant to handle the technicalities and capabilities of your electronic equipment and to educate you about them.

21. Be organized, and require everyone in your office to be the same. The goal is retrievability, not elaborate filing systems. Live by the advice in Margaret Spencer Dixon's *So Little Time, So Much Paper* (ABA, 2000 (CD/MP3)). Organization starts at the top.

22. Subscribe to *Law Office Administrator* (www.ardmorepublishing.com) and read every issue.

Your Attorney Trust Account:

1. Have written rules for use of the attorney trust account, and periodically review them with the bookkeeper, staff, and colleagues. At a minimum:

   a. No check can be written on the trust account without *cleared* funds on account for *that particular* matter.

   b. Spot-check deposit slips for the date and time that funds were deposited, and compare to those the dates and times that checks were written.

   c. Know your trust account bank's rules for clearing checks. Never let go of a trust account check until the funds for it have *cleared* into your trust account. Either have the client deliver the funds to you in advance with enough time to clear or pay the sums from your operating account and reimburse yourself from trust once the client's funds have cleared into the trust account.

2. Honor all commitments to hold checks and documents in escrow until they are released therefrom.

3. Use a bank for your trust account that is different from that for your operating account.

Your Law Practice as an Employer:

1. Require all job applicants, including attorney-applicants, to submit a signed job application in addition to submitting their résumé. On the application, ask about previous positions, reasons for leaving, references,

professional credentials, disciplinary history, and all prior names used. Call and talk to prospects on the phone before scheduling face-to-face interviews to trim the short list of candidates. In interviewing, demonstrate that you are someone worth working for and also that the applicant is worth hiring.

2. Conduct a professional background check on anyone to whom you are going to offer employment. Check under all names the applicant has used, and do your own Internet search.

3. At the time of hire, require proof that the person has the right to work in the United States, and fill out the appropriate paperwork.

4. Have a written employment manual that describes your policies on (for example) vacation, sick days, health insurance, retirement plans, permitted deductions from pay, lunch breaks, pay periods, accrual of benefits, confidentiality regarding clients and their legal matters, use of cell phones, computers, and the Internet during office hours, and the use of social media at any time. Go over the manual item by item, and have the employee initial the important provisions. Have the employee sign the confidentiality agreement and the receipt for a copy of the handbook.

5. Keep employee records in a separate folder for each employee.

6. Use a reputable payroll company for your payroll, and spot-check the accuracy thereof. You are responsible for any inaccuracies.

7. Require that all staff including attorneys sign a confidentially agreement that forbids disclosure of work activities, especially via social media.

8. Spot-check your employees' use of office equipment (especially computers, e-mail, Internet connections, and social media).

9. Require that everyone maintain written office procedures about work items that they handle. This information is essential in training new employees.

10. Keep an open door. Always keep your cool. You are responsible for making sure your instructions are understood and that everything is in its place.

Billing and Invoicing:

1. Cross-check the matters in your practice management system with those in your accounting system to prevent files from languishing and billings from escaping deposit into the firm account.

2. Keep an accurate inventory of all hard copy files with their location.

3. Personally review every bill before it goes out, looking at it from the client's perspective for form, content, and tone. Double-check the billing rate.

EILEEN E. BUHOLTZ is the sole member of the firm Connors & Corcoran PLLC in Rochester, New York, where she focuses on insurance defense liability and coverage litigation. She graduated from law school in 1979 and acquired sole ownership of the firm in 2009. *www.connorscorcoran.com*

- CHRISTINE C. FRANKLIN -

---

*"An Andy Warhol quote perhaps will have meaning for you as well:
'They always say that time changes things, but you actually have to
change them yourself.'"*

A Firm of One's Own

In 1929, Virginia Woolf published her famous essay "A Room of One's Own,"
urging that a woman needed money and a place to truly call her own—
financial and personal independence if you will—to develop intellectually
and flourish as a writer.

My response to the financial crisis some 80 years later was to start "a firm
of my own." I like to say that I was "institutionalized" for the first 30 years
of my legal career: I had worked for large institutions and, for the most part,
represented institutions. In fairness to those institutions, I got wonderful
experience and was able to affect the public good along the way. But the economic downturn impacted me negatively in 2009, and starting my own firm
seemed the best alternative despite the challenges. Solo and small firms can
truly service clients and do so much more nimbly than larger firms with their
entrenched salary structures and hourly requirements.

I had done the paperwork to set up a law firm in the form of a limited liability
company in 2004, so that already was in place. It was activated in 2009,
and articles of organization were added. Many of the mechanics of my firm
evolved on ad hoc bases as needs arose. In retrospect, this was good because
it avoided doing and paying for things that may have been inappropriate and
unnecessary at the time.

Frustratingly, what my accountant has dubbed the "rule of two" inevitably
sets in, meaning that it takes two or three attempts to get most things done.
For example, my initial effort to get malpractice insurance yielded a policy
with an exclusion for title agent activities although I specifically applied for
that coverage. Luckily, the Illinois State Bar Association offered the coverage

I wanted, and I was able to switch. But then the final hurdle of waiting for the state to approve my actual registered title agent application extended from three weeks to three months. Eventually, it all got done.

Computer issues have been too numerous to detail. Suffice it to say that I have heard worse and that a certain sense of survivability sets in when one's hard drive dies the week before Microsoft's Windows 7 is launched and it is virtually impossible to do anything other than wait. Good tech support is an ongoing challenge for small businesses, and that extends to finding a developer for a website.

Finding clients, of course, is the primary challenge, and marketing occupies a significant amount of time and energy. Referrals have been important in launching my solo practice and remind me of an experienced large firm lawyer whom I met years ago through networking. He established his own very successful firm on the basis of conflict referrals, always returning the client to the referring attorney.

Diverse experiences in my 30 years of practice have given me something akin to a general counsel perspective and enable me to offer clients pragmatic strategic advice. I am a former government prosecutor, business litigator in private practice, and in-house attorney. I have taken on many unique legal issues, ranging from criminal arguments to the California Supreme Court and insolvency questions regarding Executive Life Insurance Company to the human and property losses suffered by a business on 9/11.

These were wonderful experiences, which gave me valuable skill sets, but I am fond of saying that I never would wish the serious problems my previous clients had on others. This firm is starting from the bottom up, focusing on individuals and businesses for whom I can provide quality legal services and with whom I can build a relationship of trust, which will yield more opportunities to serve them either in their individual or business capacities. Because agreements are at the core of most personal and business relationships, and a significant part of my career has been spent litigating or negotiating contracts, part of my initial focus has been on all the financial agreements individuals and businesses need. I also remain a business litigator and point person for developing best practices for electronic document management, electronic discovery, and social media usage before and during litigation. Admissions in multiple jurisdictions enhance my capabilities.

Beyond referrals, how do individuals and businesses who will value the skills I bring and the services I can provide discover me? As you can imagine, networking occupies a significant amount of time. Some of it is purely social. Some involves writing and speaking on timely topics, which, most recently for me, has been on the financial crisis and electronic discovery. Opportunities to do this occur through the ABA's Section of Administrative Law and Regulatory Practice, of which I have been an active member for more than 15 years, through business contacts, and through my own firm.

A website also enhances discoverability, so creating a website is a focus of my efforts. A related goal is to include a blog to share thoughts on developments in a timely manner with a wider audience.

At the same time this outreach has been going on, there have been interesting "lessons learned." Pushing ahead on efforts to share ideas and widen my audience has meant learning to say "no" more readily, as difficult as that is. I have effectively said "no" to some referrals by giving realistic assessments of the costs and demands of legal services. It also has meant being less responsive to well-meaning friends or family, as well as turning down some charitable and professional opportunities. In each instance, the realization prevailed that it was just not worthwhile to take on, or continue on with, a project when balanced against the demands of developing my firm and practicing law.

Happily, other serendipitous opportunities came along that more than compensated for the doors that closed. For example, after writing a book about e-discovery and data mapping became incompatible with building a solo practice, the e-discovery conversation broadened to include social media, and opportunities to speak and write shorter pieces on those developments arose. In addition, other opportunities presented themselves, such as writing this piece and a chapter on financial and banking developments for the annual survey published by the Administrative Law Section.

Frankly, for me, one of the main attractions of the legal profession always has been the ability to continue practicing. This "firm of my own" is very much a work in progress, but it is important to me to try to stay the course and build a business to sustain myself. Meantime, an Andy Warhol quote I read in early 2010 resonated with me and perhaps will have meaning for you as well: "They always say that time changes things, but you actually have to change them yourself."

CHRISTINE C. FRANKLIN is principal at Franklin Law, LLC in Chicago, Illinois, where she focuses on commercial disputes and transactions, as well as regulatory issues. She graduated from law school in 1979 and founded her firm in 2009.

- Suzanne Villalon-Hinojosa -

"There must be 50 reasons to leave a law firm. But for me, there was only one: the ugly realization of a glass ceiling."

Kicking and Screaming...Hardly

There must be 50 *reasons* to leave a firm. But for me there was only one: the ugly realization of a glass ceiling.

After years of devoted service, board certification, CLE presentations, managing an increasing number of associates, and creating training, briefing, marketing, and performance review materials, I had a rather abrupt and surreal departure. It was like Heidi Klum's mantra, "One day you're in, and the next day you're out."

Flaky partner behavior should have clued me in. But I was not planning on going solo. I didn't see it coming. Long story, plenty of good old-fashioned greed, too. But this is not my memoir. I intend to provide some practical advice to female lawyers, whether or not you are planning to leave. Because whatever the reason, there is ultimately only one *way* to leave a firm: well-prepared.

1. Manage your personal finances well
I have been working with a financial advisor for years. I highly recommend it.

To find the right expert, your quest for someone with the right chemistry may be singular. Consider your own unique needs. I was a single mom for many years; an oddity in my culture, family, and even my firm. Search for a licensed investment professional with the Financial Industry Regulatory Authority (FINRA) BrokerCheck tool.

Credentials matter. Look for the proper state and/or federal licenses and designations such as ChFC (Chartered Financial Consultant), CFP (Certified Financial Planner), etc.

A comprehensive service is a must. Your advisor should provide guidance in many areas—health insurance, life insurance, disability insurance, wills, estate planning, mortgage, real estate, investments, retirement planning, college savings accounts, etc. A good advisor will be aligned with equally knowledgeable referrals—accountants, insurance agents, mortgage brokers, etc.

When you are ready to start your new business venture, your advisor should introduce you to the right banker, discuss a line of credit, retirement account, etc.

2. Be tech savvy

I'm not advising a mindless jump on the Internet bandwagon. But the Internet can hardly be called a craze anymore. The first dot.com domain name was registered in 1985. Success today will require expertise in social media. Consider also going green, becoming virtual and paperless. These aren't fads. It's about saving money, having total control, and the realities of today's consumer of legal services.

Let's face it, as lawyer types we may feel that having alphabet soup behind our name means we can act like big shots. But diva behavior won't help you develop the skills to go it alone.

If you hire a PR guru you won't quickly reap the rewards from your practice. In the meantime, your competition will be attracting prospective clients via the network of networks that is the World Wide Web. So learn what you can from the IT guys while at your firm. And pay attention to what they are doing to your computer.

Participate in firm marketing endeavors (easier said than done). I'll never forget the day I was told the firm was going to saturate the market (where I grew up) with our newest associate's image. Our PR guru said a young male Hispanic face would bring in Hispanic clients. I persuasively urged that a home town face wouldn't hurt either. Thereafter I became keenly interested and conspicuously intrusive on all things "marketing." I had to let go of my dream of graying gracefully, too. Oh, well, a girl's got to do what a girl's got to do!

I know. You don't have time to do it all. And your expertise is in law, not marketing. But when solo, you have to get the word out. Don't be at the mercy of the gurus. (Ca-ching for them!)

If you followed my advice at step 1 you should have saved and invested well. And you may find yourself surprisingly well poised to invest in a home office with a laptop and a multifunction printer. Start Googling to find the answers to these elusive questions:

How am I going to attract clients? Create your own website. Start at Google Sites or pay a nominal fee for a service with customizable templates. Other important features include domain registration, bandwidth, hosting space, web listing, and SEO (search engine optimization) services. Supplement performance with Google Analytics.

I settled on Intuit because of their site builder tool and 24-hour tech support. It was tedious, but now I can modify my site. I add new videos from my webcam, create new pages, change old ones, change key words, add new HTML text, etc. All free.

To optimize web hits, go beyond your own site. Enhance visibility with a sitemap, H1 tags, and links to sites like LinkedIn, Avvo, YouTube, Facebook, and Twitter. Or pay at directories/lead generators like ExpertHub. For quicker results consider Google AdWords or a comprehensive service like Yodle.

As your business grows consider cyber tools like e-mail mass marketing. The best referral sources are prospects and former happy clients. They spread the word for free. (Ca-ching for you!)

Are you still an Internet skeptic? I confess, in the beginning, referrals were from other lawyers (nice). But I can't live on my colleagues alone. It took a few months, but eventually, my website began to generate business. And it is a great calling card, something anyone can access to "get to know" me.

Make sure you comply with your state bar advertising rules. I recommend you read:

1. "Law Firm Websites That Work," *ABA Journal*, pgs. 33–37, Vol. 95, April 2009

2. "The Attorney and Social Media," *Texas Bar Journal*, pgs. 178–220, Vol. 73, No. 3, March 2010

Last, invest in marketing materials, and find options on your computer. Check out the templates on Microsoft Word. You can take branding to a new level at Vistaprint (very affordable).

Who will answer the phone? My college buddy was appalled when he called, and I said: "Hello?" He replied, "Get yourself a Virtual PBX system [virtual receptionist]…they aren't expensive."

Start at Onebox. Their demo is self-explanatory. After that, move your virtual shopping trip to PBXCompare. I needed unlimited minutes more than extension so I settled on RingCentral. But your business model may require other features.

How will I manage my calendar, files, and deadlines without staff? If you must have a paper file, hire someone. If not, shop for case management software at Capterra. Prevail had what I needed and is expanding their training materials (which will be vital when I do add staff).

Don't clients want to actually meet you? Truthfully, some don't. E-mail (with a standard disclaimer) and unlimited minutes fit my Social Security disability law practice. Other privacy issues are routinely discussed at lawyerist.com. When I am away from my laptop, phone calls are directed to my smartphone. Many clients like to get my text messages, too.

For face-to-face meetings with clients I have a virtual office. I found lawyers who own their own buildings and like my niche associated with them. If you travel to meet clients consider Regus or Davinci Suites for affordable and tailored options.

When you do hire help, consider Skype. Make sure your case management software, multifunction printer, and Virtual PBX system are all network ready!

3. Don't burn bridges

If you went straight from school to work, you may not have learned this workplace lesson. Thankfully, it's never too late to modify behavior. If you treat support staff, colleagues, opposing counsel, clients, judges, friends, and family as you want to be treated, you may be surprised when you decide to go it alone. You may not be alone at all.

Family is the foundation of my business venture. It's an odd leap of faith for a Hispanic family to have a wife/mom/daughter/sister/cousin as a business owner. But they have embraced my decision to relinquish my slavish career path to independence.

Finally, as I happily and gracefully go gray, prospective clients *are* finding me in cyberspace organically (free). You can, too, at www.southtexasdisability-lawyer.com (notice the branding).

Suzanne Villalon-Hinojosa is the owner of the Law Offices of Suzanne Villalon-Hinojosa in San Antonio and Edinburg, Texas, where she focuses on Social Security disability claimant representation before the Social Security Administration and in the Texas federal courts. She graduated from law school in 1989 and founded her firm in 2009. *www.texasdisabilityadvocates.com*

- JODI L. ROSENBERG -

"[W]hat was the worst that could happen? I would fail and have to renew the job hunt. What I did not imagine was the best that could happen: I would feel an enormous sense of accomplishment."

Dear Firm:

I am writing to thank you for laying me off in August 2009. Although it was unsettling for me to lose my position of nearly 15 years, I am now truly grateful for the outcome. I am now the owner of the Law Office of Jodi L. Rosenberg LLC.

As a member of Firm's litigation department, I was exposed to a multitude of matters and became a seasoned litigator. I was trained by Firm's top trial attorney. He came from a small practice and kept that mindset when he joined Firm. He taught me how to evaluate, work up, and try a case. He let me practice on my own unless I asked for his help. In short, he gave me the tools and the confidence to practice independently. He helped me become Firm's first part-time litigator.

Working a reduced schedule, I had to stay on top of our clients' needs. This made me self-sufficient, as I kept my own calendar, worked remotely, and did much of my own typing. I did everything necessary to fully service a client. I had enormous freedom and flexibility. This made me feel both competent and confident. My experience was so great that all three of my children were born during my tenure at Firm. I probably would not have had a third child if I did not have such a great setup.

Although I received superior performance reviews every year and the adoration of our clients, I could not save my part-time position. We were in a recession.

What next? I had never seriously considered hanging my own shingle. As a large firm veteran for my entire 17-year legal career, I looked down on solo practitioners. I loved my fancy office, all the office supplies I could ever need, and the support staff. I thought that solos were attorneys who could not get jobs on their own. Further, with three school-age children and a successful husband, I was more likely to become a stay-at-home-mom, an actress, or a yoga enthusiast than start my own firm. As counsel to Firm, I was already able to be a bit of all of these and still collect a paycheck. I had to find a way to make that continue.

With help from Firm, I immediately began talking to every attorney who would see me. Most attorneys I spoke to at other firms were scrambling to stay afloat. The more firms I visited, the more it became apparent to me that I could work for myself. I set up an LLC on my laptop late one night and didn't look back.

I had no idea that over 60 percent of attorneys in New Jersey are solo practitioners. These numbers were encouraging. I was not concerned about how to practice law, but rather how to run a business. The last time I was an entrepreneur, I was 11 and selling handmade barrettes at a local flea market.

As a lawyer and a member of the New Jersey and New York bars, what was the worst that could happen? I would fail and have to renew the job hunt. What I did not imagine was the best that could happen: I would feel an enormous sense of accomplishment, I would develop my inner accountant and business persona, and I would make my own schedule. No longer would I have to miss the first day of school. I cleared out the kids' toys and set up shop in my basement.

Setting up the practice was surprisingly simple. I went to the bank and opened the required business and trust accounts. Next, I applied for malpractice insurance. Since I was planning on working from home but did not want to give out my home address to clients, I rented a mailbox at the local UPS Store where I could receive mail and packages and make copies. I ordered business cards and letterhead. With the help of a friend, I set up a website for under $100.

At just the right time, since I was by no means the only senior attorney out of work, the New Jersey State Bar Association held a program entitled "Suddenly Solo." At this workshop, we were given a checklist of steps required to start a firm. The timing was perfect.

Also during this time, I was performing in the New Jersey Volunteer Lawyers for the Arts production of *Bye Bye Birdie*. Firm had encouraged me to pursue my outside interests, which included acting. Who would have thought that by enjoying a hobby I would make friends and contacts that would help me as a solo practitioner? One of the other performers was a solo who showed me the ropes in the criminal court system and kept me busy with contract assignments. Another performer introduced me to the New Jersey Lawyers listserv for solo attorneys, where I found mentors who could answer all of my questions.

Active in my community through my children and my outside interests, I made a point of telling every person I came in contact with what I was up to. I found that the work was finding me. I had to open my mind to new practice areas and to the business of being a business owner. I volunteered to represent friends with their traffic tickets in order to get more comfortable in municipal court. I took on a divorce case at a reduced rate in order to learn the ropes in family court. Every dollar I receive has been earned by my actions. Every decision I make directly impacts my practice. It is truly thrilling.

I do not worry about my ability to do the work. I only worry that I will have no work. However, in the middle of a recession, every single lawyer and law firm in New Jersey has the same fear. I find that having Firm as my prior employer gives me instant credibility. Prospective clients are happy to get large firm representation at small firm prices.

There is no better time than now to hang a shingle. There are so many free or inexpensive resources out there, such as Google Voice, Gmail, Solosez, and Fastcase.

There are definitely downsides. I spend an incredible amount of time on nonbillable and administrative tasks. After being with hundreds of people every day at Firm, I find solo practice to be lonely. I miss being able to pop my head into the next office and bounce ideas. Vacations are more complicated to schedule. When I used to be able to leave my work thoughts at work, now I spend every free minute thinking about my practice. But I have no regrets.

The first weekend after I learned I was losing my job, I spent the weekend with a close friend in Massachusetts. My friend encouraged me to open my own practice and told me that in one year, I would be ready to send a thank you note to my former firm for forcing me to take this path. I am sure I laughed then, but now, I know that she was right. Thanks again for letting me go.

JODI L. ROSENBERG is the owner of the Law Office of Jodi L. Rosenberg LLC in Millburn, New Jersey, where she litigates, mediates, and arbitrates a broad range of disputes, including commercial, matrimonial, custody, employment, and municipal matters. She graduated from law school in 1993 and founded her firm in 2009. *www.jodirosenberglaw.com*

- JESSICA J. KING -

"I love my firm because I have the guilt-free ability to see my parents. I still serve in my local community and am currently the deputy mayor of the city of Oshkosh."

When I graduated from law school in 2001 in San Diego, California, I would have never believed that by 2010 I would be the sole shareholder of Compass Law, S.C., a law firm in Oshkosh, Wisconsin. I picked the name of my law firm in part because its creation helped me pursue the direction of my priorities while moving my clients in a positive direction.

My first attorney position after graduating from law school was with a medical receivables management company in Northern Virginia. For 18 months much of my work focused on contract review and appeals on behalf of facility providers. I spent my average day reviewing information and drafting appeal letters.

In 2003 I realized I wanted to place my family first, and I decided to return to Oshkosh to be closer to my disabled parents. Unfortunately, I did not have any connections within Wisconsin's legal community. I was concerned the experience from my first attorney position would not be transferrable in serving the legal needs of a community with a population of 65,000. I had no litigation experience.

Legal career networking was a challenge because I didn't know any attorneys in Oshkosh, and I had only lived in Oshkosh for the five years I attended my undergraduate college, the University of Wisconsin Oshkosh (UWO). I began my career search by making a list of administrators and professors whom I knew while attending UWO. I picked individuals whom I had worked whom on collaborative projects or extracurricular activities. Looking back, I believed it helped me a great deal that I kept in touch during the six years I had lived away from the community. I called these individuals and explained my desire to return to Wisconsin to participate in my parents' lives and that I needed to find an attorney position to make the transition possible. A positive aspect of a community of 65,000 is that residents are more likely to know their neighbors, community members, and attorneys, in comparison to the DC Metro area.

After several phone calls and e-mails I had managed to arrange two interviews with two of the larger law firms, five-to-seven attorney offices, in Oshkosh. I was up front in the interviews that I did not have litigation experience and that I was moving to Wisconsin to participate in my disabled parents' lives. The first interview was short, and it was clear that I did not match what the firm required of its associates. I was fortunate that during the second interview I would be meeting my mentor. He explained that there would be a lot of learning on my feet and that I would have to earn my keep. He also indicated that I would be taking a salary cut from my current job but respected my priorities and my desire to assist my family.

I immediately felt the positive change of moving from the DC Metro area to Oshkosh. The firm fostered my desire to participate in professional associations, including the local county bar, the Wisconsin Young Lawyers Division, and the American Bar Association's Young Lawyers Division. The firm also encouraged me to participate in the local service clubs. For the first time I had clients who were people whom I got to meet, whose stories I got to learn. I will never forget my amazement when I received holiday cards and thank you notes from my clients. My firm also helped me manage my work schedule around my parents' medical appointments. My return from the DC Metro area to Oshkosh was a success for my family, myself, and my employer.

During the Spring of 2009, I faced new challenges, which meant I needed to find new answers. My father's health had taken a turn in Fall of 2008, which required him to transition into a nursing home. My mother lives approximately 20 minutes from the nursing home and does not drive. It became apparent that I needed to make choices between family and career. I realized that my firm had other associates, and there was a limit as to how flexible the firm could be with my hours without impacting my compensation. I did what I had thought previously unthinkable. I started to plan my law firm.

I began to realize that after five and a half years in Oshkosh, I had made a professional name for myself. I developed a primary practice as a consumer bankruptcy attorney. All of the professional connections I had made during my work with bar associations on the local, state, and ABA levels transitioned into attorneys outside of the bankruptcy realm providing bankruptcy case referrals to my office because they knew me. All of the community work that I participated in transitioned into that same communication tool for me to spread the word that I was available to help people and small businesses with their financial problems.

I have been operating my firm for almost one year. During this time I have been added to the Chapter 7 Bankruptcy Trustee Panel for the Eastern District of Wisconsin. I have kept a close relationship with my old firm. I refer large cases or alternative practice area cases to them. My former partners always answer the phone when I have a question or when I am in need of an "ear." To this day I consider them my uncles! My firm has alternative hours of business operation. I schedule appointments after 5 p.m. and on some Saturdays. My clients love the flexibility because they usually have to work from 8 a.m. to 5 p.m. Compass Law, S.C. still requires additional growth as I attempt to learn more about technology and business planning. I purposefully started out small and have only two part-time assistants. Both of these individuals have other full-time jobs.

I love my firm because I have the guilt-free ability to see my parents. I still serve in my local community and am currently the deputy mayor of the city of Oshkosh. Some Fridays you may find me on the riverfront at 4 p.m., happy that I had the courage to follow my priorities and wondering what's next.

JESSICA J. KING is the sole shareholder of Compass Law, S.C. in Oshkosh, Wisconsin, where she focuses on small business and consumer bankruptcy and is a member of the Chapter 7 Trustee Panel for the Eastern District of Wisconsin. She graduated from law school in 2001 and founded her firm in 2009. *www.compasslawyers.com*

- ANGELA FRANCO LUCERO -

"Women . . . are forced to walk a fine line or a tightrope between being too polite and passive. . . and being perceived as overly forceful. [L]earn how to best walk the tightrope, all the while being professional and maintaining your dignity."

The single most important factor in my success as an attorney and co-member/manager of Kranovich & Lucero, LLC has been mentoring. It is critical that those of us who have established ourselves and enjoyed success in the legal profession continue to "pay it forward" to young women and minority attorneys newly entering our profession.

I graduated from Lewis & Clark Law School in 2003, having moved to Portland, Oregon, from my home state of New Mexico. I attended college at New Mexico State University, from which I graduated with bachelor degrees in criminal justice and Spanish. Although I had wanted to be a lawyer from a very young age, I had long expected that my career would focus on criminal law. Before entering law school, to the extent possible, I tailored my education and work experience around criminal law, even interning with a public defender's office as a legal assistant/Spanish interpreter during college. Much to my surprise, however, my legal career as a law student and attorney has focused exclusively on civil litigation. Throughout law school I clerked for the in-house litigation department of Safeco. Upon graduating from law school I became a civil litigation attorney focusing on insurance defense litigation. Today, I am a partner of Kranovich & Lucero, LLC.

My law partner, Tom Kranovich, was a former managing attorney for Portland's legal department of Safeco Insurance Company. Tom hired me as a law clerk following my first year of law school. During my tenure at Safeco, Tom left the corporate world and opened up a solo practice focusing on insurance defense. After graduating from law school, I worked as a contract attorney for Tom, and then in January 2004, I became a full-time associate for the Law Office of Tom Kranovich. After five years as an associate I made partner. Today I am the majority partner of our firm, Kranovich & Lucero, LLC.

During the early years of my career, Tom proved to be the kind of supervisor who is sadly all too rare in the contemporary legal profession: not just a boss but a true mentor, champion, and friend. Tom gave me progressively greater responsibility, always making himself available as a resource, insisting that there were "no stupid questions." In the beginning, I was responsible for legal research and document review and learned from observing Tom during depositions, arbitrations, and trials. Eventually, I started taking my own depositions and second-chairing Tom in trials. Thanks to Tom's guidance and careful development of me as an attorney, today I handle a varied caseload of my own civil litigation matters and try my own cases to juries with confidence and success.

Being mentored by an experienced male attorney was in many ways especially helpful to me as a young female minority attorney. Despite the increasing number of women and minorities in the legal field, the practice of law is still heavily dominated by men and in many professional circles considered a "good old boys" network. While I have never felt that my clients lack the confidence in my abilities as a lawyer due to my age or gender, I have too many times found myself being treated dismissively by some of my grey-haired male colleagues. However, through Tom's mentorship I learned to develop confidence in myself and my abilities to practice law. I learned to not let negative treatment of me as a female attorney discourage me from succeeding. Due to the strong mentoring I received as a young female attorney, I know as an attorney and partner of my firm I will strive for further success in my field. I will continue to mentor and encourage other women and minority law students and attorneys to strive for success in the legal field.

If I had to offer advice to young women entering our profession, particularly in the litigation field, it would be this: never be ashamed to ask questions, develop confidence in yourself and your abilities to practice law, and be prepared to encounter some negative treatment along the way. Unfortunately, chauvinism continues to exist in the legal field. Female attorneys are bound to have interactions with more experienced attorneys (men as well as women) who will insist that you "pay your dues" as they had to when they were young and will at times make things more difficult than necessary. Women, particularly early in their careers, are forced to walk a fine line or a tightrope between being too polite and passive, and thus allowing themselves to be walked over, and being perceived as overly forceful. (Have you noticed that you never hear the adjectives "shrill" or "strident" used to describe men?) As a female attorney, learn how to best walk the tightrope, all the while being professional and maintaining your dignity.

Mentoring was invaluable for me as a young female attorney and continues to be in my career. It is for this reason that I believe it is critical that all women and minority attorneys seek out mentors. My partner Tom will be retiring in the not too distant future, and it will become necessary for me to take young lawyers under my wing, just as Tom took me under his. I challenge myself to be the kind of leader and advocate for those under my supervision as Tom was for me. In the meantime, I will continue to mentor law students and women lawyers as they strive to enter the legal field.

ANGELA FRANCO LUCERO is a partner of Kranovich & Lucero, LLC in Portland, Oregon, where she focuses on insurance defense litigation. She graduated from law school in 2003 and co-founded her firm in 2009. *www.tkatlaw.com*

- HOLLY ROARK -

"It's nice to be able to say you own your own firm. . . .
The reality is, it's gritty and tough, and there are a lot of long
hours away from family and friends. Nevertheless,
I am ecstatic about my choice to go solo."

On Becoming a Rock Star

From my earliest memory I wanted to be a rock star. I wanted it all: the glitz, the glamour, the music, the lifestyle, even the groupies. I wanted to be as cool as cool gets. No one ever told me that girls can't be rock stars, and at that time, The Runaways were a big deal. So I practiced my drums, wrote songs about how I hated my parents, and screamed out the vocals as I rode my bike around my rural town. One of these days I would move to Los Angeles, join a band, and get signed to a lucrative record deal.

Ten years later, in 1987, I did move to Los Angeles, right after high school graduation, but life had other plans for me. As it turned out, I was a very good student, and at some point I came to a crossroads and had to make a choice. I chose security over an uncertain future as an artist. At 18, I began my education at UCLA and gave up on music and that was that. But I never stopped wanting to be a rock star.

Fast forward more than 20 years. I am the principal lawyer at my solo law firm, practicing consumer bankruptcy and loving it. How I ended up here is a very long and sordid tale, most of which shall not be recounted in polite conversation. Perhaps over a cognac in the corner of a dimly lit bar I will tell you the whole story, but not here in the light of day.

Why did I go solo? I have often asked that same thing about various rock stars. Was it personal differences? Was it creative differences? Well, for me it was definitely both personal and creative differences that influenced me to make the leap. After four years of burning the candle at both ends at three different law firms, feeling undervalued, mocked, and abused, I realized that the only way I was going to get any respect and break the chains of white collar slavery would be to strike out on my own.

How would I do it? I knew I didn't want to be anyone's partner. I also knew I was a leader and an entrepreneur, having already started up and failed at several businesses in my early twenties. I was born ambitious and had always risen above and beyond my circumstances, propelling myself from a childhood on welfare to UCLA.

What did I want exactly? I had felt so stifled and strangled in the law firm environment. I felt like they wanted to make me into a zombie, but I just didn't have what it took to be some kind of pod person. I am far too angry. Too punk rock to sit down, shut up, and be a good girl. I wanted artistic freedom, respect, and to earn according to my work ethic and value. So, rather than wait around for years in a law firm hoping for daddy's approval and a raise, I decided to give myself a promotion by crowning myself Queen of My Own Law Firm. It was so easy. Why wait around hoping to make partner at a firm where you don't even like the people, when you can just start your own firm? Life is too short. Take the bull by the horns already.

It took me a good six months to develop and start implementing a business plan. I wrote out exactly what I would need, from office space, to insurance, to software, etc.; developed a budget and a marketing strategy; and nailed down the area of law I would make my focus. You need to map out your course in writing. Don't just jump ship without a solid plan.

It's also really important as a woman not to sell yourself short. Bill yourself out at at least the rate your last law firm billed you out at, if not more. Do some market research, find out what you are worth, and insist on getting that. The beauty of having your own firm is that you can always discount from your standard rate if you choose to. Just don't start out at a discount.

My previous practice experience definitely influenced the direction and structure of my new law firm. When I was an associate, I had very little client contact and once even worked in a mill type of setting, cranking out the same type of motion 20 times a day in a windowless office. At the firms, upper echelon males could be really sexist, while senior women attorneys were sometimes cutthroat. (You may have heard about the lobster theory, where male lobsters build a ladder out of their own bodies to help each other get out of a pot, while female lobsters actually pull the ones who are trying to escape back down into the pot to die. I don't know if any of that's true or not, but I saw it on an episode of the *L Word* and quite frankly, I wouldn't be surprised if it were true. We need to knock off that kind of crap and help out our sisters.)

At big firms it often appears that clients suffer because nobody is focusing on their interests, what with all that whip-cracking to bill, bill, bill. That's why I decided to structure my firm to be truly client-centered, much like a nonprofit, except for the fact that I did need to charge the client in order to pay my own bills. I wanted to truly help people and not just be some kind of billing robot.

I've discovered numerous benefits to having my own law firm, from making my own hours, to getting direct feedback from my clients, to having control over every aspect of business development. I get all the glory when some-thing goes well (but I also take all the blame when it doesn't).

Although just a year after going solo, I have more business than I could have ever imagined, the business development aspect of my business never ends, nor should it. You should always be marketing, no matter what you do, where you go, or whom you talk to. I am constantly going to lunch and dinner with female friends and colleagues. These women have been a great source of referrals for me. I rarely have to advertise my services, which keeps my costs down. Your women colleagues are your greatest resource. Never turn down an opportunity to lunch or have drinks with another woman, no matter what line of work she is in. You never know whom people know or what kind of insights they can give you.

Although I never fulfilled my childhood dream to become a rock star, I have learned that glamour isn't all it seems anyway. It's mostly just perception. Much like a rock star, the only really glamorous part of being a lawyer is when you are at a cocktail party telling people what you do for a living. It's nice to be able to say you own your own firm and to let people imagine what that must be like. The reality is, it's gritty and tough, and there are a lot of long hours away from family and friends. Nevertheless, I am ecstatic about my choice to go solo and am thrilled to recommend to other women lawyers that they experience the joy of opening their own firms. For me, my solo endeavor represents a lot of points in my life converging all at once. I am helping people who are in financial distress, just like my family was when I was a kid;

I am independent and running the show, like the leader I have always been; I am being creative in my approach to my business and my practice of law, like the artist I always hoped to be. I am a rock star in my own right.

HOLLY ROARK is the founding member of Roark Law Offices in Los Angeles, California, where she focuses on bankruptcy law. She graduated from law school in 2004 and founded her firm in 2009. *www.roarklawoffices.com*

- TAMARA S. FREEZE -

"I was bombarded with new clients and cases and found myself working too many hours. I hired an associate to help me out, but I am still learning how to manage my firm's expansion."

The first time I began thinking about starting my own practice was when I was still working for a big law firm. I was a labor and employment associate, representing management, and I started to feel that I was in the wrong place. Besides, I felt that my career and financial opportunities at a big firm were strictly limited and predictable. The only thing holding me back was that I could not figure out a way to leave the firm and then finance my own practice for the first few months. Fortunately for me, I was laid off in February 2009 and provided with a generous severance package. This was a much-needed boost to my new career. I opened my own solo practice, focusing exclusively on plaintiff-side employment law, in March 2009.

Before I opened my own firm, I practiced employment law (defense side) for four years. I felt prepared to handle my own clients and cases, especially having the experience of being on the other side and representing management.

The benefits of starting my own solo practice were numerous. The career opportunities were far beyond what a big law firm could offer. A few months down the road, I was managing my own clients, filing and mediating cases on my own. Typically, such a high level of responsibility is not given at a big law firm where junior associates do preparatory work of little significance, rarely go to court, and have low visibility with clients. An added bonus was better compensation as a solo attorney. Even though I did not make much money in my first year, I remained cash-flow positive, and then I quickly surpassed my law firm salary in my second year of practice due to several high value settlements I was able to obtain on behalf of my clients.

The most valuable asset of starting my own solo practice was, of course, the newly found unilateral discretion and independence. At a big law firm, your work is always checked and, sometimes, redone; the partner makes all the decisions and strategy planning, and you are in a supporting role most of the time. I felt severely constrained by the firm's politics, the personalities of certain partners I worked with, and my inability to make my own decisions. As a solo practitioner, however, I became the primary decision-maker, the leading attorney.

Another added benefit was tremendous flexibility. I could take days off during the week, design my own travel schedule, and schedule depositions and hearings on more convenient days. I was still working hard but only when I needed to and at the time I wanted to. I answered to no one but myself and my clients. This change was a very empowering experience.

The biggest challenge came a year later in the form of high volume of work. I was bombarded with new clients and cases and found myself working too many hours. I hired an associate to help me out, but I am still learning how to manage my firm's expansion and handle the high volume of client work.

Another challenge was learning how to spot and turn down problem clients. This part of practice cannot be taught but rather comes with experience.

My business model was to develop a reputation as an excellent plaintiff-side employment attorney, build a referral network among local professionals, grow my practice, and provide my clients with winning solutions. I focused on extensive valuation of my cases and planned my litigation strategy and my financial goals accordingly. Since most of my cases are contingency-based, it is very difficult to plan ahead, as I do not exactly know how long my cases will take to resolve, how they will be resolved (by settlement or trial), and what is the exact amount of compensation I will receive. To maintain a continuous cash flow, I built a healthy share of hourly work, billing my clients every month for the work I have done on their behalf. This mixed workload approach has worked out very well so far.

I kept the exact same billing rate I had at my former firm. I do not believe that small and solo attorneys with comparable experience should charge less than big law firms. I, however, was sensitive to my clients' needs and created numerous incentives for them to see the value of my services. I did not charge for any telephone conversation less than 10 minutes or short e-mails. As a former law firm associate, I can attest to the fact that no one likes to get a $20 charge for a simple question. And because I do not have any billable hours, there is no pressure to bill as much as possible.

Starting a solo practice was indeed expensive, but I tried to keep my costs low. I had to borrow money from my emergency fund to buy books, as well as to finance my expenses and marketing efforts. This was a good investment. Within a year, I was able to repay the money. For the first few months, I worked at home. I got virtual offices in three different cities (Los Angeles, Irvine, and San Diego), as I was trying to figure out where most of my client work would come from. I met all my clients at local executive suites, where I rented conference rooms for the meetings. As my clientele grew and as I started getting paid for my work, I rented a physical office and, a few months later, another office for my new associate.

I created a website almost immediately, and this was a huge boost to my marketing campaign. My website is currently in three different languages and has all the necessary information about me, my firm, and my practice areas. I am able to see, through Google Analytics, that I am getting a good share of visitors every week.

I did not envision opening my own practice when I was a law student. I aspired to become a partner at a prominent law firm. When I became an associate, I realized that the traditional path to partnership is long, unpredictable, and may not be as rewarding as I thought. I wanted to be in a leadership position but without the professional limitations, the office politics, or the robotic nomenclature of a law firm. The solo practice was a natural progression for my career. The leap from junior associate to a managing attorney of my own firm was challenging but extremely rewarding.

My own firm is growing and building a solid reputation in the community, as I envisioned. I am anticipating growing pains and possible staffing issues, but these are inevitable in any firm's expansion. I am now learning how to assign work, how to manage associates, and how to delegate my caseload. I am planning to continue as a solo business model, but I do not preclude the possibility of partnership with another attorney who has a solid book of business. My business model is extremely flexible and highly adaptable to the changing market, client demands, and financial fluctuations. At the moment, I am extremely satisfied with my career choice. And I plan to keep it that way.

TAMARA S. FREEZE is a founding partner of the Law Offices of Tamara Freeze in Irvine and Beverly Hills, California, where she practices plaintiff-side employment law. She graduated from law school in 2005 and founded her firm in 2009. *www.freezelawoffice.com*

- Francine Friedman Griesing -

"I finally launched my own firm when I had outgrown working for others who did not support my efforts. At that point. . . I had a core team that I trusted to undertake the challenge."

Nothing feels as good as being my own boss. After nearly 30 years of law practice, principally at Am Law 200 firms in New York and Philadelphia, with a three-year stint in public service as litigation chair of the Philadelphia City Solicitors Office, I launched my own firm in January 2010. Since going out on my own, I have been asked the same two questions over and over again. It just depends on who is asking. Those who have done this before me ask "Don't you wish you did this sooner?" while the intrepid wonder, "Are you ever sorry you did this?" Neither captures my perspective, and I welcome the opportunity to share it. I do not wish that I did this sooner nor do I regret doing it now. The timing feels right for me.

For many lawyers, the possibility of starting their own firm is a dream long pursued; for others, unexpected circumstances leave them no other choice. For me, it was the logical next step of a gradual professional progression. Over time, it just became clear that this was the right path to take. It was not something I ever anticipated. It did not cross my mind when I entered Penn Law School or when I began my career as a first-year associate at a Wall Street firm. In fact, for most of the 28 years that followed, I insisted that I would never go out on my own. I liked being part of a big institution where the day-to-day administration was handled by others. I finally launched my own firm when I had outgrown working for others who did not support my efforts. At that point, I was sufficiently established to be successful on my own, and I had a core team that I trusted to undertake the challenge.

Over the past 30 years I have read dozens of articles and books about the state of women in the profession, attended and presented at countless programs designed to support and promote women lawyers, and have been advised by and given advice to an unending parade of others. The most valuable lessons I take away from those experiences are simple and straightforward. Here are the pointers I wish someone had shared with me even before I started law school.

First, whether you start your own firm, build a practice within an existing firm, pursue an in-house counsel position, or enter public service, you need to develop your craft as a lawyer. Being an excellent lawyer is the lowest common denominator for success in any path you pursue, but professional excellence is nothing more than the threshold.

Second, you should not abdicate control of your career to others or expect that someone else is going to make things happen for you. No one else can protect you from the challenges you will face, save you from downsizing, or prevent you from being passed over for partner. You need to take and keep control of your professional life as much as possible. It is up to you to decide what type of practice you want to build, where you want to practice, what you want to get out of it, and how you are going to accomplish those objectives. Expecting others to take care of your career, promote you, or make your professional dreams come true is only a crutch. You need to be able to stand alone.

Third, create a strategic plan designed to accomplish the professional goals you set for yourself. But a plan is only effective if it does not just collect dust. To succeed, you need to set aside time to focus on it. In my experience, that means you need to follow your plan consistently, evaluate it often to assess its effectiveness in bringing you closer to your goals, and update it to adapt to changes in your circumstances or objectives.

Fourth, surround yourself with people who support you unconditionally but care enough to tell you the hard truth. There are many challenges and disappointments in any career, and the law has its fair share of unexpected obstacles. In addition to having a core group of family and friends you can count on, there is great value in assembling a range of people who can serve as your professional cheerleaders, connectors, sponsors, mentors, and protégés. My advice is to seek out those people in your organization and outside of it. Become involved in professional groups where you are likely to meet others in your region and your practice area who are in positions to guide you, recommend you, and encourage you. And it must be a two-way street. Reciprocity is essential to benefiting from a relationship. Demonstrate to those helping you that you appreciate their efforts, and make sure that you give back to people who help you along the way. When you are in a position to do so, help others coming after you. If you invest in others, you will be surprised how supportive your network will be if and when you decide to strike out on your own.

Specifically, build a team you can trust and rely upon. Then, empower them to advance your shared goals. I invited two colleagues to join me in this new venture—Kate Legge, the associate with whom I was working most closely, and Jessica Mazzeo, our mutual executive assistant. They have been essential to the success of this new venture. As a start-up, we encountered unexpected challenges from the outset, but instead of regarding them as setbacks, my team turned them into opportunities. I had very high expectations for my founding colleagues, and they have exceeded them. I credit this achievement to their abilities and to the way we work as a team. Working collaboratively brings out the best efforts in everyone. We are not distracted by the competition to log in more billable hours or generate more business than our colleagues. By pulling in the same direction, rather than constantly looking over our shoulders to protect our turf within the firm, we are better able to serve our clients.

Finally, treat people the way you want to be treated, and treat yourself well. As a firm manager, you will deal with clients, employees, vendors, and others. Each of these groups deserves to be treated as valued partners in your firm. Without them, you cannot succeed, and you should never forget that. Our clients followed us from a mega firm to a two-lawyer operation; making that transition takes hard-earned trust. We work everyday to make sure we keep it by responding quickly, billing fairly, and doing our best to get results. When we are the client, we follow the same standards. Our vendors are just as important to our success. They have offered us credit, worked creatively to solve our problems, and treated us as valued customers. We show them respect by always paying our bills on time and thanking them for serving us well.

And, of course, no one can take care of you if you do not take care of yourself. For the first several months after I started my firm, I could barely tear myself away from work, for fear I might miss the call for the case of a lifetime. Starting a new firm is exhilarating and exhausting, and it is easy to forget to breathe. If you want to achieve success and to be well enough to enjoy it, stop and catch your breath. Take time to reflect, exercise, and eat well. Spend downtime with the people you care about and who care about you. You are your firm brand now, so make sure to nurture yourself so your brand flourishes. Good luck.

FRANCINE FRIEDMAN GRIESING is the managing member at Griesing Law, LLC in Philadelphia, Pennsylvania, where she focuses on hospitality law, commercial litigation, and employment law. She graduated from law school in 1981 and founded her firm in 2010. *www.griesinglaw.com*

- MARCY H. KAMMERMAN -

"Women . . . when in a position of strength were generally viewed as difficult and destructive instead of aggressive and productive like their male counterparts. I do not sense those distinctions today, and that is a huge change that I embrace with open arms."

When I graduated law school in 1986, starting my own law practice was completely out of the question. The truth is that I was fortunate enough to graduate law school at a time when those, like myself, who did well in school and had secured an editing position on law review were hired for the high- paying New York City associate positions at the large, prestigious law firms. Ultimately, I became a partner at a well-known Florida firm after moving there in 1997 and then secured a general counsel position for a well-known development company. I became accustomed to doing the "big deal" with the "big players," and that was the kind of legal work I wanted to always continue to do. That was my experience and my comfort zone, so never did I dream that nearly 24 years after graduating law school I would venture out on my own. Solo practitioners would never be able to get the "big deal" with the "big players," right? Wrong.

The decision to start my own law practice came fairly recently and not because I woke up one day and thought, "having my own law practice would be a great idea; let's do it!" On the contrary, the development company I was working for was in Chapter 11 and decided a legal department in Florida was a luxury not a necessity. Yes...I lost my job, and for the first time in many years, I was unemployed. I tried for a short time to enter the job-seeking world. It was very different from anything I was used to. Of course there is always the networking angle, but I was also introduced to the ever-annoying Internet employment market, where you send numerous résumés daily into a black hole never to be heard from again. Why bother, I began to say.... Then one day during the last few days at the development company, my two paralegals approached me about the idea to start my own practice. They were convinced it was the only way to go and completely wanted in on it. The economy was terrible, especially in South Florida. Jobs were scarce, and even when there was a job, the salaries were in most cases significantly less than what we were being paid. I began to think about it, and as more and more résumés went into that black hole, it did not take me too long to decide. I thought, "what do I really have to lose? I'll try it for a year, and then the economy will get better, and I'll get that job doing the 'big deals' with the 'big players.'"

I have now been practicing in my own law practice since February 2010. Although it has been a relatively short time, I have secured nearly 20 clients, and I could not imagine ever going back to the big firm and big business life. Don't get me wrong, the last several months have been petrifying. I have had numerous sleepless nights (I really like Tylenol PM these days), and I keep asking these questions over and over again: How will I make a living? How will I get clients? What if I go to the office and have nothing to do? As a single mother of two young boys, how will I be able to manage financially?

However, my ever-continuing fears become overshadowed by the real life events that have been emerging. I cannot tell you that there is a magic formula that makes this work, but I can say that dedication, hard work, trust in your colleagues, and never giving up are probably the key ingredients. We began as a team of three: me and my two paralegals from the development company. Prior to our departure, we started regular meetings and gave ourselves six weeks to "open up" for business. Thankfully I have been a saver over the years and agreed to be the financial backer of the company. We put together a detailed forecast-ing budget that we stick to as much as possible to keep operating costs low. Additionally, I wrote a business plan that in my heart I truly believed would, and still believe will, make this a successful venture based on a strategy that we would provide big firm, high quality legal services at a fraction of the cost.

Unfortunately, there have been and continue to be challenges. Prior to our opening date, one of my paralegals decided not to go forward. For me, she was one of the pivotal reasons I was sure we could be successful, and her energy and belief in what we were undertaking were contagious. This 180-degree turn by her made me question what I had started. Nevertheless, my other paralegal was more committed than ever. The departure of one became the strength of the other. Thank goodness for her.

One of my other main challenges, which will probably persist in perpetuity, is the ever-existing anxiety of the necessity of having clients. Unfortunately, without them, you cannot pay bills, afford a practice, or put food on the table. I do admit, it becomes an obsession that overtakes you, but at the same time, it motivates you. I am fortunate in that during the last few months I have had the pleasure of representing nearly 20 clients, some of whom truly are the "big players" doing the "big deal." Call it luck, call it a reputation, call it an intelligent marketing strategy in a challenging economy—I call it a mixture of it all and then some. The truth is you need to distinguish yourself and make sure your clients know they can count on you. It's a 24/7 mentality and a willingness to do what it takes for a reasonable fee. I started, fortunately, representing my prior development firm; sent out announcements; made (and continue to make) lunch, dinner, and happy hour appointments; and simply have made and continue to make everyone I know aware of what I am doing. One thing leads to another, and it does materialize.

What does the future hold? No one can know for sure, but I can tell you that I am committed to keep on going. I do believe that the economy will continue to improve, which will inevitably grow my practice. As a woman, that is an immensely gratifying feeling. When I graduated law school in 1986, women were generally not in charge, and when in a position of strength, they were generally viewed as difficult and destructive instead of aggressive and productive like their male counterparts. I do not sense those distinctions today, and that is a huge change that I embrace with open arms. Simply put, the majority of my nearly 20 clients are men.

I would like to conclude this letter by encouraging all women lawyers to always remember: "anything you want bad enough can be yours if you really want it." Believe in yourself, and know that we all have children, a husband (or in my case an ex-husband), family, friends, and others. However, all of that and more is what makes us great and ensures our success, even if it means sleepless nights, stress, and challenges. For without all of that, we would not strive to be what I tell my kids everyday is their most important job in life, and that is, "Be the best person you can be."

MARCY H. KAMMERMAN is the senior attorney at The Kammerman Law Group, P.A. in Fort Lauderdale, Florida, where she focuses on commercial and residential real estate and business transactions. She graduated from law school in 1986 and founded her firm in 2010. *www.kamlawgroup.com*

- Johnna M. Darby -

"Make the decision early regarding whether to have a paperless office or not. . . . I decided on a cloud-based system because of its flexibility and cost over time."

So you want to start your own law firm? If you are just starting to think about it, or are in the thick of it, I hope you find the advice I provide below helpful to you during this exciting, frustrating, exhausting, and most rewarding journey.

I am not a *Late Show with David Letterman* fan (I can't stay up that late!), but I believe the "Top Ten List" segment of the show lends itself to the presentation I make here (space limitations prevent a list of 10 pieces of advice). So, here goes: the Top Five pieces of advice I can impart to you (please do not assign any significance to the numbering sequence):

1. *Listen to the voice in your head, the beat of your heart, or that feeling in your gut (or whatever you want to call it) that is telling you, "You can do it!"* Never, ever let anyone tell you that you cannot open your own firm. You had the fire and desire to attend and complete law school. You then had the tenacity to take and to pass the bar exam. You are now qualified to represent clients; you may lack the experience to do so (more on that later). Do not, however, let that stand in your way. You have trusted your inner voice/heartbeat/gut in many different contexts in your life. Trust it now: you can do it!

2. *Get a business coach/certified public accountant.* You might say, "OK. That's great. But *how* do I do start my own firm?" There is no one right answer to this question. I can only tell you how I did it. The first step I took and the most important thing I did was to hire a business coach/certified public accountant—especially in this banking climate. The press reported that banks were favoring small business and new start-ups. Despite those news stories, I found obtaining bank financing to be difficult. I could not have imagined trying to obtain financing without my business coach/ CPA. If you need financial help, devote much time to defining which

financial institution is a good fit with your firm (my business coach/CPA assisted greatly with this task). The relationship you forge with it will be one of the most important relationships your business has over its life. My business coach/CPA also arranged and facilitated meetings with banks; prepared the numbers for the anticipated financial outlook for the firm that were given to the banks; and, last but not least, acted as my ally and support when I thought my firm was going to remain a dream. Also, having someone handle the financial end of the firm will free you up to attend to the business end of the firm, i.e., form your entity, find your office space, purchase furniture and technology, begin marketing, and most importantly, obtain clients.

3. *Surround yourself with mentors—many, many mentors.* I cannot emphasize this enough. You absolutely need people around you who are willing to help. Align yourself with senior practitioners in the various practice areas in which you intend to practice. These lawyers have the wisdom and experience to provide you with general advice about the practice area and can lend support when you need it. In addition, join your bar association's solo/small firm section to become part of an incredibly supportive community of other solo/small firm practitioners who have been where you are about to go (or are) and can advise you on the various challenges you are about to (or are) face(ing). I also highly recommend the website www.myshingle.com. It is the creation of Carolyn Elefant and is a site dedicated to providing information and tips to solos and small firms. It is an invaluable treasure trove of information. You also need to surround yourself with mentors who are not lawyers. I have a close circle of trusted friends who have helped me with everything from sending out firm opening announcements to setting up the office. And, of course, it does not hurt to have a significant other like my husband, who has spent countless hours delivering furniture, running errands, painting the office, listening to my concerns, holding me when I cried, etc. To all these people I am and will be forever grateful.

4. *If you talk yourself out of opening your own firm because you have convinced yourself you are too inexperienced, you are doing yourself a great disservice.* I had this discussion with myself many times. It is difficult not to listen to such self-talk. Up until the time I started thinking about opening my

own firm, I had always been an associate doing work "behind the scenes." What was I thinking, opening my own firm?! But here's the thing, and there's no getting around it: you went to law school to do this! You may not know everything there is to know about a particular client's problem, but you figure it out. And if you cannot figure it out, the mentors with whom you have surrounded yourself will help you.

5. *If I knew then what I know now...*

   a. I would have made the decision about a practice management/billing system much earlier. Make the decision early regarding whether to have a paperless office or not, a manual or electronic conflict check system, and an electronic or paper calendar—these decisions affect your entire practice. Some practice management/billing systems can perform all of these functions. I decided on a cloud-based system because of its flexibility and cost over time. I looked at a few, such as Rocket Matter and Clio, but decided on Clio and have not looked back. It has been an invaluable practice tool for my calendar, files, billing, and operating/trust accounting functions.

   b. I would have had a more concrete marketing plan in place. For example, I believe it is not enough to conclude that you intend to obtain clients through referrals from other lawyers. What is the basis for that conclusion? What is your plan to obtain the referrals? How will those lawyers know you and/or know you left your firm? Know prior to opening your firm that you intend to obtain referrals by advertising in the local legal press, by sending out firm announcements, or by lunching with lawyers in your chosen practice area(s). Do not wait until your firm opens to make this move. It takes time to obtain referrals. The sooner you reach out to those people from whom potential referrals will come, the sooner potential clients will begin to come in the door.

   c. Hire an assistant as soon as you can—even if she or he begins on a part-time basis. You will be amazed at how much of your time is taken up with tasks that can be performed by an assistant. While a certain part of my day is administrative (given my role as managing member), too much of my day was being taken up with tasks that could have been performed by an assistant, such as dealing with vendors, checking supplies and ordering same, copying, and sending correspondence.

Your attention should be solely focused on practicing law and growing that practice. Anything that takes your attention away from your practice will, in the long run, cost you more than will an assistant.

I hope you find this information helpful. Good luck!

JOHNNA M. DARBY is the member of The Darby Law Firm, LLC located in Wilmington, Delaware, where she practices in the areas of Chapter 11 bankruptcy and family law. She graduated from law school in 1997 and founded her firm in 2010. *www.darbylawllc.com*

- STACY N. LILLY -

---

*"I wanted to work exclusively. . . on a freelance basis.
My mission is to provide a flexible, strategic business resource
that enables law firms to provide high-quality service while
decreasing overhead and costs to their clients."*

I could write an entire book on the reasons why I started my own practice.
The desire to have control over my life, calendar, and future is certainly at the
top. Flexibility is a close second. I also wanted to be able to give back to my
community in ways a large law firm could not appreciate due to the emphasis
on the billable hour. I was in private practice for nine years before I decided
to go out on my own. It was admittedly one of the scariest times of my life;
but it was also one of the most exciting and personally rewarding. I have not
looked back and would choose to do it over again tomorrow.

The business model I had in mind for my new practice was very different from
a traditional law firm. I wanted to work exclusively for other attorneys on a
freelance basis, helping with overflow projects and otherwise filling the gap
when firms need the extra hand of an experienced attorney. My mission is to
provide a flexible, strategic business resource that enables law firms to provide high-quality service while decreasing overhead and costs to their clients.

The ultimate decision to open my own practice was made during a long car
ride with my husband. I knew his full support would be necessary in order
to turn this crazy idea into a reality. I didn't realize it at the time, but that
seven-hour road trip laid the groundwork for the backbone of my practice:
the Business Plan.

The Business Plan
I had very little personal knowledge about starting a law firm or operating
a small business. But I knew that thousands of attorneys had done it and
had done it successfully. So why couldn't I? I was amazed at the resources
available on the Internet for new business owners. The U.S. Small Business

Administration has a wealth of information, the most important of which was guidance on putting together a business plan. At the time, I had no idea how important the exercise of drafting a business plan would become.

I quickly learned that a business plan is much more detailed than just determining what specific services I would offer and at what price. I was forced to analyze the legal market, identify my competition, and articulate why my services were different and better. The financial worksheets of the plan, which required a detailed budget and breakdown of anticipated business expenses, were critical to determining how much capital I needed to start my business and sustain it until the receivables began. Perhaps the most important part of the plan for me though was the marketing aspect, which included setting specific and measurable goals with respect to identifying my ideal clients, determining how and when I would contact them, and how and when to follow up with new leads and prospects.

I spent several months researching, talking with colleagues, and drafting my business plan. I decided to use personal savings to start my business, so I did not need to apply for financing. However, being the cautious person that I am, I felt that I needed additional feedback before I launched. So, I put together what I now call my "board of advisors." My board had two levels. The first level consisted of people close to me and included an uncle who has been a small business owner his entire adult life, an aunt with extensive marketing experience, a brother-in-law who has an MBA, and a long-time attorney-friend. Once I received constructive feedback from each of them, I submitted my revised business plan to the second level of my board, which consisted of a counselor at the Women's Business Development Center, an attorney who has been successfully practicing as a freelancer for many years, and a personal career coach. This entire process—from the car ride to completing my plan—took approximately four months. After the second round of reviews and further tweaks to my plan, it was time to prepare for my launch!

Preparing to Launch My Practice
Before I officially launched my new practice, I wanted a professional website. This was critical for several reasons. First, I believe that a website is a no brainer for any business. It's like having an ad in the phone book 20 years ago. Second, as a consumer, I know that if a website is poorly designed or difficult to navigate, the user will just move on to the next site. Therefore, a

user-friendly site was imperative. Finally, I wanted to be taken seriously by prospective clients. A professional website is proof of the financial investment and commitment to my practice and reflects the pride I put into my work.

I briefly thought about developing my own site. Again, I was amazed at the do-it-yourself web design resources available on the Internet. But I ultimately decided that my time could be better spent elsewhere, like compiling and updating my list of personal and professional contacts. So, I hired a marketing expert to help me develop my personal brand. She designed my logo, letterhead, business cards, and website. It was by far my largest start-up expense, but it was well worth it.

Notably, the very first thing I gave my marketing professional was my business plan. Before she began any substantive work, I wanted her to fully understand what my business was all about. Although I had little to do with the design and layout of my website, the actual content came largely from my business plan. As a result, when it came to putting together my footprint on the World Wide Web, a lot of the legwork was already done.

The Launch

Because I work out of a home office, I did not have a "grand opening," so to speak. My announcement to the world that The Law Office of Stacy N. Lilly was open for business consisted primarily of a press release, which was distributed to various legal and business media with the help of my marketing professional. I did not receive a lot of media attention, but my release played a very important part in opening my practice. I sent the release, along with my new business card and a handwritten personal note, to my professional contacts letting them know about my new venture. This was an excellent opportunity for me to become reconnected with some people I had lost contact with over the years and also a terrific way to introduce myself to many of the target clients I had already identified in my business plan. The traffic to my website grew exponentially after my press release was issued and mailed.

Today

I am now six months into my solo practice. I still look to my business plan on a regular basis to make sure I'm on track. But I've also learned to have an open mind to new opportunities I did not anticipate. The best part of my practice is that I have the control and flexibility I wanted and the time to commit to philanthropic activities. I recently took my first vacation as a solo practitioner. The only person needed to approve the time off was me. And I had no problem whatsoever saying yes.

Warmest regards.

STACY N. LILLY is a solo practitioner in Philadelphia, Pennsylvania, where she focuses on business litigation and serves the needs of other firms as a freelance attorney. She graduated from law school in 2000 and founded her firm in 2010. *www.thelillylawoffice.com*

- MICHELLE BEDOYA BARNETT -

"I did not leave large law firm life to work less, to achieve less, or because I could not hack it. Rather, I left large law firm life to chart my own path, to scratch my entrepreneurial itch."

I sit in my office as I write this and look up, right across the street, at the 39th floor office I left behind. I left behind the national law firm where I had started my career as a summer associate, worked myself up the ladder, received several appointments to firm committees, and traveled to top law schools to recruit on the firm's behalf. I lived and devoted several years of my life to that 39th floor office. In that office, I e-flirted with my now husband, planned my wedding, designed my child's nursery, and received the news that my grandmother Maria had passed away. I have a lot of good memories from that office and will always carry with me the incredible, life-changing opportunities that were given to me that helped mold me as a lawyer and as a person in more ways than I can count. Yet, something was missing in my large law firm life.

I am proud of my time, my contribution, and my affiliation with that firm. While I was there, I billed the right number of hours and in recent years origi-nated a good bit of business. I had been told that I originated more business than anyone else at my same level. Every indication was that I would make partner. Somewhere along the way it was engrained in me that to achieve the status of partner at a major national law firm earns membership into a club that many hope for but few actually achieve. All these years I spent my time accumulating my chips so that I could cash in at the end for the title of partner. But as I got closer and closer, I seemed to get less and less excited at the prospect of being partner, and I found myself pushing the chips away. So why did I decide to throw away my nontransferable chips instead of sticking around a little longer to cash in on the big prize?

There is not an easy answer to why I left large law firm life. I am not really sure that even now, having taken the jump, I know all of the reasons why I left. Yet I still find myself identifying new benefits and perks in small firm life, reasons I did not initially consider. The business reasons are easy. With respect to clients, the legal services climate is changing, and a smaller firm allows us to provide the same superior client service with greater flexibility in billing and fee arrangements. The reasons I gave to my sister, my mother, and my best friend are much different. Plainly and simply—I did not leave large law firm life to work less, to achieve less, or because I could not hack it. Rather, I left large law firm life to chart my own path, to scratch my entrepreneurial itch. Large law firms have a fine-tuned formula for success. As long as you bill a certain number of hours this year, you will be promoted to the next level and make slightly more money. The path is charted for you, and assuming that you follow all of the directions and achieve all of the goals set for you, you will be successful. I have likened large law firm life to a boxed cake mix. As long as you follow the directions, you will end up with a cake. I wanted to make my own cake, not the first cake, but my own kind of cake. I wanted to have the flexibility of altering the recipe for that cake from year to year. Maybe it was something as simple as the selection of drinks in the refrigerator (or the absence of a Coke machine), the selection of the office furniture, or the color scheme in the office. At a large law firm, you inherit what is there, and these are all things that are taken care of for you. I have quickly come to realize that it is such seemingly small and insignificant things that help you to feel a sense of ownership in your own firm. My new law firm of Alexander DeGance Barnett would not be the same without me. At the very least, it would only be Alexander DeGance. While it is not being a named partner that drives me, it is the fact that I have a say in so many things, down to the name.

I have learned that you trade some things for others. I still value, and quite frankly miss, a lot of the things that I was so proud of at my large law firm. As I traveled, recruiting law students for clerkship positions, I was repeatedly asked, "what was it that attracted you to the firm?" It wasn't just one thing. It was the firm's reputation, the quality of work, the mentorship, the training, the opportunities for advancement and travel, the firm's commitment to diversity. All of these things were important to me. If the interviewee was a woman, I would add, they have a great maternity leave policy and are truly committed to the advancement of women. My answer still holds true today.

Was making the jump the right choice? Only time will tell. So far, my gut tells me it was the right choice, and from past experience, I suspect it is not a choice that I will regret. I have found that small law firm life does not necessarily translate into more time with my family. However, I feel a true sense of ownership and feel more personally and professionally fulfilled because I, along with my partners, have created our own recipe for success. I would not trade my large law firm experience for anything. However, I am happy to be living my dream of building my own enterprise.

MICHELLE BEDOYA BARNETT is a partner at the boutique labor and employment firm of Alexander DeGance Barnett, P.A. in Jacksonville, Florida, where she represents employers inside and outside the courtroom. She graduated from law school in 2004 and founded her firm in 2010. *www.adblegal.com*

- Jayne Sykora -
&
- Jennifer Santini -

"So as we stand at the precipice of taking on our first clients, our final word of advice is: do it. We did and are more excited than ever about our careers, our profession, and the endless possibilities ahead of us."

So you're thinking about starting your own law firm? If we were writing this 20 years down the road, we know we would have volumes of advice to offer. But you see, we are not that far into the process of starting our own practice, having just filed our partnership papers only last month. So, we know all too well that the decision, from thinking about starting your own firm to actually doing it, is extremely daunting. However, because we only recently faced those feelings ourselves, we do believe we can be valuable voices speaking to all the angst, uncertainty, hesitation, and fear that accompany this life-changing decision.

If you are asking yourself: How can I do it? Will I succeed? Where do I even begin? Realize that hundreds, thousands of others have asked all those same questions, including us. We believe that asking those questions is the first step to show you are qualified to start your own practice because you're already taking the time to think through the answers and make the process easier. The attorneys who pursue having their own firm without even an afterthought of how difficult the process can be will face a startling realization that the success of a law firm requires not only a law degree and bar admission, but also a great deal of business savvy, social competence, and extensive pre-planning.

To better understand from where our advice comes, let us briefly share our stories that led to our partnership as a law firm. We are newly minted, having just graduated from law school in May 2009 and having been admitted to the bar in October 2009. As most know, 2009 was not an ideal year to enter the job market as an attorney. Very few jobs were being offered, and for the few positions that were available, either hundreds of other qualified entry-level applicants also applied or these positions were offered to the hundreds of experienced attorneys who had been laid off in 2008 and 2009.

Additionally, people usually advise that you should go to law school in the place where you want to live because you will become more familiar with that state's law, you'll develop your network, and presumably, you'll find it easier to find a job there. For better or worse, neither of us followed that path. So on top of graduating when the economy was at an all-time low, we both decided to move to a new state and to a city that is home to four law schools that generate hundreds and hundreds of new graduates each year.

Neither of us had any desire prior to, during, or even immediately following law school to hang out our own shingle. We both wanted employment that provided consistent work, a steady income, and a challenging atmosphere. Given the economy and new city, we were optimistic that, if not immediately, eventually such positions would be made available. Unfortunately, fast forward to February 2010, and both of us were still unemployed.

Slowly we began asking, what if we opened our own shop? We both contemplated this idea for quite awhile, grappling with those aforementioned questions: How can we do this? Will we succeed? Where do we begin? At our first business meeting we shared our concerns, our fears, our hopes, and our ideas and tackled those notorious questions. Eventually, by the end of that lengthy meeting, we were cautiously optimistic, extremely excited, and felt for the first time in a long time back in control of our careers.

Law school teaches you the law, but even more importantly, it prepares you to think rationally and methodically about a problem in order to find a solution. For both of us, that is exactly how we established our firm. Our problem was that we were both unemployed and could not find work. Our solution was to create our own firm and become our own bosses. We don't know what the future will hold for either of us, or our firm, but we are inspired and motivated to build our firm into a business that will support us, challenge us, and inspire us. We know that there will be tough times, a lack of immediate steady income, and an enormous amount of work, but we also know that the hard work will lead to priceless rewards.

Throughout this initial process, there are a few qualities that we know have primed us for success. We offer them here merely as reminders because, while they may seem intuitive, they are certainly not qualities everyone possesses.

- Be outgoing and charismatic. You cannot be humble and shy when you need to interact with others and, more importantly, when you need to instill in your clients confidence in your capabilities.

- However, don't be too arrogant. There is a fine line between confidence and arrogance, and depending on your audience, both will be perceived differently. It is essential to respect opposing counsel, clients, staff, bankers, accountants, and insurance agents because one never knows from whom the next referral will come; a display of arrogance will ensure from whom that next referral will not come.

- Recognize that your network of family, friends, acquaintances, and colleagues want you to be successful. Our network has been nothing but excited, supportive, and encouraging as we started our firm. This network has led to developing more contacts with others that can help us with the intricacies of our business or provide a source of potential clients.

- Don't be too proud. Remember to solicit assistance whenever necessary. Requesting guidance from experienced sources saves money, time, and effort, which might be better spent on something else to further your business.

- Maintain a sense of humor. This profession is challenging and requires occasional laughter to survive the stress.

- Remain patient. This is an endeavor that requires both time and care.

It is essential to file the proper formation documents with the proper authorities according to your state's statutes. Create an initial budget and a strategic business plan before opening the doors to clients. Tend to the business details of your practice, and once all of that is completed, then you can focus on providing your legal expertise to your clients and marketing for new ones.

So, given all this, as we stand at the precipice of taking on our first clients, our final word of advice is: do it. We did and are more excited than ever about our careers, our profession, and the endless possibilities ahead of us. Starting our own firm has reinvigorated both of us not only professionally, but personally as well. Answer those lingering questions. Openly discuss your fears, hopes, worries, and big ideas. You won't regret it. We certainly don't.

JAYNE SYKORA and **JENNIFER SANTINI** are partners and founders of Sykora & Santini PLLP located in Edina, Minnesota, where they focus on estate planning and general business law. They graduated from law school in 2009 and founded their firm in 2010. *www.sykorasantini.com*

- Charna E. Sherman -

"My personal strategy, in short, was to stay vigilant about
my future in every way that has made me successful in the past:
to stay stridently focused on my visions, without losing sight
of rigorous attention to the details."

I launched my own firm—Charna E. Sherman Law Offices Co., LPA—on one of the most auspicious dates on the calendar: 1/1/11. To be sure, I sought to bolster my soaring optimism and exhilarating sense of empowerment by scouring the New Year's press for mystical musings about this cosmically masterful moment in time. But, in retrospect, just as consequential was the pragmatic import of this date: indeed, buried in the voluminous partnership agreement of the Am Law 100 firm I was leaving were onerous exit provisions, imposing severe financial penalties were I to resign on any other day.

So my most earnest advice to any woman in the certain-to-be-anguished throes of whether to leave BigLaw is necessarily twofold. At the most transcendent level, I am genuinely buoyed every day by believing, deeply, that my new independence—along with a growing tide of others'—is really part of something bigger . . . of a turning point in our profession—finally—for fabulously talented women to compete seriously *and successfully* in the uppermost echelons of the law. And yet, at the same time, it is incumbent to share a practical observation: I am privileged now to leave the trappings of BigLaw success precisely because I so relentlessly applied myself to achieving that success . . . and not only in my practice, but also as a mother, wife, and daughter. I now have earned the confidence to bank not only on my record, but also on the extraordinary records of more and more women in our profession who demonstrate time and again the determination and ability to succeed simultaneously in multiple realms. In truth, we really need only do what we do best: apply our considerable talents and incredible dedication to our own futures, just as we always have to representing our clients, caring for our families, and pursuing our passions.

The Inspiration of "Defying Gravity"

Before I could even begin to contemplate the looming challenges (let alone the fine print) of leaving BigLaw, I had to convince myself that I should. Since so few women really make it up the ranks in BigLaw, every success only magnified the gravitational pull just to stay and persevere. Given my passions for advancing women in the law, I was weighed down even more by the prospect of disappointing—and the guilt of abandoning—women in my firm and others. But I experienced a moment of inspiration in, of all places, a Broadway theater, watching my struggle brilliantly played out on stage in the musical hit *Wicked*. As a career litigator, I have long combatted being typed a "witch." So I was especially enthralled by the poignancy of the musical duel between two witches—and also two close girlfriends—over what really is good and right—and what really makes us happy—in a complex world ridden with unfair bias:

> Something has changed within me
> Something is not the same
> I'm through with playing by
> The rules of someone else's game . . .
> It's time to trust my instincts . . .
> It's time to try
> [D]efying gravity![1]

For me, their melodic debate gave not only real voice to mine, but also flight to my dreams.

Leaving Kansas

As we all know, Dorothy's abrupt departure from home proved rather tumultuous and quite scary. So I would be remiss not to stress that leaving BigLaw required much more than inspiration; it's been a journey that required resilience to a degree I wasn't even sure that I had and a lot of detailed thought and planning. But in those moments when it all seemed overwhelming and more than I believed I could do well, I had to be even more vigilant in reminding myself that women from the beginning of time have changed history by successfully multitasking. And since the moment law schools opened the doors to us, we not only have zealously represented our clients, but all the while have also reared our children, spoiled our spouses, cared for our par-

---

1 Stephen Schwartz, *Defying Gravity*

ents, paid our bills, fixed our homes, planned our social lives, fit in exercise, and dressed ourselves in style to boot. And precisely because we insist on doing it all well, we do exactly that. So amongst the most compelling advice I got before starting out on my own is the simple truth that starting a law firm is no different: it takes time and hard work . . . just like all the other things we've had to learn and achieve in our lives.

The Ruby Slippers

The life lesson of *The Wizard of Oz* was that Dorothy always had the power: the ruby slippers were with her *all along*. But we shouldn't overlook that so was the "Good Witch of the North," who watched and guided her along her new path of self-awareness. And for me, one of the most precious treasures of my new independence has been discovering that I never was alone. Throughout this process, I turned for advice to some of the most fabulous women I know and some other incredible trailblazers I didn't; and true to form, they were all always generous with their time, their tips, their inspiration, and mostly, their extraordinary support.

And more, regardless whether we formally partner together, the legal profession increasingly has created—and even demanded we create—opportunities to "virtually" partner with one another. We each can augment our own firm capabilities with powerful and effective external networks and nimbly compete on the terms that matter most to our clients: effectiveness and value.

Over the Rainbow

For me, independence was the only way I could see my way to practicing law actually according to the principles I was raised to cherish and which I truly believe. More, my decades of work on diversity issues in the law convinced me that even the most successful women lawyers need special support to reach, stay, and excel at the very top echelons of our profession. My own experience illustrates that need, as so many helped me discover the hidden meaning of Dorothy's ruby slippers—that I always had it in my power to succeed. Indeed, the power to change our world and reach our potential lies in each of us.

So simultaneously with launching my own firm, I also decided to mark my new milestone with—and commit a percentage of my firm's profits to—a new philanthropic cause: *The Ruby Shoes Fund* supports new initiatives to empower women on the ladder of success in the legal profession, particularly strategies to help us overcome the unique challenges engendered, ironically, by our success. As Bette Midler once said, "Give a girl the right shoes, and she can conquer the world." And as one of my mentors once counseled me: "If you are going to go about the business of breaking glass ceilings, wear sharp shoes."

Thus, as the sand in the hourglass reached 1/1/11 and I embarked on this exciting journey down a new yellow brick road, my personal strategy, in short, was to stay vigilant about my future in every way that has made me successful in the past: to stay stridently focused on my vision, without losing sight of rigorous attention to the details. And too, just like Dorothy, I experienced the joy of returning home but seeing it differently: indeed, ironically, this "witch of the Midwest" leased office space not only in Cleveland's highest tower, but above my old firm. So now that I am literally building my new foundation atop their glass ceiling, I enthusiastically invite you to learn more about my new ventures at www.charnalaw.com and to defy gravity with me and so many others.

Warmest wishes.

CHARNA E. SHERMAN is president and founding partner of Charna E. Sherman Law Offices Co., LPA in Cleveland, Ohio, where she focuses on complex commercial litigation. She graduated from law school in 1985 and founded her firm in 2011. *www.charnalaw.com*

Conclusion

These 101 letters show that, on a profession-wide basis, more women—of all ages and levels of seniority—are stepping onto the road to independence—to found, fund, and run law firms. No longer is the start-up decision reached because the profession won't have her, as our first letter from a 1954 founder conveys. Feeding into the current decade, the distribution of women choosing to step into a woman-owned practice has swept in seasoned lawyers across the four decades of women in active practice.

This historically arranged compendium of letters, by women to women who wish to found their own law firms, yields an overriding theme: the profession has not yet acknowledged or used the power that women lawyers carry, and can carry, as successful counselors, advocates, and co-owners of practices.

Focused on practicing without artificial constraints in their opportunities to own and win at the practice of law, women lawyers use their ambition, their drive, their vision, and their dedication to the profession. They are creating business models that provide productivity, profit, and professional longevity.

ABA Resources for Women Lawyers

For information on resources within the
American Bar Association to assist women
lawyers, visit the website of the ABA
Commission on Women in the Profession
at *www.americanbar.org/groups/women/
resources.html*

Editor Biography

KAREN M. LOCKWOOD, based on deep experience as an AV-rated trial lawyer and arbitrator, works every day to articulate the issues and find solutions in the puzzles of the professions' efforts to diversify.

As CEO and founder of The Lockwood Group, LLC, Ms. Lockwood advises professionals on the strategies and practical means "to achieve sustained diversity" by focusing on the business of their professional practice. Springing to her consulting practice from law practice as a partner in complex commercial litigation, she knows that firm leaders often recognize the problems and wish to solve them. "The question is *how*," she says. "I founded The Lockwood Group to answer that question." Based in Washington, DC, Ms. Lockwood works with firm and corporate leadership or with groups of lawyers who seek to improve their own access or to make change in the profession. Her approach is fact based, educational, tailored to the particular firm and key issues, and innovative. She advocates for transparent gateways for women and minority professionals to access the opportunities that translate into their business success.

A thought leader, speaker, facilitator of difficult conversations, and strategic advisor, Ms. Lockwood developed this expertise through law practice. A member of the U.S. Supreme Court and 10 federal circuit bars, she was a trial partner for a decade at Howrey LLP, where she served as global co-chair of its women's initiative. With a decade as trial partner also at mid-sized Collier Shannon Rill & Scott, PLLC and previously having co-founded a boutique litigation firm, Ms. Lockwood has observed and advocated the advancement of women throughout her practice.

Ms. Lockwood was president of the Women's Bar Association of the District of Columbia (WBA) in 2005-2006. She devised a new "exchange method" in creating the groundbreaking WBA Initiative for Advancement and Retention of Women. Her first Initiative event drew over 230 lawyers and managing partners for 16 hours of frank exchange on the obstacles women face, how firms attempt to meet those issues, and why those best practices were not enough. The seminal report, *Creating Pathways to Success*, available at *www.wbadc.org*, galvanized change and is joined by the WBA's two succeeding Initiative publications on women of color and women in corporate practice.

Ms. Lockwood is a leader in bar associations. She represents the District of Columbia Bar in the ABA House of Delegates, serves as liaison to the ABA Commission on Women in the Profession, and has belonged to the boards of the Women's Bar Association of the District of Columbia, the WBA Foundation, and the National Conference of Women's Bar Associations.

Ms. Lockwood also practices as an arbitrator and mediator and uses experiential learning to teach trial advocacy to trial lawyers as a National Institute for Trial Advocacy (NITA) program director and faculty member. She is an associate professor (adjunct) at American University Washington College of Law, teaching dispute resolution.

Working for new solutions in the business of the professions that impact diversity–defined broadly–Ms. Lockwood frequently presents and writes on issues of diversity in the professions. She was featured in the front-page lead feature by the *New York Times* entitled "Up the Down Staircase" (Mar. 5, 2006). She has received numerous awards including the 2009 Annice Wagner Pioneer Award (Bar Association of the District of Columbia), the 2007 Women's Bar Association Stars of the Bar Recognition, and the 2006 Women in the Law Leadership Award and 2004 Woman to Watch Award from American University's Washington College of Law.

Ms. Lockwood's curriculum vitae is available at *www.lockwoodgroup.com*.

About the Commission on Women in the Profession

As the national voice for women lawyers, the ABA Commission on Women in the Profession forges a new and better profession that ensures that women have equal opportunities for professional growth and advancement commensurate with their male counterparts. It was created in 1987 to assess the status of women in the legal profession and to identify barriers to their advancement. Hillary Rodham Clinton, the first chair of the Commission, issued a groundbreaking report in 1988 showing that women lawyers were not advancing at a satisfactory rate.

Now in its third decade, the Commission not only reports the challenges that women lawyers face, it also brings about positive change in the legal workplace through such efforts as its Women of Color Research Initiative, Women in Law Leadership Academy, women in-house counsel regional summits, and Margaret Brent Women Lawyers of Achievement Awards. Drawing upon the expertise and diverse backgrounds of its 12 members, who are appointed by the ABA president, the Commission develops programs, policies, and publications to advance and assist women in public and private practice, the judiciary, and academia. For more information, visit www.americanbar.org/women.

Author Index